UNINTENTIONALLY MINE

A Birch Crossing Novel

STEPHANIE ROWE

Authenticity Playground, LLC

COPYRIGHT

For further information, please contact
Stephanie@stephanierowe.com

For all the non-biological families created by adoption, remarriages, and other beautiful ways of coming together. Family is created through the heart and the soul.

CHAPTER ONE

THE NIGHT WAS FINALLY dark enough.

Harlan Shea eased through the thick jungle, moving in precise and lethal silence. The air was heavy and wet, and insects buzzed around his head. But he didn't react to them. He just kept his focus on the decrepit, dark shack sitting alone in the hostile zone. His right hand was locked around the heavy knife that was the only weapon he dared use in the dangerous stillness of the night.

Even a silencer would be too loud, with the kidnappers just on the other side of the trees, reveling in the fact that their ransom demand had been agreed to.

Or so they thought.

Behind him, he could feel the breath of his teammate Blue Carboni, but the other male was equally undetectable as they slipped into the deepest shadows of a land that didn't welcome people like them: mercenaries who worked for no government. They were private hires who snuck in and plucked the bounty from the hands of kidnappers before anyone even knew they were there. The last hope for families who had nowhere else to turn.

1

He damn well never got tired of that moment when strung-out families got their first sighting of the person they'd feared they would never see again.

Harlan reached the front door and looked over his shoulder.

Blue's face was painted black, and his clothes were dark. In the darkness, the whites of his eyes glowed brightly, but everything else about him faded into the night. Blue grinned nodded his readiness.

Two men were not enough for this job, but as usual, it was all that could be afforded by the client. In Harlan's world, clients wanted miracles for nothing, and he and Blue had to find a way to deliver and keep themselves alive in the process. Not easy, but what else was he going to do? This was who he was.

Harlan eased the front door open, and then leapt inside, striking before his presence could be detected. The man standing guard slumped to the ground, not expecting the attack. Harlan caught him before he hit the floor, and there was a muffled scream. Harlan glanced across the room as the young woman cowered against the wall, hugging a small boy to her chest, shackles binding them both. They were covered in dirt, and their eyes were wide with terror.

For a split second, Harlan could only stare at them, the sight of the mother protecting her boy catapulting him back into his past. How many times had that been him with his stepmother, cringing against the wall as his father lurched through the door, ready to punish the world for the hell he was living? Memories raked at Harlan, and the woman scrambled backward away from him, dragging the boy with her. "Stay away from us," she hissed. "Get away!"

Harlan blinked as her panic jerked him back to the present, and he shook his head to dismiss her fears. "We're here to rescue you," he told her as he shoved the dead guard out of the way. He moved swiftly toward them, but she scrambled even further back, not trusting him. He stopped, unable to risk her getting scared and raising an alarm. "Keep quiet," he warned. "We're on your side."

"Stay back!" She held up a small knife she'd gotten from who the hell knew where. "I won't let you touch him."

Shit! They didn't have time for this!

"Hey." Blue moved past him, heading directly toward the victims. "My name's Blue Carboni. Your dad hired us. Let's go."

Instantly, the resistance seemed to leave the woman. She shoved the knife into her pocket, trusting Blue without further words. Shit. What was up with that? It happened this way every damn time. The victims ran from Harlan and threw themselves into Blue's arms. No one seemed to believe Harlan was one of the good guys until Blue reassured them.

Not that he cared whether anyone liked him, but sometimes it was a pain in the ass to have to wait for Blue to calm everyone down.

As Blue knelt before the duo, skillfully freeing them from their shackles, Harlan turned away from the tearful rescue, easing back to the door and watching outside for signs that they had been heard. There was still low conversation and celebration from the kidnappers, but Harlan didn't buy it.

The shadows near the cabin were too still. They'd missed someone.

Blue came up behind him with the woman and the boy, but Harlan held up his hand to still them. Everyone froze, and Harlan searched the night. Then he saw a slight movement in the bushes to the right of the cabin. The soft brush of footsteps moving carefully. Investigating.

Harlan indicated with a quick gesture to Blue. They knew the plan.

They all waited as the footsteps neared. A shadowed

3

silhouette appeared out of the bushes, a rifle raised high, aimed right at the front door. Swearing, Harlan eased back against the wall, Blue and the two victims behind him, using him as a shield.

They waited, each step taking a lifetime.

Finally, the front step creaked and a shadow moved across the entry. Harlan reacted quickly, striking hard while Blue and his charges rushed past him, heading for safety. The man's rifle hit the ground, but he got off a shout before Harlan silenced him.

With a curse, Harlan leapt through the front door. Blue and the others were heading north, but Blue was slowed by his cargo. Harlan knew he had to give them time to get a lead. He took off south, running loudly, breaking branches, drawing the rest of the kidnappers after him. They were on his trail instantly, a good twenty men, too many for him to take on alone.

He had to outrun them, and give Blue time to get the others to safety.

Harlan put on a burst of speed, sprinting toward the distant cliff, toward the escape that he'd already mapped out. Bullets sizzled past his shoulder, and he let out a shout, just to let them know they'd almost hit him. It was too dark for them to see he was alone, and he ran hard and long, drawing them farther and farther away from Blue.

Another shot blistered too close, and he felt the sting on his right arm. Swearing, he bore down, sweat pouring off him as he ran. He fired off a few shots, and shouts of pain told him he'd taken a couple out. Progress. Then he heard the roar of an engine, and knew they'd gone mobile. Not surprising, but not exactly the cooperative bad guys it would have been nice to run into for once.

He reached the edge of the cliff and ran alongside it, drawing it out for as long as he could. Five minutes. Eight minutes. Over rocks. His lungs burning. Firing behind him as he ran. Seventy feet below him, the river ran hard, churning violently over rocks.

A bullet bit into his shoulder and he stumbled, hitting the ground.

Dirt kicked up all around him, and he knew it was time to bail. Not even bothering to get up, he rolled to his left, straight over the edge of the cliff.

He twisted in the air as he plummeted, as bullets whizzed by him. He just managed to get himself perpendicular as he hit the surface of the water. The impact was brutal, but he immediately kicked back to the surface, fighting for air among the violent rapids. He had just gotten his head above the surface when he hit a rock, his skull cracking against the hard surface.

Pain rang through him even as he grabbed a log careening past. He locked it under his arms and hung on, fighting with all his draining strength to stay afloat. His mind quickly assessed his options as he was tossed ruthlessly, as the jungle flashed past in a blur. A wave swamped him, ripping him off the log, and he was dragged under, filthy water pouring into his mouth.

He kicked off a rock, and launched himself to the surface. His injured shoulder slammed into another rock, and then he was thrust again into the middle of the river.

With a roar of fury, Harlan fought for the shore, losing half his progress with each yard he gained. It felt like hours, days, years, but finally, he was almost there. His feet hit solid ground and he threw himself onto the mud. He landed face down and didn't move, gasping for breath, his muscles spent beyond exhaustion, his shoulder throbbing.

There was no sound of an approaching helicopter coming to pick him up. He'd gone miles past where they'd be looking for him. The only sound was the roar of the river, overwhelming all other noise.

As he lay there, a grim awareness began to dawn on him, his mind filling with a memory that had been triggered by the woman huddling protectively with her son, like his stepmother had done with him so many times. An image flashed into his mind, a memory of the night so many years ago when he'd gone out into the woods behind his house, trying to find the family dog that had gone missing. How he'd come across his father, face down. Dead. His leg was broken, and he'd been unable to walk for help. So he'd lain there in those woods until he'd died.

He'd been dead for weeks, and no one had gone looking for him, not even Harlan.

No one had wanted to look for him. No one in the whole damn town had wanted to find him. Not even his own son. But the sight of that old man crumpled in the woods, forgotten in death, had been brutal.

His father had lived for sixty-one years, and he'd died a nothing. No one had cared.

As Harlan lay there, sucked into the grisly reminders of his past, he became grimly aware that if he died here, on the bank of this river, no one would know. No one would care. He'd never turned in a next of kin form, so the small-time private outfit he worked for had no one to call if he didn't come home from work today.

Even his sister wouldn't know. He barely knew Astrid, though they lived in the same town now. Even she would have no idea what happened to him, and probably wouldn't even notice for a long time that he was missing.

Just like his father.

Son of a bitch.

He would not die forgotten like that scum had.

He would not.

With a growl of pain, Harlan shoved himself to his feet, staggering with weakness. Gritting his jaw against exhaustion and pain, he began to head up the river. He was going to make it home, and when he did, he was going to tell his Astrid what he did all those times when he was out of town.

Someone had to know.

Someone had to know enough to notice when he died.

"CONGRATULATIONS!"

Emma Larson blinked in surprise as she walked in the front door of the charming lakeside home of her friend Astrid Munroe...now Astrid Sarantos. Astrid had called her over at the last minute to babysit her infant Rosie, but instead of a baby, Emma was greeted with dozens of helium balloons, streamers, and the grinning faces of her two best friends, Clare Friesé and Astrid. She stopped in confusion. "What is this?"

Astrid's outrageous auburn hair was tucked up in a colorful scarf, and she held up a champagne bottle. "Girl power, sweetie. You survived!"

Emma was still confused. The dark wood beams had glittering stars hanging from them, and the huge stone fireplace was draped with a rainbow-colored "Congratulations" banner. "Survived what?"

Clare held out two champagne glasses as Astrid popped the cork. It careened across the living room and smashed into the ceiling. "Getting divorced, of course!"

"Getting divorced?" Emma echoed as Astrid poured the champagne into the glasses. She'd just received the final paperwork from the court in the mail that afternoon, but she hadn't even told her friends that she'd received it. She'd moved back to Birch Crossing more than two years, but the divorce had dragged out for a long time. Now that it was over, celebration was not what she'd had on her mind. It still felt too weird, not exactly celebratory. Yes, her ex-husband was not a good man, but to have the final nail in the coffin of her dreams was a strange, desolate feeling. "How did you know?"

"I told them," announced a voice from the kitchen.

Emma started to smile. She knew that voice. Everyone in the small Maine town of Birch Crossing knew that voice. "Eppie?"

"Of course it's me," the gravelly old voice called out. "Who else would it be? I wouldn't miss a party with my girls!"

A feeling of warmth began to seep through Emma's sadness over the divorce as Astrid handed her a glass of champagne. She hadn't thought of calling her friends with the news, but now that she was with them, it felt good. Right. "And how did you know, Eppie?"

"Oh, I was at the post office today chatting with Rick, our oh-so-handsome postman. He had to run down the street for a moment, so I filled in at the counter for a few minutes. I happened to be putting your mail away and saw the return address, and I knew exactly what it was." In from the kitchen strode Eppie Orlowe, the seventy-something gossipmonger who ruled Birch Crossing. She tapped the side of her head, her fuchsia and violet beret sliding dangerously to the side on her gray hair. "Just because I'm old doesn't mean I can't figure things out."

Emma started to laugh at the sight of Eppie and her outrageous hat. There was no privacy in Birch Crossing if Eppie was around. "Well, that explains why the envelope had been re-taped shut."

Eppie gave her an innocent blink. "What? You're accusing me of opening your mail? You youngsters are so impertinent." She set a tray of brownies topped with chocolate-dipped strawberries on the dining table, which Emma noticed had been set with a beautiful lace table cloth and the new china that she'd helped Astrid pick out for her wedding six months ago. "I laced all of these with generous amounts of my finest rum. Chocolate and alcohol are important for days like this. It's not every day a woman gets liberated to go forth and live the rest of her life the way she sees fit."

"Here you go." Astrid handed a glass of champagne to Clare, and then gave a glass to Eppie. "Happy Liberation Day, Emma."

"Happy Liberation Day," Clare and Eppie repeated, raising their glasses.

As Emma looked around at her dear friends, suddenly being divorced didn't seem so lonely anymore. With her friends around her, she could get through anything, right? For the first time since she'd received the envelope officially freeing her from Preston Hayes, she smiled. "Thank you, my darlings," she teased as she raised her glass. "I can't think of anyone I'd rather celebrate a failed marriage with than you guys. Cheers!"

"Cheers!"

The champagne was dry and bubbly, absolutely perfect, and Emma grinned as the girls led her to the table, where a few gift bags were set out. "You guys didn't have to do this," she protested as Astrid held out the chair for her.

"Of course we did." Astrid sat down next to her, her brown eyes suddenly serious. "Both Clare and I know what it's like to become single after you thought you'd never be single again."

"As do I," Eppie chimed in as she wedged her bottom into the chair at the head of the table. "I thought George would outlast me, but the poor dear couldn't keep up with me in the end. It's tough to be as much of a hot ticket as I am, I'll tell you that right now."

Emma smiled, knowing full well that Eppie had been dearly in love with her husband, despite the fact she had adjusted remarkably well to becoming single in her sixties.

"Hey." Astrid touched her hand, drawing her attention back. "My point is that even when the guy isn't the right guy and you're better off without him, it's still pretty terrifying to be on your own when you thought you were set for life."

Emma's throat tightened at Astrid's empathy. "It's fine—"

"No, it's not." Clare smiled, her eyes soft with understanding. "You don't ever have to admit it to us, but we've both been there, so we know. Anytime you're feeling down, just say you need a hug, and we'll be there for you. We'll know what it's about."

Emma blinked hard several times, not quite able to say the words she wanted to say through the tightness in her throat. So she simply nodded.

Astrid put her arm around Emma and squeezed gently. "And just remember, men come and go, but girlfriends are forever."

"Men come way too fast actually," Eppie said. "Most of them need to learn to slow it down a bit, you know?"

Emma burst out laughing at Eppie's outrageous comment. "Eppie!"

"What? You think I haven't been around?" Eppie picked up her champagne glass and waggled it at them. "I know you girls talk about sex when I'm not around, and I want in. I can't go around having proper conversations all the time, you know." Then she leaned forward, her eyes piercing as she turned serious. "You listen to me, Emma. You married a bad man, but all men aren't like that. You've been like a damn nun since you moved back to town, and it's time for that to end, or you're going to shrivel up and die like an old raisin."

Emma stiffened. "I'm not a raisin, Eppie."

"No, not yet. But you've got that look in your eye that

says you'd rather get old and wrinkly than ever let another man near you. It's not healthy. Women need men. They need them for more than sex, but, I'm not going to lie, the sex is critical." She shrugged. "We have to accept it. It's the way we're hardwired."

"Okay, okay." Astrid held up her hand to cool Eppie down. Not that they didn't love Eppie, but sex advice from a senior citizen with a better sex life than she had was just depressing. "Let's give Emma a break, shall we? Today is about celebrating liberation, and that's what we're going to do." She handed Emma a package wrapped in gold and silver polka dots. "Open this first."

Grateful for the distraction, Emma tore open the package. Inside were ten tubes of paint. The most expensive, most beautiful paint available. She had only three tubes of it, and she rationed it carefully. The tubes were resting on seven canvas boards that she could already tell were of the highest quality, far beyond what she ever bought for herself. A dozen paintbrushes were tied with a pretty red ribbon. Not just any paintbrushes. The best that money could buy. Stunned, she looked at her friend. "It's an incredible gift. I don't even know how to thank you."

Astrid beamed at her. "Painting is your salvation, so I figured you should do it in style."

Emma ran her hand over the art supplies, still amazed by Astrid's thoughtfulness. Her day job was a museum curator in Portland, but her first love was painting. "Thank you." She cocked her head. "Are you sure? It's so expensive."

"Of course. What's the point of falling madly in love with a rich guy if you don't spend his money on your best friends?" Astrid patted her hand. "Enjoy."

Emma grinned at Astrid's generosity. After watching Astrid struggle financially for so long, it was great to see her being able to afford the things that mattered to her.

Clare set a gift bag in front of her. "You'll like this."

Emma opened it, then grimaced when she saw it was an array of decadent lace underwear and bras. She held up a light pink nightie that was pure silken elegance...and sex. "I thought we agreed I didn't have to start dating—"

"It's not for men." Clare grinned. "It's for you. A girl doesn't need a man to feel sexy."

How long had it been since she'd worn anything sexy? Years. Since before her marriage ended. Would she dare wear it now? Even for herself? Temptation called to her, but fear was stronger. She managed a smile. "They're beautiful."

"No man is going to jump you just because you're secretly wearing a pair of sexy underwear," Clare said. "Try it. You'll like it. You'll be like this giant tease. Every man will know there's something about you...but he won't know what it is."

Emma laughed then, and gave up the pretense of pretending she wasn't terrified at the mere idea of doing anything that could attract a man's attention. "How do you know me so well?"

"Because we've been friends for twenty years. You can't hide from me," Clare said, holding up a pair of the lace undies and flipping them toward Emma. "I know you don't feel like it now, but someday you'll be happy to have some sexy lingerie to show off to the right guy."

A cold chill rippled over Emma, and she shook her head. "No way. I'm done."

Empathy flickered in Clare's eyes, and Emma had to look away. She didn't want her friends looking at her in pity, or seeing her as a lonely spinster. She was fine being single. It was so much safer than dating, so much safer than putting her trust in another man, and in her own judgment. She remembered it hadn't been that long ago when both her friends were claiming to prefer single life as well. Now that they had met the loves of their lives, they seemed to have forgotten that being single could be a great gift.

"And mine." Eppie pointed to another bag, this one covered in huge red cartoon lips on a gold background. "This is for you."

Ignoring the silent exchange of glances between Astrid and Clare, which Emma knew was about her ongoing refusal to consider dating again, Emma unwrapped the hot pink tissue from Eppie's present. It was a six-inch, framed watercolor of two hummingbirds drinking from the same pink petunia, their green, yellow and blue bodies vibrant against the white background. Exquisitely painted, it was elegant in its simplicity. It brought to life the nature that abounded in Birch Crossing, the same nature that gave Emma so much solace when she was struggling emotionally. It was as if someone had painted serenity itself onto the canvas and captured it just for her. "It's beautiful," she whispered in awe.

"It was my first anniversary present from George," Eppie said.

Emma was shocked and tried to give it back. "I can't take this—"

"Of course you can. I have forty-two anniversary presents from him. I want you to have this one." Eppie pushed it right back to her. "It shows how even hummingbirds can stay still long enough to fall in love with each other. That's what he used to call me, his hummingbird, because I was always on the run so much he thought he'd never catch me." She smiled, her cherry red lips stretching wide and deepening the wrinkles on her skin. "He never tried to slow me down. He just always made sure to be there when I paused." She leaned forward. "That's the kind of man you need, Emma. A man who will let you buzz around, but who will be there when you are ready for him. Not a scum-sucking pig who tries to rip you down and destroy the light in your soul before the final vows are even read." She held up her champagne glass. "Remember that, girl, and you'll be all set."

"I appreciate the reference to Preston as a scum-sucking pig." Emma couldn't help but smile. "I'm not going to date anyone, but I will cherish the hummingbirds."

"I know you will." Eppie winked. "Just enjoy the art. That's enough for now. The rest will come."

After the gifts, the evening began to descend into a bawdy girls' night of terrible dating stories, fashion trends, and an examination of Astrid's latest jewelry line. By the time an hour had passed, Emma's tension about joining the divorced world had faded. She felt comfortable and at home in her world with her girls—

"Are we interrupting?" The front door opened, and in walked Jason Sarantos, Astrid's new husband. He was carrying their baby Rosie in his arms, and beside him was his eight-year-old son, Noah, who was wearing a Red Sox hat.

"Jason!" Astrid's face lit up, and she jumped up from the table. The kiss she gave her husband was so intimate and sweet that Emma felt an ache of longing in her own chest. She was happy for Astrid, but it was so clear from the way that Astrid's face softened at the sight of her family that she was definitely no longer someone who would sit up late nights with Emma enjoying some popcorn and Netflix.

Behind him was Clare's husband, Griffin Friesé. He was carrying six large pizzas from Jason's cafe, a broad grin on his face. "Dinner has arrived for the party."

"Fantastic!" Clare leapt up, her own face illuminating at the sight of *her* husband. "Thanks so much. We're starving."

Emma sank back into her seat, retreating from the excitement that the men brought into the room. She glanced across the table at Eppie, and then was startled to see the older lady was gazing across the room with a gleam in her eye. She followed Eppie's gaze and saw Astrid's stepfather, Ralph Hutchins, walk in the door, carrying Rosie's diaper bag.

Eppie immediately straightened her hat, gave Emma a wink, and then rose from her chair. "I'm going to the kitchen for some napkins," she announced.

"I'll help." Ralph immediately changed course and hustled after her, the door swinging shut behind them almost before they'd even made it through. Eppie and Ralph were getting it on? How had she missed that?

"Is this the party?" Through the front door stepped another couple, Jackson Reed and his wife, along with their toddler. The noise and energy of the room began to rise as people hugged and kissed, welcoming each other into Astrid's home. So much warmth, so many kids, so much connection, so many families, it was almost overwhelming.

The pizza was set on the table and drinks were poured, as everyone hugged Emma and celebrated her liberation day. The noise began to close in on her, the joviality too much. She caught Clare's arm. "Clare, I think I need to get some air—"

"No, wait." Clare grinned as the front door opened again. In walked the new bartender from Johnny's Swill and Grill, the best pub in town. He was still the well-muscled specimen he'd been at Astrid's botched going away party, and the tattoo on his biceps was partially visible below the sleeve of his black tee shirt. He looked around the room, then saw Clare. He nodded at her and headed toward them, his eyes fixed with too much interest on Emma.

Emma stiffened. "What is he doing here? I don't even know him."

"He's new to town. None of us know anything about him. Griffin decided we needed to change that, so here he is. Smile and be nice." Clare beamed at him as he approached. "Glad you could make it, Brady. This is Emma Larson. You remember her, don't you? Emma, this is Brady Foster. Don't let the tattoos fool you. He's actually a good guy. Oh, wait, Eppie's got the wrong dishes. Eppie!" Clare hurried off, leaving Emma alone with Brady.

He loomed over her, large. Too large. Too powerful. Too strong. He smiled at her, a smile designed to rip her heart right out of her chest, just like Preston's practiced good looks had done for her that damned July day when he'd finally noticed her after years of coming to Birch Crossing as a summer resident.

"Hey," he said. His voice was low and reserved, but it had a muted edge that told her he wasn't entirely comfortable at the party either.

She swallowed, and clenched her palms. "Hi," she managed, her mouth dry. She looked around the room, desperate for an escape, but everyone was occupied with a significant other. Smiles that were so genuine, filled with so much love, so much connection. Children being hugged. Families.

Aside from Brady, she was the only single one there, standing beside a stranger with huge shoulders. She swallowed, fighting against the panic. She couldn't do this. She simply could not do it. "I have to go—"

"Wait." He caught her arm, his touch light, but Emma jumped anyway at the familiarity. "Stay a sec." His dark brown eyes flickered over her face. "Griffin wanted me to meet you. He's a good guy. Let's give it a chance."

Emma swallowed, her heart pounding. She glanced over at Clare, who was cuddling baby Rosie. Astrid was laughing with Jason and Griffin. It was a scene of pure domestic bliss, a world that her two best friends lived in, a lifestyle she wasn't a part of, not anymore. Where was she going to escape to? She had nowhere to go. This was her life. She had to find a way to make peace with it and to belong. She managed a smile at

Brady, even though her stomach was churning. All she wanted to do was leave, but it was her party. How could she? "Yeah, okay."

"Okay." Releasing her arm, he leaned against the wall, his body too muscled and appealing for comfort. "Tell me, Emma Larson, what is it that makes you tick?"

She was surprised by the depth of that question and shifted uncomfortably. "You can't just ask me about the weather?"

His dark eyes were brooding. "I don't care about the weather."

The moment he said those words, she knew he wasn't a man she could control. He was a man who would consume whatever woman he was with, stripping her of her defenses and demanding access to every one of her private thoughts and feelings. He was a man who would fight for all of a woman, and never be satisfied with halfway. Once, too long ago, that was the kind of man she burned for.

Now? He was the kind of man who terrified her.

CHAPTER TWO

ASTRID LIVED HERE? The house was incredible, a lakeside retreat nestled at the edge of the woods with a two acre yard, a carriage house, and a view of the mountains on the other side of the lake. And this was his sister's house?

Harlan pulled his truck up behind a silver Mercedes and four other cars. Scowling, he studied the vast home that Astrid had mentioned in her last email to him, the one where she'd told him that she'd gotten married and had a baby. He'd known this was Jason's house, but logically, he'd never actually comprehended that his sister had landed in a place like this. As he studied it, a slow grin began to dawn on his face, and the most tremendous sense of relief seemed to fill him as he shifted his truck into park.

This was good. She deserved this. His little sister had finally found someone to take care of her and make sure she was all right. He wanted to fist pump the air for her. *You go, Astrid.*

He got out of his truck, grimacing at the pain in his shoulder from his latest mission. He rubbed his jaw as he strode up the walkway, past all the cars lining the circular drive. Five cars. Was she having a party? He slowed his steps as he neared the front door, feeling out of place in this domestic scene.

It had been almost a year since he'd been back in Birch Crossing. A year since he'd consorted with people who lived normal lives. He glanced at his reflection as he walked past a shiny black SUV, and then grimaced. His face was a grizzled mess. Once he'd been dropped back in the States, he hadn't bothered to even change, let alone shave or shower. He'd just come straight here, still haunted by the image of his father dying alone. He had only forty-eight hours until his next mission, and he needed to see his sister before he left.

The sound of laughter and music assaulted him as he reached the bottom step. Definitely a party. He vaulted up two steps, ignored the front door, and peered in the window instead. He found his sister right away. She was laughing with Jason Sarantos, the bastard Harlan had punched in the face right before he'd taken off.

The man was grinning at Astrid as if she were the very reason he took a breath every morning, and Astrid was looking at him the same way. A young boy was next to Jason, chatting animatedly to Astrid. In her arms was a small baby. Rosie? Wasn't that what she'd said? Named after their mother. The scene was pure domestic bliss, which was something that Harlan had never associated with anyone he was related to. The furniture was perfect, and the dining table even had china on it. China? His little sister had china?

Harlan looked down at himself. His jeans were stained and torn, his boots still caked with mud. His tee shirt had was streaked with dirt on it, and he hadn't shaved in days. What the hell was he doing, bringing that shit into his sister's life? She'd made it out of the hell that their mother had started them in. She'd gotten what she wanted and deserved. She was all set.

She didn't need Harlan's protection anymore, which meant his job with her was done. There was no need for him to bug her, or to inject himself into her life. He realized he'd been a fool to come back here. He didn't belong in this world. He belonged in a world where a man died alone on the bank of a river, with nothing but angels and demons around him, warring for his soul.

He was just starting to turn away when he heard a shout from the back of the room. He looked sharply as he saw Eppie Orlowe emerge from what looked like the kitchen, carrying a flaming dessert of some sort. She shot a grin at the back corner.

Harlan followed her gaze, and then he saw her. *Emma Larson*. His breath caught at the sight of her, hungrily drinking her in. Her face was drawn and haunted, her cheeks too hollow. Protectiveness surged through him and he gripped the window frame. What was wrong with her? Her hair, that gorgeous blond hair, was curling around her neck, softening her face, but the shadows were still in her eyes.

Two years ago, he'd been there the first day she'd walked into Wright's General Store after being away for half a decade. Everyone in the store had leapt up, welcoming her back to town, but he'd seen the depth of suffering in those green eyes, and he'd seen the effort it had taken for her to graciously accept all the attention. But gracious she'd been, reaching out with warmth to all, despite the weight in her soul. She had been haunted by something, and even now she still carried it with her. Harlan saw her grief, he felt her struggle. He wanted to reach out to her, to tell her that someone understood, but she'd never looked in his direction.

Of course she wouldn't. Emma Larson was purity at its best. Her smile was always kind. She was always there with a hug for anyone who needed it. She had a softness, a vulnerability to her spirit that called to Harlan, that made him want to get down on his knees and beg her to share it with him, to show him what it was like to have one minute, one second, of that kind of beauty in his life.

Not that he'd ever do it. He would never contaminate Emma with who he was. Ever.

Then a man, a tall, big man walked over to her, carrying a glass of champagne. Emma started with obvious nervousness, and Harlan fisted his hands, moving closer to the window. Who was he? What was he doing with Emma? The man was too strong, too dangerous for Emma. He'd crush her. What the hell? Why wasn't anyone in there looking out for her?

Harlan glanced around the room. Astrid was still engaged with Jason and the kid. Clare was talking to Eppie. No one was watching out for Emma. Shit. It was up to Harlan to go in there and run interference for her—

He looked back at her, but she was gone.

Harlan stopped, his hand halfway to the doorknob. Emma was no longer in the living room. The behemoth who'd been bugging her was still there, now being cornered by Eppie. Where was Emma?

Harlan dropped his hand from the doorknob, a sudden sense of loss assaulting him at the disappearance of Emma. Shit. What had he been thinking, rushing in there like some ass to save a damsel in distress, who clearly was capable of extricating herself from a situation she didn't like?

He had no role here. He was done. It was time to go back to his life.

∿

EMMA HURRIED down the back steps of Astrid's house, desperate to get away from the party. She could barely breathe, and her chest hurt. She just needed a minute to regroup, to find her space. Ditching her sandals by the pot of pink geraniums at the foot of the deck stairs, she jogged down the cobblestone path toward the lake and into the merciful silence of nature.

Clouds were thick in the sky, blocking the moon. The lake and the woods were dark, swallowing up light and life, like a soothing blanket of nothingness coating the night. She needed to get away from the world she didn't belong to, the one that had no place for her. Tears were thick in her throat, her eyes stinging as she ran. The stones were wet from the rain earlier in the day, and the cool dampness sent chills through her.

She reached the dock and leapt out on the damp wood. Her foot slipped, and she yelped as she lost her balance—

Strong hands shot out and grabbed her around the waist, catching her before she fell into the water. Shrieking in surprise, she jerked free, twisting out of range. The evasive move sent her off balance again, her feet went out from under her, and she was falling—

And again, someone grabbed her. "Hey," a low voice said. "I'm not going to hurt you."

Emma froze at the sound of the voice she knew so well, the one that had haunted her for so many sleepless nights. The voice she thought she'd never hear again, because he'd been gone for so long. "Harlan?"

"Yeah."

Emma spun around in his grasp, and her breath caught as she saw his shadowed face. His eyes were dark and hooded in the filtered light, his cheekbones more prominent than they had been the last time she'd seen him. Heavy stubble framed his face, and his hair was long and ragged around the base of his neck. He was leaner than she remembered, but his muscles were more defined, straining at his tee shirt. He looked grungy and real, a man who lived by the earth every day of his life. He exuded pure strength and a raw appeal that ignited something deep within her. She instinctively leaned toward him, into the strength that emanated from him. His hands felt hot and invasive where they clasped her hips, but she had no urge to push him away.

Damn him. After not seeing him for a year, he still affected her beyond reason.

"You're back," she managed.

"Yeah."

Again, the one word answer. He had never said much more than that to her, but she'd seen him watching her intently on countless occasions, his piercing blue eyes roiling with so much unspoken emotion and turbulence. She managed a smile, trying to hide the intensity of her reaction to seeing him. "Astrid didn't mention you would be here."

"She doesn't know." Again, he fell silent, but he raised one hand and lifted a lock of her hair, thumbing it gently. "Like silk," he said softly. "Just as I always thought it would feel."

Her heart began to pound now. There was no way to stop it, not when she was so close to him, not when she could feel his hands on her, a touch she'd craved since the first time she'd seen him. It had been two years ago, the day she'd walked back into her life in Birch Crossing. He had been leaning against the deli counter in Wright's, his arms folded over his chest, his blue eyes watching so intently.

And now he was here, in these woods, holding onto her.

His grip was strong, but his touch was gentle in her hair as he filtered the strands through his fingers. "You've thought about my hair before?" she asked. Ridiculous question, but it tumbled out anyway. And she wanted to know. Had he really thought about her before? Was she not alone in the way her mind had wandered to him so many nights when she hadn't been able to sleep?

His gaze met hers, and for a second, heat seemed to explode between them. Then he dropped his hands from her

23

and stepped back. The loss of his touch was like ice cold water drenching her, and she had to hug herself to keep from reaching out for him.

"Tell Astrid I was here," he said. "I'm leaving again—"

"What?" She couldn't hold back the protest. "Already? Why?"

"I have a job."

That job. That mysterious job. He had never told Astrid, or anyone else in town, where he went when he disappeared. Sometimes, he was in town for months, playing at his real estate business, taking off for only a few days at a time. Other times, he was absent for longer. This last time, he'd been gone for almost a year, which was the longest that anyone could remember him being out of town. And he was leaving again already? "Astrid misses you," Emma said quickly, instinctively trying to give him a reason not to disappear again. "You can't leave without saying hi."

Harlan's gaze flicked to the house, and his mouth tightened. He made no move to join the celebration, and suddenly she realized that he felt the same way she did about invading that happy little world. He didn't belong to it any more than she did. Empathy tightened her chest, and she looked more carefully at the independent man that no one in town had ever been able to get close to. "You can stop by and see her tomorrow," she said softly.

He didn't move, and he didn't take his eyes off the house. "She's happy? Jason's good to her?"

Emma nodded. "He treasures her. They're so in love." She couldn't quite keep the ache out of her voice, and she saw Harlan look sharply at her.

"What's wrong?" he asked. "Why did you say it like that?"

"No, no, they're great. Really." She swallowed and pulled back her shoulders, refusing to let herself yearn for that which she did not want or need in her life. "She would kill me

24

if she found out I let you leave town without seeing her. How long do you have until you have to go?"

He shifted. "Forty-eight hours." The confession was reluctant, as if he hadn't wanted to reveal it.

"So, then, come back here tomorrow and see her," she said, relief rushing through her at the thought he wasn't leaving town immediately. For at least two nights, she could sleep knowing that he was breathing the same air as she was.

"No, not here." He ran his hand through his hair, and she saw a dark bruise on the underside of his triceps. "You guys still go to Wright's in the morning for coffee?"

Emma's heart fluttered at his question. For a man who had held himself aloof, he seemed endearingly aware of what his sister did every day...and he knew that she was always there as well. "Yes. We'll be there at eight thirty."

He nodded. "Yeah, okay, I'll try to make it then." He glanced at her again, and just like before, heat seemed to rush through her—

Then he turned away, stealing that warmth from her before she'd had time to finish savoring it. "No." She grabbed his arm, her fingers sliding over his hard muscles. Shocked by the feel of his body, she jerked her hand back, but not soon enough.

He froze under her touch, sucking in his breath. Slowly, he turned his head to look back at her. "No?"

"Don't *try* to make it tomorrow morning," she said quickly, trying to pretend her panic had been on Astrid's behalf, not her own. "You *have* to make it. Astrid needs to see you. She wants you to meet Rosie. She's happy, Harlan, but she needs her brother, too. Jason is her family, but so are you, and you know how she needs to be connected."

Harlan closed his eyes for a long moment, and she saw emotions warring within him. For a man so stoic and aloof, he was fermenting with emotions in a way that she'd never seen before. She looked again at the bruise on his arm. "Are you okay, Harlan? What happened to you while you were gone?" There was no way to keep the concern out of her voice, no way to hide that her heart ached at the thought of him being hurt.

His eyes opened again. He said nothing, but he suddenly wrapped his hand around the back of her neck.

She stiffened, her heart pounding as he drew her close to him. "What are you doing?"

"I need this." Then he captured her mouth with his.

She had no time to be afraid, no time to fear. His kiss was too desperate for her to be afraid. It wasn't a kiss to seduce or dominate. It was a burning, aching need for connection, for humanity, for something to chase away the darkness haunting him...everything she needed in a kiss as well.

Her hands went to his chest, bracing, protecting, but at the same time, connecting. She kissed him back, needing the same touch that he did, desperate for that feeling of being wanted. She didn't know this man, and yet, on some levels, she'd known him for so long. She'd seen his torment, she'd felt his isolation, and she'd witnessed his unfailing need to protect Astrid, even if he had never inserted himself fully into her life.

Somehow, Harlan's kiss wasn't a threat the way other men's were. He was leaving town, so he was no more than a shadow that would ease into her life and then disappear. He wouldn't try to take her, to trick her, to consume her. He wouldn't make promises and then betray them. All he wanted was the same thing she did, a break from the isolation that locked him down, a fragile whisper of human connection to fill the gaping hole in his heart.

"Emma!" Astrid's voice rang out in the night, shattering the moment. "Are you out here?"

Harlan broke the kiss, but he didn't move away, keeping

his lips against hers. One of his hands was tangled lightly in her hair, the other was locked around her waist. Somehow, he'd pulled them together, until her breasts were against his chest, their bodies melted together. It felt so right, but at the same time, a familiar anxiety began to build inside Emma at the intimacy.

"Do not fear me, sweet Emma," Harlan whispered against her lips. "I would only treasure what you give."

His voice was so soft and tender that her throat tightened. How she'd yearned for so many years, for a lifetime, for someone to speak to her like that...until she'd finally become smart enough to relinquish that dream. And now, here it was, in the form of a man who would disappear from her life in forty-eight hours, maybe never to return. Which was why it was okay, because she didn't have to worry that he would want more than she could give, or that she would give him more than she could afford. Maybe she didn't belong in the room of couples and families, but for this brief moment, she belonged out in the night, with a man who lived the same existence that she did.

"Emma?" Astrid's footsteps sounded on the deck, and Harlan released her.

"Don't tell her I was here," he said. "I'll come by Wright's in the morning. Now is not the time." Then, without a sound, he faded into the darkness, vanishing so quickly she almost wondered if she'd imagined him.

"Emma!"

"I'm on the dock," Emma called out. She ran her fingers over her lips, and then hurried up the path, heading toward the party that had driven her out only moments earlier. But as she emerged from the shadows and waved to Astrid, she didn't feel quite as desolate as she had before, her mouth still tingling from the first kiss she'd had in a very long time.

Harlan Shea was back in town. For forty-eight hours. No longer.

She wasn't ready for a man. She wasn't ready to date. She wouldn't *ever* be ready for a man again, but Harlan wasn't going to stay around long enough to threaten her. He'd kissed her in a moment when they'd both needed it.

That was all.

Nothing more.

But as she hurried up the steps to head back to her party, she couldn't help but think about the fact she was going to see him in the morning. Nerves assaulted her at the idea of seeing him again, and she stumbled on the top step. The man was leaving town. There was no reason to clutter her memories of that kiss with an awkward morning after. Maybe she would skip out on the coffee.

No. She wasn't that pathetic. The man had kissed her, a kiss that had been so beautiful she'd forgotten to be afraid. There was no way she was going to miss the chance to see him in the morning.

Absolutely no way.

CHAPTER THREE

AT EIGHT TWENTY-FIVE the next morning, Harlan was
leaning on the hood of his truck, watching people go in and
out of Wright's General Store, a classic old New England
building with white boards, green shutters, and a rambling
front porch. Many of the patrons were people he knew, but
there was also a large segment of unknowns. Their nice cars
and well-matched outfits told him they were summer folk,
here to steal time with nature and hand over their dollars to
the locals.

He'd parked across the street, keeping his truck out of
sight of the windows in case Astrid was sitting by them, not
wanting to be drawn into the reunion before he was ready.
He'd pulled his black cap low over his head, and he knew that
his overgrown hair and beard would hide him well. Usually,
coming back to Birch Crossing was a relief, a welcome
respite, but today he felt restless and unsettled, not ready to
walk in there and be assaulted by twenty townspeople
wanting to know where he'd been for the last year.

Last night at Astrid's had made him realize he didn't fit in
here anymore, if he ever had.

And then... Emma... For the hundredth time, he replayed that kiss in his mind. Why had he kissed her? He'd fantasized about it often since the day he'd first seen her, but he'd never even considered approaching her.

But last night, when she'd been so close, her troubled green eyes staring up at him with such emotion, he'd been lost. He'd been utterly consumed by her gaze. He'd come back to town for Astrid, but after that kiss, he didn't want it to be Astrid who would notice when he died.

He wanted it to be Emma.

Hell. That was a damned dangerous way to be thinking. He wasn't doing that, he wasn't going to pretend he could play this game anymore. He needed to get out of town—

"Harlan?"

Swearing, he looked up. Walking toward him was Jackson Reed, one of the few men in town that he could call a friend. Jackson broke into a huge grin. "Hey, man, it's been too damn long. Good to see you."

Harlan relaxed and grinned, the familiar face restoring his ease. Jackson was a good guy, a man with enough shadows in his past not to be bothered by Harlan's reclusiveness. He suspected, on some level neither of them mentioned, they got each other. "Yeah, it's good to be back."

"You going in for coffee?" Jackson asked.

Harlan glanced at the store, and sudden resolution filled him. He could talk to Astrid for five minutes to reassure himself that she really was in a good place, and then say good-bye, releasing her from any obligation to worry about him. Then, he would be cleared to move on and stop fixating on her, this town...and Emma. He needed to cut his ties and get out. He shoved himself off his truck. "Yeah, you?"

"You bet. Can't start the morning without some Wright's coffee."

Harlan fell in beside Jackson as the other man headed up

the steps to Wright's. Last time he'd been in town, Jackson's wife had been pregnant. "How's Trish? The baby?"

Jackson beamed at him. "I haven't slept through the night in eight months, but I gotta admit that it's been the best damn time of my life."

Harlan couldn't help grinning back. The dude looked so damned happy. "That's great."

"Yeah." Jackson grabbed the front door of Wright's. "Trish is pregnant again. I need a bigger house. Can you find one for me? You know my budget."

Harlan's smile faded. "Sorry, man. I'm only in town for two days."

"You can find me one in two days. You always do." Jackson opened the door. "Harlan's back," he yelled into the store.

Harlan barely suppressed a grimace as the place erupted. Hands slammed down on his shoulders, people asking where he'd been, reporting on the state of his cabin, which the townspeople had taken upon themselves to keep up. Apparently, they had plowed him out all winter and even picked the lock to turn off his water so his pipes wouldn't freeze. All that well-meaning gossip and attention that proved he had no privacy in this town.

When had he lost his privacy here? He'd moved to Birch Crossing because no one knew him, and no one knew his past. This was the place he came to when he didn't want to be who he was, when he wanted people to look at him and see something that he wasn't. A nice guy. A guy who would get you the house of your dreams. A man who didn't have the blood of a thousand people on his hands.

But now he felt like being here was a lie, and he didn't feel comfortable anymore. Managing affable smiles with the crowd, he looked over their heads to the corner.

The table where his sister and her friends usually sat was

empty. No Astrid. No Clare. And no Emma. Disappointment surged through him, a feeling of infinite loss.

"Harlan Shea, you look too damned thin." Ophelia Wright, the wife of the former proprietor of the store, strode up to him, carrying a cup of coffee and one of her famous blueberry muffins. She was wearing a black blouse and her gray hair had gotten longer, tied up in a hairdo that looked a little fancier than she used to wear. A scarf was woven into her hair, which he suspected was Astrid's touch. "I'm whipping up your favorite omelet, so you have a seat. Your sister will be along shortly. She's always late now that little Rosie slows her down." Ophelia gave him a gentle shove toward the empty table, and Harlan let her push him.

He eased down into the seat, gripping the cup of coffee as he took a gulp. Straight black with a shot of something stiffer. He almost spit it out when he realized Ophelia had spiked it. He glanced back at Ophelia who gave him a thumbs up. "You look like you needed it," she said cheerfully.

Yeah, he did, but even he had limits. Eight-thirty in the morning did not go with whiskey—

"Harlan?" Astrid's startled voice interrupted his thoughts.

He spun around. She was standing at the front door, a look of absolute shock on her face. Her hair was tumbling down around her shoulders, her eyes were bright, and her skin was flushed with energy. She looked alive and vibrant, albeit somewhat startled to see him. Her baby was asleep against her chest, a tiny little thing that was too damned small to survive in this world.

He stood up. "Hey."

"Harlan!" Astrid hurried across the room toward him, her free arm held high for a hug. The hug was awkward, something they hadn't done much of, and she stepped back, her face was a little wary. "Welcome back."

"Yeah, thanks." For a moment, they sort of looked at each other, and then Harlan pulled out a chair. "Have a seat."

"Okay." Astrid sat down across from him, her dark brown eyes studying him. "Where have you been? It's been almost a year. I've sent you emails and—"

"I know. I got them. Sorry I didn't reply." He sat down across from her, suddenly wishing he hadn't come back. "I was caught up in stuff."

"In *what*?" She leaned forward, her hand cupping the back of the baby's head, the heart-shaped pendant of her blown-glass necklace brushing gently against the baby's shoulder. "What could possibly be so important that you couldn't send even a two-word reply to me? I thought you were dead."

Harlan shifted restlessly. Three years ago, Astrid had reached out to him when she'd been in a desperate place. He'd bailed her out and brought her to Birch Crossing, but before that day, he'd met her only twice before. They had the same mother, but Harlan had grown up with his dad with no memory of the woman who had been his mother as a baby. She'd abandoned him, and he'd been fine with leaving her behind, until he'd been contacted by a teenage Astrid claiming to be his little sister, making him realize that he'd left behind a sister who'd had no one to protect her from the life their mother had thrust upon her. He still didn't know how to be a brother to her, to offer her the family she'd wanted so badly, but he'd done all he knew how to do. "Yeah, well, about that—"

"Harlan!" Clare Gray sat down at the table. No, he reminded himself. It was Clare Friesé now that she'd gotten married. She was wearing a tee shirt that boasted the name of her new cupcake shop, and she was wearing silver earrings that had Astrid's signature flair to them. He liked seeing Astrid's touch on so many people. It meant that his sister was connecting with the town, that she'd found her place. "I can't believe you're back. It's good to see you."

Harlan nodded at Clare. "Yeah, you look good, Clare."

She smiled, her face positively glowing. "Thanks. You, however, look like you were dragged under a truck for about twenty miles and then spit out to crawl back here."

Harlan ground his jaw at her honest assessment of him, keenly aware of how he didn't fit into this small town where everyone was considered family, even if they were almost strangers. Why had he ever thought he could play this game? He felt rough and dirty. "Yeah, well, that's what I do in my free time, so it makes sense."

Clare raised her eyebrows. "Do you now? That's the glamorous job you've been hiding from us all this time?"

"Yeah, of course." He looked back at Astrid, who was still watching him. "You happy, sis?"

A smile broke out over her face, and she nodded. "So happy, Harlan." She turned the baby so he could see her better. "Her name is Rosie. I named her after Mom. Isn't she beautiful?"

Harlan leaned forward, studying the tiny face. Her little hands were balled into fists, and her eyes were tightly shut. She didn't have much hair, but he could already tell that the auburn wisps were going to match Astrid's. She was wearing a light green tee shirt and matching sweatpants, like she was ready to go play soccer for a team of green beans. "She's really small. Is she okay?"

Astrid smiled. "She's completely healthy. This is how small babies are, Harlan."

"Oh." He examined the baby more carefully. Her hands were clenched, but he counted the right number of fingers, so that was good.

"She's your niece," Astrid said softly. "Rosie, that's your uncle Harlan."

Uncle? Unexpectedly, something seemed to tighten in his chest. "Are they always that quiet?"

Astrid laughed. "She's still asleep, so she's quiet. When she wakes up, she'll be plenty loud." She held her up. "Do you want to hold her?"

Harlan sat back quickly, fisting his hands. "No. I'll hurt her."

His sister rolled her eyes. "You won't hurt her—"

"No." He folded his arms over his chest. "How's Jason? Is he good to you?"

Astrid sighed and tucked Rosie against her chest again. "Of course he is. He doesn't even hold any grudges against you for when you punched him."

Harlan ran his hand through his hair, remembering all too well the incident that had driven him to leave town for this last trip, the one that had reminded him of who he really was. "Yeah, well, that's good, I guess."

"Do you want to come for dinner tonight? You can meet him properly."

Harlan thought of the beautiful house that his little sister had made her home, and he knew he had no place in it. He'd helped her find her place and her safety, and now he needed to step away so she could go forward with the life she wanted. "No, I have some things I need to take care of."

Her brow furrowed. "You do? What kind of things?"

Harlan leaned forward, suddenly knowing what he had to do. He couldn't dump his life on her and tell her that he was going to get himself killed one of these days, and he wanted her permission to list her as next of kin. How could he bring that into her life? She'd been through so much. So, he simply said. "Some work stuff."

She sat up quickly. "You aren't leaving again, are you? Not so soon?"

He opened his mouth to answer her, then shut it when he

saw the anguish in her eyes. How could he do that to her? Tell her that he wasn't coming back? He couldn't. He would just drift away, easing seamlessly out of her life without causing her any more anguish. She was good now. She had the life he wanted for her. She was all set. It was time to free her. "You turned out good, sis. I'm really glad you found Jason." He touched her cheek with his hand. "I gotta go. I'll...I'll be in touch." Then he turned and strode out without looking back. He couldn't look back. If he did, he would never do what was right.

But it was hard as hell, harder than he'd expected it to be, to walk out the door of Wright's and free his sister and this town from who he was.

It wasn't until he got back in his truck and was halfway to his cabin that he realized Emma had never arrived for breakfast. He wasn't going to see her again before he left.

Suddenly, his bad mood got even darker.

MATTIE WILLIAMS WASN'T in class.

The five-year-old's empty seat haunted Emma for the entire two hours, though no doubt her mood wasn't helped by the fact she couldn't help thinking of the fact she'd skipped out on morning coffee to avoid Harlan. She'd wanted to go so she could see him, but the intensity of her need to see him had convinced her that she was already getting in way too deep, so she'd headed in early to work, and regretting the decision every moment since.

Emma sighed as she looked again at Mattie's empty seat. Although her day job was a curator at an art museum, Emma volunteered as an art teacher on Monday afternoons at a local youth center in Portland, Maine. In the ten months since Emma had picked up the class when the previous teacher had decided she didn't have time, little Mattie had never missed the class. Not once. Even when she broke her arm. Even when her mother had finally died after a long illness. Even the day that her brother had run away.

Even on the days when tears streaked her cheeks and her pigtails looked like no one had combed them in weeks, Mattie was always there, her canvas bag of markers and paper that Emma had given her clutched tightly in her little fist. Every time she slipped in the door, her dark brown eyes would hungrily search out Emma as she crept to her seat at the front of the room directly in front of Emma's desk.

But today, she wasn't there, and Emma couldn't think of a single reason for Mattie's absence that didn't scare her to death.

The minute the last child left, Emma grabbed her phone out of her bag and dialed Chloe Dalton, the social worker who had been assigned to Mattie.

Chloe answered on the first ring. "Em! How was your weekend? I have to tell you—"

"Where's Mattie?"

"Mattie?" Chloe repeated. "What do you mean? Wasn't she in class today?"

"No. Where is she? Did she—" Emma's voice tightened up and she had to clear her throat. "She didn't leave, did she? To South Carolina?" Ever since Mattie's mother had died, her grandparents in South Carolina had been trying to gain custody of Mattie and her brother, Robbie. Emma had heard stories from Mattie about trips to her grandparents, stories that still haunted her, as well as the little girl, and she prayed that Mattie wouldn't end up there.

"No, no, she's still in town. She's in a foster home—"

"Foster home?" Emma gripped the phone more tightly. "Why?"

"Her aunt and uncle ran into some issues and can't have

her in the house anymore. The foster home is just temporary until her future gets sorted out—"

"Where's the house? What's the address?"

Chloe hesitated. "Emma, I can't give out that info—"

"Chloe! What if she's in trouble? She never misses class, and you know it."

The social worker sighed. "Okay, look, I can meet you there in twenty minutes. Don't go in until I get there, okay?"

"Fine." Emma jotted down the address, and then was in her car two minutes later, her heart pounding. Something was wrong. Mattie was in trouble, she was sure of it.

When she reached the address eight minutes later, her heart froze. Sitting on a narrow ledge on the third story roof of the multi-family house was Mattie. A woman was leaning out a dormer, apparently talking to her, but every time she leaned out, Mattie scooted further away...and closer to the edge. "Oh, dear God."

Emma leapt out of the car and raced up the steps. "Mattie," she shouted. "Mattie, it's me. Don't go anywhere, I'm coming up!" Without even knocking, she yanked open the screen door and ran for the stairs, her feet pounding as she raced upstairs in what felt like the longest run of her life.

At the third floor, it took an agonizingly long minute for her to find the room with the open window, but at last she saw the woman leaning out. Emma sprinted over to it and shoved her shoulders out the window, not even looking at the woman. "Mattie." The word croaked in her throat when she saw the bony shoulders hunched over, her thin arms hugging her knees. "Mattie, sweetie, it's Emma."

Mattie's face was buried in her knees, the thick braids of her kinky hair dangling by her ears. She didn't move.

"Mattie," Emma tried again. "Look at me, sweetie."

Again, no response.

"She won't say anything," the woman said. Her brown hair

was slightly messy, and the lines on her face spoke of a life of too much struggle, though her eyes were kind. "I'm afraid to go out there and get her. I don't want to startle her into falling."

Emma glanced down at the ground so far away, and her stomach lurched. "I'll go." Without hesitating, she hoisted herself up on the windowsill and swung her legs over the ledge. "Mattie, hon, I'm going to come out there and sit with you, okay?"

Mattie didn't move, but she didn't jerk away either.

Holding her breath, Emma inched along the roof, along the ledge that was barely two feet wide. She reached Mattie and sat next to her. She wanted to grab her, hug her, and pull her to safety, but she didn't dare move, terrified she would spook the little girl.

For a long moment, neither of them spoke. Emma's heart was thudding painfully in her chest, she was so terrified of saying the wrong thing and spooking Mattie. "I missed you in class today," she said finally. "We did clay butterflies."

Mattie didn't lift her head.

"I painted one purple with pink sparkles," Emma added, gesturing at the woman not to come out. "I named it Tom."

"Tom is a boy's name," Mattie said quietly.

Relief rushed through Emma when she heard Mattie's voice. "He's a boy who likes pink sparkles."

"Boys don't like pink."

"Tom does."

"Tom must be a girl."

Emma smiled. "He might be. I didn't actually ask him."

Mattie finally looked up, and Emma's heart broke at the anguish in the little girl's eyes. Streaks of tears had dried in rivulets on her light brown cheeks. "You should have asked," Mattie said. "Butterflies like to be asked."

Emma nodded. "You're right. I'll ask him when I go back

to the center." She raised her brows. "Unless you want to talk to him?"

Mattie looked at Emma. "I don't want to go live with Grammy and Pappy," she whispered. "But since Aunt Lucy and Uncle Roger can't keep me, they might make me go."

Emma's heart tightened. "No one is going to send you to South Carolina—"

"They will. I heard Chloe talking about it."

"She was?" Emma had heard enough about the grandparents to know that wasn't a place for a child. Pappy had a temper that terrified Mattie, and Grammy wasn't any better. Emma struggled to keep her voice calm. "Oh, sweetie, it will work out—"

"How? How will it work out?" Mattie lowered her voice to a whisper. "I hate it there. They ignore me. It's like I'm invisible. Like a ghost they can't see. One day, I sat in the barn for a whole day to see if anyone would look for me, but no one did. I even slept there, and my skin hurt from the hay prickles in the morning. No one came to find me until my mom came back from work in the morning. She cared, but she's dead. No one thinks it matters that I'm like a ghost, or that it's a bad thing. But it is."

Emma felt like her own heart was going to fragment. "I know it is," she said. "I was ignored when I was a child, too. It makes you feel like your heart is breaking every minute of every day."

Mattie stared at her. "Yes," she whispered. "Exactly like that. Who ignored you?"

"My parents." It wasn't simply being ignored. It had been so much more than that, but that was as far as she would take it with Mattie, though she knew that Mattie was dealing with far more than being ignored as well. Mattie was facing longings that Emma's arid childhood had evoked in her, the ones that had led her into a marriage she thought would save her.

Instead, the marriage that she'd thought would be her salvation had destroyed her...but at the same time, it had also finally given her the courage to not need anyone anymore. Not a marriage, not a man—

Her mind involuntarily flashed back to the previous night, to the encounter with Harlan. To his kiss. The haunting of his dark eyes. The depth of his pain.

She immediately cut herself off from thinking about him. There was no space in her life for a man, for anyone who would betray her, the same way that life was betraying Mattie. She managed a smile. "It doesn't matter what other people think, Mattie. Ignore the ones who don't believe in you, and pay attention to the people that do care. Like me." Her voice thickened ever so slightly, and she had to clear her throat. "You matter to me."

A small smile played at the corner of Mattie's mouth. "I do?"

"Of course you do."

"Pinkie swear?"

Emma laughed and held up her hand. "Pinkie swear." They locked pinkies, and then Emma pulled Mattie into her arms, giving her a hug. "Now, will you please do me a favor and come inside so I can stop worrying that you're going to fall on your bum and squish all the flowers in the yard?" Or crack her head open, but she didn't want to put that out there.

Mattie squinted at her. "There are no flowers in the yard."

Emma grinned. "Then we should plant some."

"I don't live here. I don't want to plant any." She looked at Emma. "Can I go visit you? Can we plant some there? You always talk about how pretty the lake is. I want to go there."

Down below, Chloe's car pulled in, and Emma grimaced, hoping she wasn't going to get Chloe in trouble for giving

Emma the address. "I'll talk to Chloe and see what we can work out, okay?"

"Promise?" Mattie gave her a solemn look.

Emma knew that a broken promise would not do her any favors. Broken promises were cruel beyond words, the instruments to broken dreams and shattered hearts. "I promise I will do everything I can, Mattie."

An understanding too mature for a five-year-old settled in Mattie's dark eyes. "Okay." But there was a flatness to Mattie's tone as she stood up and walked back toward the window, and Emma knew that Mattie didn't believe the world would offer her good things anymore.

Emma scrambled to her feet and hurried after her, catching her hand and holding it tightly as Mattie carefully scooted her dirty pink sneakers along the ledge. Emma remembered when those sneakers had been new, the last present Mattie's mom had given her.

Now they were dirty, tearing at the seams. The laces were frayed, the shoes most likely too small, and yet Mattie wore them every single day. To Mattie, they were the last thing she had to cling to, the last breath of life as she wanted it to be.

Dirty, worn shoes were all Mattie had to hold her tiny, fragile heart together, and Emma knew from her own experience that it wouldn't be enough. There had to be something she could do to help Mattie, to make her life turn out differently than Emma's had. She had to find a way to give Mattie something real to believe in, something more viable than an elusive and hopeless kiss stolen on a dark night with a man who was nothing more than a passing shadow slipping through her fingers.

CHAPTER FOUR

EMMA CORNERED Chloe the moment the social worker returned to her car, after she'd settled Mattie back inside and talked with the foster mom. "Mattie says you're going to send her to South Carolina," Emma said.

Chloe sighed and pushed her dark hair back from her face. She was wearing jeans and a tee shirt, indicating that she'd been in the middle of something unrelated to work when Emma had called, which was unusual given that it was still early in the afternoon on a weekday. Chloe was relentless in her job. "It's looking possible. Her uncle just got arrested again, and her aunt hasn't shown up for work in three days. The judge doesn't want her there."

Emma glanced back at the house with the peeling paint and crooked shutters. "She can't go to South Carolina. Her grandparents aren't good people—"

"They're better than her aunt and uncle, and that's all she's got."

"Well, it's not enough! They aren't even capable of keeping track of her! Did she tell you how she spent the night in the barn and no one even noticed?"

Chloe grimaced. "I know. We had the social worker down there evaluate them." She sighed. "I'll admit, Em, that there are significant issues with them, but trust me that when I say that they're still better than a foster home."

Emma felt a chill go through her. "What issues? What *else* is the matter with them?" Dear God, what were they going to send Mattie to? Being ignored was bad enough, but what hadn't the five-year-old shared, or possibly even realized, about her grandparents?

But Chloe shook her head. "It's confidential, Em. You know I can't say, but know that if she goes there, a social worker will visit regularly to make sure she's...safe."

"Safe? *Safe?* You have to check on them to make sure she's even *safe*?" Where did loved and nurtured fall under that low standard? "There has to be someone else in the family—"

"There isn't," Chloe said, looking tired. "It sucks, but at least she has relatives willing to take her in. Otherwise, she'd be in foster care for good."

Emma tried to imagine the little girl so far away, hiding in that barn from people who ignored her. Her hands started to shake and a cold chill settled in her bones. "She can't go to South Carolina."

"Well, what do you suggest? You want to take her?"

Emma stared at Chloe in shock. "What?"

"Never mind." Chloe pulled open the door of her rusting Volkswagen. "I need to go—"

"No, wait." Emma grabbed the frame of her door. "Could I foster Mattie? Or even...adopt her?" The words tumbled out before she even meant to say them. The idea was terrifying, but at the same time, it felt right, so right. If she could help her—

Chloe sighed. "Emma, you're freaking out right now, but it's all going to work out—"

Emma gripped the car door. "I'm serious. Could I?"

44

Chloe's eyes narrowed. "Emma, first of all, Mattie has two sets of relatives willing to take her. You're not related, and you're not even married anymore. You've known her for less than a year. No judge is going to think a single, unrelated woman is a better option for her than family."

"But her family sucks."

"It's the way it is," Chloe said, her voice softening. "I know it's hard, but Mattie is luckier than some kids who lose their parents."

Emma looked up at the house and saw Mattie's face appear in one of the third floor windows, watching her. In that window, she looked so tiny and alone, a little girl completely lost. God, how many times had Emma done the same thing? Sat in the window and wished for something to be different? Emma felt her heart start to break again. "Can I at least foster her instead of this family? Or take her for a weekend?"

"Don't do it."

Emma stared at Chloe. "Why not?"

"Because Mattie doesn't need her heart broken again. If she gets too attached to you, it's one more loss she will have to suffer when she loses you."

"She won't lose me—"

"No?" Chloe tossed her purse onto the front seat. "Are you going to move to rural South Carolina to hang out with her when she gets placed with her grandparents?"

Emma's throat tightened. "Just one weekend. Just to give her a break. Birch Crossing's summer festival is coming up and she'd love it—"

"Don't do that to her, Emma. It's not fair to her to bring her into your world just because you're lonely."

"I'm not doing this for me. I'm not lonely—"

Chloe gave her a penetrating look as she slid into the driver's seat. "You just got divorced yesterday. Your dreams are shattered. You're reeling, I know you are." She managed a grim smile. "Trust me, I know. You're in no place to make decisions like this. You're not going to be able to adopt her, so don't try to foster her. Seriously. Be Mattie's friend, but you need to let her deal with her own life or she won't be strong enough to cope with it." She turned on the car. "I need to go." She pushed a tangled strand of brown hair off her face, and Emma suddenly noticed how tired Chloe looked.

"You okay?" she asked.

Chloe hesitated, then shrugged. "No time for anything but to be okay, right?"

It was a lie. Something was seriously wrong with her friend. Emma put her hand on the door as Chloe shifted into drive. "Want to get a drink one night this week? Girl time?"

"I can't. I have some stuff I need to deal with." Chloe glanced back at the house and waved to Mattie, who was still watching them. "A heart can be broken only so many times," she said softly. "Don't break hers again, Emma. It's not fair."

Emma closed her eyes. "I would never break her heart."

"Not on purpose, no, but by accident? It's very possible. There's not much holding her together right now." Chloe waved her back so she could close the door. "Go home, Emma. Give yourself a break."

Then she shut the door and drove off, leaving Emma on the sidewalk.

For a long moment, she could only stand there watching Mattie in the window of that huge house, until her mind no longer saw a little brown face with dark pigtails, but a blond-haired, green-eyed girl whose spirit was breaking day by day, night by night...the girl she had once been...

Tears burned her eyes, and with a small wave at Mattie, Emma turned away.

THE GRIEF WOULD NOT STOP.

It was long past midnight, and the tears would not stop flowing. Emma wrapped the blanket more tightly around herself, as if the weight of the wool would stop the chills from digging in deeper.

The moon was bright on the water, and her rickety dock was hard beneath her butt, which was numb from over two hours of sitting on the bare wood, but still she didn't move. What had all this been for? Five years of marriage, two years of hell trying to get out of it, and then today's terrible day with Mattie...

Isolation pressed down upon her. Failure. A sense of hopelessness. Fresh tears streamed free, and all the recent years of trying to be strong seemed to be nothing more than a great joke on her. It was too hard, seeing her friends moving into their roles as wives and mothers. How hard she'd tried to find that, how hard she'd fought in her marriage, only to have it spoil and fester in ways she could never have conceived of.

Her prince, the man who had swept her out of her life and thrust her into a fairytale, had been nothing but a monster who had nearly destroyed her. Chloe was right. There was no joy in knowing that her marriage was finally over. It was just a sense of loss. Of failure. A grim truth of what life was really like. It hadn't felt real these last two years while she'd been going through the divorce. Too much battling, too much confrontation, too much survival just to get through each day.

But now that the fight was over, she felt like she'd been left drained and exhausted on a patch of mud, with no strength or will left to pick up and start over with. And Mattie, her dear, sweet Mattie. Looking at her with those troubled eyes when no one else could reach her. How could she have let her down like that? How—

The low rumble of a motorboat engine penetrated her

thoughts. Startled, she looked up as the red bow light of a boat moved slowly toward her dock in the darkness. For a split second, she didn't move, too shocked by the sudden flashback to the night eight years ago when Preston Hayes, the out-of-town summer resident she'd had a crush on for years, had picked her up at the town dock on their first date, sweeping her off for a night on an island that had cemented her as his.

"Emma?" Harlan's low voice drifted over the water, and sudden electricity flooded her.

She lurched to her feet, her heart hammering as she saw his broad silhouette guiding the boat right toward her.

SHE WAS like an angel in the night.

Harlan couldn't take his gaze off Emma as he cut the engine, letting his boat drift in toward her dock. He'd been out for one last tour of the lake, one last night to remember the town that he'd made his home for the last five years. He'd expected to feel relief, but he hadn't. He'd felt strangely melancholy, as if he was leaving before he was supposed to. Instinct had taken him past Emma's small cabin, as he'd done on so many other sleepless nights.

This time, for the first time in two years, she'd been outside, even though it was past midnight. The way she'd been huddled up in that huge blanket had caught his attention, as if she were a broken bird stranded on land. He hadn't intended to approach. Hadn't planned to say anything. But the boat had drifted right toward her anyway.

"Harlan?" She grabbed the bow of the boat as it bumped her dock, jerking him back to the present.

He caught one of the pilings on her dock, anchoring the boat as the blanket slid off her shoulders. In the moonlight, he could tell she was wearing a white tank top with straps so thin they looked like they would snap under the faintest breeze. Her black shorts were boldly short, revealing so much more leg than he'd ever seen from the woman who wore long skirts and blue jeans every day of her life, or at least on every day that he'd seen her. Her hair was down, tangled around her shoulders, as if it were caressing the skin she'd so carelessly exposed to the night.

"What are you doing here?" she asked. Her voice was throaty and raw, and he realized she'd been crying.

"Couldn't sleep." He leaned on the piling, not daring to get out of the boat, not when the need to play the hero was pulsing through him so strongly. All he could think of was folding her into his arms and chasing away the demons haunting her. "You?"

"Same." She hugged herself, her huge eyes searching his. The moonlight cast dark shadows on her face, hollowing out her eyes and her cheeks.

"Want a ride?" He asked the question without intending to, but found himself holding his breath while it sat in the air, waiting for her response.

"To where?"

He shrugged. "Nowhere. I'm just driving."

She looked back at her cabin. "I was just—"

"Crying. I know. Going back inside will help, do you think? Or maybe getting the hell away from life for twenty minutes would be better?"

Defiance flared in her eyes, and her shoulders seemed to lift. Without a word, she grabbed the corner of his windshield and set her bare foot on the edge of his boat. Silently, he held out his hand to the woman he'd never touched in all the years he'd known her, except for last night. She met his gaze, and then set her hand in his.

Jesus. Her skin was like the softest silk, decadent in its

fragility, tempting in its strength. He closed his fingers around hers and helped her into his boat. Her hip slid against his side as she stepped in, and electricity sizzled through him.

She caught her breath, glancing at him as she moved away to sit in the passenger seat.

Harlan said nothing. He had no idea what to say. Not to her. Not to this woman. Not in this moment. So, instead, he restarted the boat, backed up until he was clear of her dock, and then unleashed the throttle. The boat leapt forward, slicing through the water with a boldness that was probably irresponsible in the dark.

But he knew the lake, every inch of it, and the moonlight was bright enough to guide him.

He didn't feel like being careful. Not tonight. Tonight he wanted wind. He wanted water. He wanted freedom. And he wanted the woman sitting in his boat.

HARLAN CRUISED the lake for almost an hour.

They didn't speak, for which Emma was grateful. She had no idea what to say to him, to this man that she'd seen around town for years, but never actually had a conversation with until last night. She knew a little about him from Astrid, knew that he'd come to Astrid's aid when she'd had no one else to help her, but even Astrid had never been able to unlock the secrets of her brother.

For a long while, Emma stopped thinking about anything. She just closed her eyes and leaned back in the seat, letting the wind whip at her. Though it was a warm night, it was chilly in the boat, but she didn't feel like stopping. There was just something liberating about being out on the water, nowhere near land, with nothing but a broad expanse of black sky and white stars above her head.

Eventually, however, she could not resist a peek at the man standing beside her. Harlan was standing up, one hand on the steering wheel, one arm draped over the windshield. The wind was whipping his dark hair, and his white tee shirt was flapping against his steel-hard body. There was no fat on him, just raw, solid muscle, as if he were a machine that had been created for physical labor. His jaw was hard as he scanned the lake, his face stoic and impassive. There was nothing soft about him, nothing approachable, but she didn't feel scared with him.

Maybe it was because she'd seen the turmoil in his eyes the night before, the humanity that was beneath his cool exterior.

He turned his head to look at her, and awareness leapt through her as she met his intense gaze. Without a word, he pulled back on the gearshift, and the boat slowed instantly, sinking into the water as it eased to a stop. He cut the engine, and there was no sound except the gentle lapping of the water against the hull.

Around them was nothing but water. Further away were the dark shadows of the wooded shoreline. During the day, houses would be visible dotting the shore, but at this hour, it was just blackness, with only an occasional outdoor light glistening in the dark. It was early July, and the summer residents were descending upon the town, opening up their houses and filling the region with energy.

But right there, on the lake, it was just the two of them.

"Why were you crying?" Harlan asked, without preamble, without any of the delicate tact that a person was supposed to have.

Weirdly, she wasn't offended. It was almost a relief not to have to pretend. Out here, in the darkness, it seemed like reality was so far away. She felt as if secrets that were whispered would disappear into the night, never to haunt the day. "Because I was sad."

"Why were you sad?" He was still standing at the wheel, one arm draped over the windshield, but he was watching her intently, so focused she could feel the heat of his gaze on her.

"Just a lot of stuff coming down on me at the same time." She shrugged, not wanting to rehash details that would just make her cry again.

"Tell me one of them."

She sighed, his insistence almost a relief. She didn't know how to bring someone else into her struggles, but somehow, he made it easier. "Because I was officially divorced yesterday."

He looked away, staring across the lake. "You loved him." His voice was flat.

"I once did, until I realized that he was a manipulative bastard."

He turned his head toward her again. "Did he hurt you?"

"Physically?"

He nodded once. "Yeah."

"A little."

His jaw ticked, and he looked across the lake again. "Do you know what that makes me want to do?"

She watched his grip tighten around the wheel. "What?"

"Kill him."

Emma started to smile, then realized he wasn't kidding. She stared at him. "You're serious."

"Yeah."

Weird emotions swirled through her, including an inappropriate rush of excitement that this man, this intensely potent man, would actually want to come to her defense. At the same time, there was a ripple of wariness that he could actually even conceive of killing another person, and then admit it so calmly. Preston had been like that, hiding his true self behind a display of glitz, charm, and wealth. Not that Harlan was glitzy, or even charming. But he didn't exactly have a tattoo on his chest that announced that killing people was his first reaction to hearing about a bastard ex-husband.

He said nothing for another moment, and neither did she. Finally, she spoke, "Have you killed people?" The moment the question was out, she was horrified. What kind of question was that? It was rude, and, if by some horrible twist of fate, the answer was yes, she did not want to know that while she was stranded on a boat with him.

Harlan didn't respond, and a cold chill burrowed into Emma's bones. She began to shiver, and she knew it wasn't from just the temperature of the air. "I think it's time to go back—"

"I have skills," Harlan said quietly, keeping his attention focused on the distant shoreline. "Useful skills. People pay me to do things."

A cold draft of foreboding began to pulse at her. "What kinds of things?"

He finally turned his head to look at her. His eyes were dark and inscrutable. "Tell me a secret, Emma. Something dark. Something terrible. Something that you've never told anyone else."

Her heart began to pound. "I don't—"

He sat down suddenly on the driver's seat, facing her. His knees went on either side of hers, and he leaned forward, taking her hands in his, his gaze searching hers. "People get kidnapped," he said. "Paying a ransom isn't always the right choice. I go find them. I get them out. I bring them home. Sometimes I fail. Sometimes I shoot people. Sometimes I get shot. At some point, I'm not going to walk away alive."

She stared at him, her heart pounding in her throat. His hands were tight around hers, like a vice. He was so intense in his body language, crowding her space with his size and

STEPHANIE ROWE

strength. It was intoxicating, even though she knew she should probably be afraid. But she wasn't. She actually wanted to scoot forward in her own seat and get closer to him, as if his intensity was calling to her, igniting her own emotions. "Why are you telling me this?"

"Because someone has to know." He leaned closer, his shoulders bunched. "Someone needs to know when I don't come back. Someone has to miss me."

She swallowed. "Astrid—"

"—has finally found peace after a life of hell," he said. "I won't bring this to her plate."

Emma had a sudden sense that he'd never told anyone, ever, what he was telling her now. "Why me? Why now?"

"Because I need to." He slid his hand behind her neck, pulling her so close that his face was against hers, his cheek just barely brushing against hers.

"Oh." She closed her eyes, trying to catch her breath. "That's where you're going tomorrow? On a mission? That might kill you?" The words caught in her throat, and unexpected grief seemed to surge through her.

"I have a feeling," he said quietly.

"Then don't go." She pulled her hand free of his and gripped the front of his shirt. "Then don't do it."

He didn't look away, didn't back off. "It's the only thing I do."

"You're a real estate agent. You're a brother. An uncle—"

"No." He wrapped his hand around her fist, holding her hand to his chest. The heat from his skin seemed to burn right through his shirt, searing her palm. She tore her gaze off his chest and looked at him. There was such haunting agony in his eyes, such tormented isolation, that she felt her own heart break for him.

He didn't belong in this world, in this small town, just as how she always felt she didn't fit into her life either. She had tried to be the good wife and failed. She knew what it was like. She understood him.

He relaxed under her gaze, and a small smile flickered at the corner of his mouth. "You get it," he said softly.

"I still think you shouldn't go. Not if you think you might die. You have to listen to your instincts." She thought back to the night of her wedding, while she'd been standing in the foyer of that beautiful church. "I knew something was wrong," she said softly. "Right before I married Preston, I was suddenly terrified. I felt like something was going to leap out of the earth and swallow me up." She managed a small smile. "I thought it was nerves, but it wasn't. My instincts picked up on something, and I didn't listen." She met his gaze. "If you feel like this mission will go bad, don't go."

He studied her, and she grimaced, bracing herself for his harsh retort that she didn't have the right to talk to him like that, or to make judgments about his life. Harlan was a man that practically bled independence. No way would he tolerate her offering her opinion—

"My father died alone," he said softly, surprising her with a confession instead of hostility and condemnation. "He died in the woods, and no one knew or cared that he was gone. I found him months later. He'd been half-eaten by scavengers, rotting away two miles from the town he'd lived in his whole life. No one cared. No one looked for him. He just lay there, injured, waiting to die, and knowing that no one gave a shit."

Her heart tightened. "That's so sad."

"I don't want that to be me."

Emma touched his face, her heart aching for him. A man like Harlan would never talk of these things, not with strangers, not with women. She knew that, and yet in the darkness, on the eve of what he thought was his death, the words came. "Astrid would look for you—"

"She didn't. I've been gone for almost a year, and she let me go."

"That's not fair. She sent emails, and you didn't answer—"

"Not the same." He gripped her wrist. "It's not the same."

"Well, you have to reach out and—"

"Marry me, Emma."

She froze, sudden terror careening through her. "*What?*" She must have heard wrong. She must have—

"Marry me." He took her hand and pressed his lips to her palm. "Let me put your name on the emergency contact form so that when I die, they have someone to tell. Someone to bring me home to. Someone who will notice."

Tears began to burn in her eyes, for his pain, and for her own fear...as well as the aching desire in her to say yes. "Harlan, we barely know each other. Astrid should be the one to take care of things if you die—"

"No. I won't do that to her." He cupped her face, his fingers rough against her jaw. "But you've been there. You've seen darkness. You understand."

"I won't get married again," she whispered. "It broke me, Harlan. It really broke me. I believed in him, and I was wrong. So wrong. I can't go back there. I can't trap myself like that. I can't make a mistake like that again—"

"No, sweet Emma." He pressed his lips to her forehead, a kiss so gentle it made more tears fall. How could this man of such darkness be so tender? "I want nothing from you. It's not a real marriage. It's just a promise to notice when I die."

"I can notice that without marrying you." Because she would notice. Dear God, in one day, this man she'd watched from afar had come plunging into her life and torn it apart. She wanted to tell him not to go on the stupid mission and die, but she knew there was no chance. He had to go. She could feel it in his words, in the weight of his gaze. He was running from demons, just as she was, and he was using his work to escape. "How can you ask me to marry you just so I can mourn your death? What kind of request is that?"

For a long moment, Harlan said nothing. He just sat there with his head bowed, his forehead against hers. Finally, he squeezed her hands and sat up, releasing her. "You're right."

"What?" The air suddenly felt so cold with him gone, a chill that seemed to burrow right into her bones.

Harlan slouched back in the driver's seat, no longer facing her, but looking forward. His left arm was draped over the steering wheel, the other resting on the gearshift that was on the side of the boat, by his right hip. "I'm a bastard," he said softly. "I should never have asked that of you." He ran his hand through his hair and glanced at her. "That wasn't my plan. I don't know why I did it. Forget it, okay? No pressure."

She managed a smile, but she didn't feel relief. Instead, she felt a sudden urge to leap and grab at the offer before he could retract it. "It's okay."

"Thanks." But he didn't start the boat. He just sat there while it floated. The air grew cooler, and Emma started to shiver.

Harlan glanced over at her. "Cold?"

She shook her head, not wanting to give him a reason to take them home. "No."

He raised one brow. "I could warm you up."

She burst out in nervous laughter, even as her body pulsed in response. "You're hitting on me?"

He shrugged. "Going away to war tomorrow, darlin'. Might be my last night on the earth." He winked at her, no doubt trying to diffuse the tension. "Show a soldier a little love, yes?"

She shoved her hands into her pockets. "You're incorrigible. Was that all the proposal was? An attempt to get into my pants?" No man had gotten into her pants in a long time, and she'd had no interest in it either. But with the way Harlan was looking at her, she was thinking of things she hadn't thought about in a long time.

"No. I'd still marry you if you'd be up for it. Getting you naked is completely different." His eyes were dark. "You do something to me, Emma Larson. You always have."

Heat pulsed through her at his confession. All those times she'd been craving his touch, he'd been experiencing the same reaction? She quickly shook her head, trying to chase away tempting thoughts that were far too dangerous. "Stop it. I don't have sex anymore."

"Why not?"

"Because I don't want to."

"No?" He moved closer. "I think you're a liar."

Her heart started to pound. "I'm not a liar. I'm terrified," she whispered.

His eyes darkened. "Of sex?"

"Of men. Of making myself vulnerable. Of failing."

"Failing at sex?"

She nodded.

He cupped her jaw, moving in closer. "Emma, babe, your ex-husband should be shot."

Then he kissed her.

CHAPTER FIVE

EMMA FROZE when Harlan's lips descended upon hers. The kiss was electrifying and terrifying, flooding her with a torrent of emotions so powerful they seemed to chase all sanity and self-preservation from her mind. He tasted like vanilla, with a hint of freshly brewed coffee—all natural, all man, and pure heat.

She couldn't have said no, even if she wanted to...but she didn't want to stop him. For the first time in so long, so excruciatingly long, the sensation of a man's mouth on hers didn't feel like an assault trying to destroy her. It was a sensual caress of delicate seduction, a decadent temptation of pure desire.

Unbidden, her hands drifted to his shoulders, to the mass of rock-hard strength beneath her palms. Heat seemed to burn through her skin where she gripped his shoulders. She felt his steel muscles shift as he raised his hand and wrapped it around the back of her neck, steadying her under his onslaught of seduction.

For a split second, she tensed, grabbing his wrist in self-defense.

He stopped the kiss immediately. "He trapped you by your hair, didn't he?"

Tears sprang to her eyes, but she still couldn't relax her grip on his wrist, or quell her need to pull his hand away from her hair. "How do you know that?"

"Because it scared you when I did that." He released her hair and ran his hand down her arm, his face still resting against hers. "I know how to scare people, but I didn't mean to scare you."

"It's okay." She realized she was trembling now. "It's not you. It's me. I have issues."

He laughed softly and pulled back, but his eyes were dark and impenetrable. "We all have issues, Emma. If you didn't, I'd think you were dull and delusional."

She laughed then, relieved that he didn't expect her to be some ray of sparkling sunshine. "Well, you don't need to worry about that. I'm fully loaded." She didn't even know why she was telling him. She worked hard to be normal, to function in society, to hide all the damage she still battled from her marriage. She didn't want to be seen as the woman who couldn't move on, as the woman who was too weak to reclaim her life.

But for some reason, Harlan made her feel like it was okay to admit it. Maybe it was because he would leave in the morning, and she'd never see him again. Any secrets he took with him would disappear from her life forever.

At the thought of never seeing him again, an unfamiliar sadness seemed to take root deep in her chest. It made no sense. She barely knew him. He was nothing more than a shadow that had flitted in and out of the periphery of her existence for the last two years, a man who wasn't hers, and who had never even drifted within reach of her fingers. So, why did it matter if she never saw him again?

"I should get you back." Harlan turned away and started

the engine. He didn't look at her as he drove the boat in a sweeping turn, heading back toward her dock.

There were no further words between them, but she could still feel her lips burning from his brief kiss. She could still feel his hand in her hair. His palm sliding down her arm in the most seductive of caresses, sending electricity tingling through her body. She hadn't thought she had the ability to react to a man anymore. Too many walls, too many shields, too much fear. Sexual desires had died long ago for her...and yet, one kiss, one sweet, magical kiss from a man who lived a life of violence, and everything had come roaring back to life.

Emma leaned back in her seat, the wind whipping her hair around her cheeks as she watched Harlan drive the boat. He was focused on the water in front of them, searching the blackness for the safe route that he had clearly memorized.

He looked over at her and smiled, and she smiled back. "There's nothing like being on the water, is there?" he shouted over the roar of the engine.

"It's amazing," she yelled back. The air was so fresh and pure, the water splashing over the sides of the boat, the night a heavy blanket hiding them from the world. Harlan grinned wider as he opened up the throttle, his body relaxed as he allowed himself to absorb the pitches of the boat with ease.

He might not fit in the small town society of Birch Crossing, but as she watched him embrace the experience of being on the water, she realized that he *was* a perfect fit for life on a lake. A man who could be at peace in the utter simplicity of nature and companionable silence. She envied him, a man who carried all that weight and darkness, but could shut it all down for a boat ride.

He looked over at her again, then held out his hand. "You drive."

"What? No. I'm fine—"

He grabbed her hand and pulled her to her feet. "Come

on." He pulled her in front of him, squeezing her between the front of his body and the steering wheel, though he did take a step back, bracing one bare foot on the seat behind him. "You're in control, babe. Enjoy it."

"I don't know the lake well enough," she shouted at him over the wind. "I can't—"

"I'll watch. You drive." He set her hand on the steering wheel. "Go for it."

Emma grabbed the wheel as the boat started to veer off to the left. The leather was cold and smooth to the touch, and she gripped it tightly. Despite growing up in Birch Crossing, she hadn't spent much time on the lake, and she'd never had an interest in actually *driving* a boat. But as the wind hammered at her face, and the boat bounced across the open water, a strange exhilaration began to flood through her. The engine was roaring, the water churning up in their wake, and the wind whipping her shirt against her body.

"Faster," Harlan yelled, taking her right hand and setting on the throttle. "Push down a little bit more."

Emma tapped the throttle with a couple fingers, and Harlan's laughter echoed in her ear. "Really? That's all you've got?"

She grabbed the gearshift and pushed down hard. The boat leapt forward so fast that she pitched backward into Harlan. He braced her fall with his body, his well-muscled arm reaching past her shoulder to grab the windshield for balance so he could support them both. He leaned forward, his face so close to hers that his cheek was against hers. "Awesome, isn't it?" he yelled. "Total freedom."

She nodded, her eyes watering from the wind. It was incredible. They were going so fast, screaming across the black lake, hidden by the darkness of the night. She had no idea where they were going, or what they might hit, and she felt crazily wild and reckless, like she was throwing herself off a cliff on a stormy day and letting the winds hurl her around for an exhilarating, dangerous ride.

Harlan inched closer, his body against hers, moving in perfect tandem as the boat lurched beneath them. The heat from his body, the dampness of the water, the violence of the wind... "I feel alive," she shouted. "It's incredible!"

"I know!" Harlan tapped her shoulder and pointed ahead to the right. "Your place is in there. Start heading that way."

Regret filled her as she turned the boat, slowing it slightly as they began to head toward the dark shapes of the wooded land. The wind began to die down, and the boat slid more deeply into the water as she slowed further. The white of her dock was up ahead, barely visible in the water. With a sigh of regret, she slowed the boat all the way, until it was drifting, momentum still carrying it toward her home.

Harlan hadn't moved away from her, his body framing hers possessively. "I always forget how much I miss the lake until I come back," he said. "Then once I take the boat out, I remember why I keep coming back."

Her house loomed in the night. It was a small, one-bedroom cabin that had been so ramshackle that she'd been able to afford it on the small amount she'd saved from her job. Preston's prenuptial agreement left her with nothing, but she didn't want his money tainting her cabin anyway. It was her sanctuary, a place for art and solitude, but now, with the energy of Harlan circulating around her, it seemed empty and lonely, a place that was missing life.

The boat bumped against the dock, and Harlan leaned past her to grab the pilings. He held onto the post, but she didn't move to get out. Sitting on the dock was the blanket that she'd wrapped around herself when she'd been out there crying, before Harlan had appeared. She'd been crying because she was alone, and because the little girl she'd dreamed of saving would never be coming home. It hadn't been treasured solitude; it had been devastating loneliness...which had been completely chased away by a boat ride with Harlan.

"How come you don't have a boat?" he asked.

She shrugged, finally pulling herself together. "I don't know. I never thought about getting one. Money."

"You can use mine while I'm gone." He took her hand to help her out of the boat. "It will be good for it to get some use. Just make sure to have someone pull it out of the lake before the ice comes in."

The dock was cold and damp under her bare feet, and Emma shoved her hands into her front pockets.

Harlan nodded at her. "You're losing something."

She looked down and saw a black thread from her shorts was hanging partway out of her pocket. It had twirled around her bare finger like a ring... She froze, her heart starting to pound as she recalled Chloe's words about why she would never get selected to adopt Mattie. *You're a single, unrelated woman—*

She couldn't change the fact she wasn't related to Mattie, but what if she had a family? A husband? A real home? Would that help?

"Don't let the bastard win," Harlan said quietly, as he shifted into reverse. The engine hummed as the boat began to slide away from the dock. "Do more than survive, Emma. You deserve it."

Emma looked up sharply as a strip of moonlight swept across his face. His features were dark and hooded, his mouth tight, his body tense. He was going back to hell, and they both knew it. He wasn't coming back. He would go on missions until he died, whether it was this one, or a later one. *He would never come back to claim her...* If she married him, he would never come back to destroy her as her husband. "Harlan!" She ran to the edge of the dock. "Wait!"

He shifted into neutral, but the boat continued to drift away. "What?"

Her heart started to pound, and fear swirled around her. "I—" She stopped, her breath tight in her chest.

Harlan shifted the boat into forward gear. The boat jerked, and then switched direction, moving ever so slowly toward her. He put it back in neutral as he neared and caught the piling again. His gaze met hers, dark and foreboding. "Tell me."

She stared at him. "Okay," she whispered.

His brow furrowed. "Okay, what?"

Oh, God. Could she really say it? She gripped the string, twisting it so tightly around her hand she knew it was cutting off the circulation. "You're really going to go on this mission?"

Disappointment flared in his eyes. "That's what you wanted to ask? Yeah, I'm going." He shoved back from the dock—

"Wait!" Emma ran forward and jumped onto the boat. Her foot slipped, and Harlan grabbed her arm, yanking her into the boat before she fell into the water. His strong grip was like a manacle around her wrist, but she didn't let herself stop to think, to realize what she was saying. "I'll do it, Harlan."

His face darkened, and his grip tightened. "Do what?"

"Marry you."

"HELLO! NED! WAKE UP!"

Emma shifted restlessly on the front porch, waiting nervously as Harlan pounded on the door. It was three in the morning now. Three in the morning! What were they doing?

A light went on in the house, and Harlan stepped back, waiting for the door to open.

His face was inscrutable, and it had been since the moment she'd said she would marry him. She couldn't tell if he was happy or mad or even insane. He had simply gotten serious about making it happen, which is why they were on the front steps of the town clerk at three in the morning.

The door finally opened, and the front porch light illuminated the night, almost blinding her. Wearing a pair of faded red flannel pajamas, Ned Hartmann peered through the screen door, his gray hair askew and his eyeglasses not quite straight. "Harlan? Emma? What's going on here?"

Harlan didn't waste time. "I'm in town for two days, and I don't know when I'll be back. I leave town at eight tomorrow morning. Emma and I want to get married."

Emma's heart jumped at the words, and her hands started to tremble. Oh, God. Get married again? A cold chill seemed to settle on her skin, and she lost track of the conversation between Harlan and Ned as a weird buzzing started to fill her ears.

A strong hand clasped her upper arm, and a low voice filled her. "Hey, sweetheart, it's okay. I've got you."

Her heart seemed to stop when she saw Harlan looking down at her. He was unshaven, his hair too long, his tee shirt old. He was rough and dangerous, a man she should run screaming from. But instead, his roughness seemed to ease her fear. He wasn't trying to be perfect. He wasn't putting on a façade to hide who he was. He was just *him*, and he'd told her exactly what he was about and what drove him. No lies. No secrets. Just ugly truths, which actually made her feel better.

He didn't smile, but his brow furrowed. "Ned has all the required paperwork here. He can certify our marriage license without even going into the office. He's already gone to get his wife up to witness it."

She stared at him, her mouth suddenly dry. "We really can do this? Get married legally in the middle of the night?" But of course they could. This was Birch Crossing. Things like that could happen here.

"Yeah." He grasped her other arm and gently turned her toward him, his grip firm but not threatening. His brows were knit, his expression unreadable, but not harsh. "Listen, Emma, you don't have to do this. It's fucked up, what we're doing, what I'm asking you to do. I know that, and I can't ask you to—"

"No." She covered his mouth with her fingers. "I want to. I need to get married, too."

Questions flared in his eyes. "You do? Why?"

"Because—"

"Come on in," Ned interrupted. "I woke Iris up. Even after fifty-two years of marriage, my dear wife still gets all emotional at the idea of two young people beginning a new life together." He was now wearing jeans and a flannel shirt that looked amazingly similar to his pajamas. He grinned, looking much more awake. "She thinks it's so romantic. It's been a long time since we've had young lovers show up at our door in the middle of the night." He smiled at Emma, a smile so kind that she wanted to cry. God, how vulnerable was she feeling? A smile from an old man could make her cry? "We've been worried about you, Emma. The whole town has. You'll be in good hands with Harlan. He's got good morals." He held the door open. "Let's get this done. I'm sure you kids want a little time alone as newlyweds before Harlan leaves in the morning."

Emma stared at the front hall, with its bare wood floor and its charming little entry table, afraid to take that final step across the threshold. Could she really do this? Young lovers? They weren't young lovers. They were two messed up people who needed each other for reasons that no one else would ever understand. "I don't think I can do thi—"

"Emma!" Iris Hartmann hurried down the stairs, wearing a slightly wrinkled sundress with pink tulips on it. Her hair was hastily put up in a bun on the top of her head, with a few strands still hanging down. "This is so exciting! I've told Ned for years that you and Harlan were sweet on each other, but he never believed me. It's so obvious from the way you two look at each other."

Emma swallowed as Harlan glanced at her. A quiet smile seemed to be hovering at the corners of his mouth. "I don't—"

"Here you go." Iris handed her a pale blue silk item. "It's actually a hair scrunchie, but I think if you stretch it, it will work as a garter. It's mine, so that takes care of borrowed and blue, right?'

The silk was cool and soft in her hand, and Emma clenched it in her fingers. Sweat was trickling down her back, and she felt faint—

Harlan slipped behind her and wrapped his arms around her upper body, folding his forearms across her chest and pulling her against him, into the shield of his body. "It's perfect, Iris," he said, resting his chin on Emma's shoulder. "Thanks for being so thoughtful."

He sounded so warm and kind, and his body was so strong the way it was wrapped around her, that suddenly Emma's tension faded. This was nothing like her wedding to Preston, which had been in a huge church, with a ten-thousand dollar gown, and five hundred strangers in attendance in the hot Florida sun. Tonight, she was wearing shorts and a tank top, and her feet were in flip flops instead of two-thousand dollar stilettos. A used hair scrunchie for a garter. Seriously. Wasn't there some humor here? It wasn't the same. Harlan wasn't the same. He was strong and protective, a man who spent his life rescuing others. What kind of man did that? A good man, right? And she wasn't even really getting married, not really, not in the way that would strangle her, right? It would be okay. *It would be okay.*

Iris sighed and put her hand over her heart. "Oh, did you see that, Ned? Emma's whole body relaxed when Harlan took her in his arms. That is love, my dear, such beautiful love." She leaned forward, lowering her voice to a stage whisper. "A marriage will never work until the man makes the woman feel safe. You guys will be perfect for each other."

Emma looked back at Harlan. Across his left temple was a small scar, and his nose was crooked, as if it had been broken more than once. He exuded violence, and yet, Iris was right. The moment he'd wrapped his arms around her, her fear had seemed to fade. "Thanks," she whispered.

Harlan winked at her.

"And here is something new." Iris held up a box of Kleenex. "I'm afraid it's the only thing I had in the house that hadn't been opened yet." She handed it to Emma. "Just open it and tuck a few of them in your bra. That should do it."

Emma couldn't help but laugh as she took the box. "Really?"

"Of course really." Iris held up an ivory headband with a few bits of yellowed lace dangling from it. "This was my veil when I was married. I'm afraid that one of our dogs ate it a few years ago, but it will still work." She set it on Emma's head, tucking it behind her ears. "And there we have your 'old.' Now you can get married!"

Harlan grinned at her. "You look beautiful, my darling." He flicked the dog-eaten veil out of her face, an amused and amazingly endearing smile on his face.

"You think so?"

"Absolutely." He squeezed her hand, and then led her down the hallway toward the back of the house.

Emma's heart was still racing as she followed everyone into the living room. At Iris's urging, she tore open the tissue box and pulled out a couple. With the three of them watching with expressions ranging from Iris's delight, to Ned's well-humored tolerance, to a heated smolder in Harlan's eyes, she quickly shoved them past the neckline of her tank and into her bra. "Okay, ready."

Ned walked them through the documents, winking as he signed the form stating that he'd seen both their birth certificates. "You both were surely born, so I'm okay with it." Both she and Harlan signed their own names, and then Ned was ready.

Iris thrust a bouquet of slightly wilted flowers into Emma's hand, and then stood by her husband beaming as Ned married them. It happened too fast, and suddenly Ned and Iris were staring expectantly at them. "Where's your ring?" Ned asked.

"We don't have any," Harlan said. "We didn't really plan ahead."

Iris set her hands on her hips. "You can't not give her a ring—"

"No, it's okay." Emma realized that not having a ring was perfect. A ring was like a trap, and she didn't want the symbol of it. "We'll get one. We have time for that. We want it to be perfect," she added, not wanting Iris to decide to rush off and pluck one from her own collection.

Iris tsked her disapproval, but Ned seemed satisfied, and minutes later, he was commanding Harlan to kiss his bride.

His bride.

She was a bride again.

Fear started to ripple through her, but Harlan's kiss was swift and cursory, not demanding and proprietary like

Preston's had been at their wedding. She barely had time to register it before Iris was hugging her and offering cookies, chattering with delight. And then, before she knew it, they were back in his truck, two copies of the wedding certificate in her hand.

Married.

Again.

~

HE WAS MARRIED.

To Emma.

To the woman who had haunted him since the day he'd first seen her in Wright's.

Harlan gripped the steering wheel as he drove them back toward her house, his truck bumping over the old roads. Her scent seemed to fill the car, that delicate fragrance of fresh soap and spring. He couldn't believe the surge of protectiveness and connection that had filled him the moment that Ned had pronounced them a couple. It had raged through him, a need to claim her for his own, to seal her as his so that even when he left her, even when he lay dying in some hell-hole, a part of him would always be there with her. He'd barely brushed his lips over hers for the post-wedding kiss, knowing that if he got even one taste of her, he would have carted her off to the nearest closet and taken her right there.

Which was totally fucked up, but at the same time, he couldn't shut the emotions off.

She was fidgeting beside him, playing restlessly with their marriage certificate. She was pale, and her breathing was still shallow. Protectiveness pulsed at him. "You okay?"

She looked up, her face shadowed by the dim light of his dash. "I'm a little freaked out."

Her honesty made him relax. He liked that she didn't play

games with him or try to be what she wasn't. "Second thoughts?" Weirdly, when he asked the question, he didn't want an answer. He was afraid she would say yes.

She met his gaze. "No."

Relief rushed through him as he turned the corner onto the dirt road that led to her house. "Good."

He pulled up in front of her cabin too soon, not wanting to walk away from her yet. He felt like it was unfinished, like there were things he should say to her before he walked away to die. She didn't get out, as if caught in the same trap that had him.

For a moment, they sat in silence, but it wasn't the same companionable silence that they'd had on the boat. This one was heavy with tension, with the stark reality of what they'd done, and what they were heading towards.

"I never thought I'd get married," he said finally.

She looked over at him. "Why not?"

"Because my father destroyed my stepmother when he married her. I always swore I wouldn't do that to a woman." He looked at her. "I still won't. I promise not to stay around long enough to do that to you."

Her face softened. "You wouldn't destroy anyone, Harlan."

"Sure I would." He leaned forward, draping his arms over the steering wheel. He knew now why he had asked Emma to marry him when he had. It was because he wouldn't be around to strip the light from her. "I'm not a good guy, Emma. I only know violence. I protect. I kill. I rescue. That's what I am. I'm not the husband type." He looked over at her. "You know that, don't you? That I'm leaving tomorrow?"

"Of course I do." She pulled her knees to her chest and wrapped her arms around them, still making no move to get out of the truck. "That's why you're safe for me to marry. Because you'll be gone."

He laughed softly as he reached out to trace his fingers over her hair. "We're a perfect match then, aren't we? You want a husband who will take off and never come back, and I want a wife who will take the call when I die, but not be around for me to destroy her."

She turned her head to look at him. In those green depths, he saw something he didn't understand, something that had never been directed at him. An emotion that seemed to reach inside and grab him. "I hardly know you," she said, not pulling away from his touch. "I've spoken to you more in the last twenty-four hours than in the last two years combined. You're dangerous and a little scary. But I think," she said softly, "that I will cry for you if I ever get that phone call."

Her words were starkly honest, and they went right to his heart, opening up a wound that had been festering inside him for decades. He had no words to reply, no sentences to express, no ability to articulate how her words had made him feel.

So, he told her the only way he could.

With a kiss.

CHAPTER SIX

HARLAN'S KISS was tender beyond words, a kiss that a hardened man like him should never be able to deliver. It dove straight past Emma's fears and her worries, shredded her shields, and softened the razor-sharp edges that had protected her heart for so long.

He paused in the kiss, as if offering the chance to end it and pull away, but she didn't want to. She wanted another moment with him, with the way he made her feel. It was safe with him because he was leaving. She could drop all her guards, tumble into his arms, and succumb to his magic. She would never have to fear that he would take advantage of her or use her need for him to chisel away at her foundation and tear her away from her life and who she was.

Harlan's kiss was a breath of restoration in her life, a reassurance that she was still a woman. It showed her that fire could burn in her and sustain her when she woke up in the morning with battles to fight. A one-night stand for a woman who had slept with only one man before her husband. Could she do it? Did he even want to? Or was she imagining it? What man would want her? She knew she was—

"Let's go inside." Harlan's voice was a whisper against her mouth, a desperate wish swallowed up by a kiss that had turned deeper and more urgent. His hand went to the back of her hair, but he quickly moved it to her lower back before she could tense, pulling her against him as he deepened the kiss.

Intense need and longing rushed through her, and she almost said yes. But how could she? Marrying him was one thing, but to surrender herself to him so completely, to make herself vulnerable to him—

He unsnapped her seatbelt with a click, and with one swift move dragged her across the bench seat onto his lap. Excitement and desire rushed through her as she sank down onto him, the bulge of his jeans digging into her inner thigh. He wanted her? Just like that? In the front seat of a car? For no reason? Raw, untamed need built inside her, and she wrapped her arms around his neck, taking over the kiss, unable to contain her own need for what he gave her.

With a soft growl, he fisted her hair, only to let go with a muttered apology the moment he did it. "I keep forgetting," he said, breathing soft kisses across her forehead and her eyelids. "I will never let myself hurt you," he said, "but I know you don't know that."

Then, before she could respond, she heard the click of the car door opening. Still kissing her, he stepped out. He took her with him, anchoring her thighs around his hips, one arm secured around her waist as he kicked the door shut.

His body was hard and lean against hers as his boots thudded up the steps of her back porch. His kisses were a relentless assault that seemed to dizzy her senses as he opened the door that she never locked. He shoved it shut behind them, and the darkness of her sanctuary buzzed with electricity that had never been present before. "Where's your room?" he asked between kisses.

"Lakeside," she whispered, the word coming out before

she'd even made the decision to tell him. But when his arms tightened around her and his kiss grew fiercer, she knew that she'd made the decision several minutes ago, when she'd chosen not to leap out of his truck and run for safety when he'd pulled up in front of her house.

Harlan made her feel alive. He made her feel like a woman. He gave her hope that her heart could start beating again someday. He could offer her so little, only one night and then he would be gone forever, but that was exactly what she needed: a gift of life with none of the terrifying repercussions of a long-term connection.

She counted his steps and knew the moment he'd crossed the threshold into her bedroom, into her world that had never been invaded by a man, and she'd thought never would be. But there was no fear as he crossed the small room, as he eased her onto the double bed that was barely bigger than a twin.

Emma propped herself up on her elbows as Harlan stripped off his shirt. His body was chiseled with muscle, but there were also dark bruises, as if someone had beaten him badly.

A cold chill ripped across her and she sat up, palming one of the large ones on his left side. "What happened?"

But Harlan didn't answer. He just went still and closed his eyes, setting his hand over hers. He breathed deeply, as if inhaling the moment into his very soul. "Kiss it," he said quietly.

Her heart tightened at the request, and she bent her head, lightly pressing her lips to the darkened flesh. His hand eased over her back as she did it, a touch so light it was as if he were trying to memorize the curve of her body. "So beautiful," he whispered.

She looked up as he knelt before her, taking her face into his hands. "You are my angel," he said.

"I'm not an angel. I'm a mess." She didn't want to pretend to be something she wasn't. She didn't want to be the beautiful woman who looked good in an expensive dress. She wanted Harlan to see her as flawed, imperfect, and grungy. If he saw her that way and still wanted to make love to her, then she would know that the connection she felt to him wasn't one-sided.

"I know you're a mess. It makes you real and compelling." Suddenly, his kiss grew more heated, igniting an answering desire inside her. He shoved her back on the bed as he moved over her, ripping at his belt and tearing his jeans over his hips. His boots hit the floor with a thud, and then he was on top of her, more than six feet of male, pinning her to the bed as he consumed her with kisses more dangerous than she could even conceive of.

"I need you naked." His words sent a shiver of anticipation through Emma, but when he gripped her shirt and pulled it over her head, it became more than anticipation. It became wild, desperate desire. She fumbled with her bra straps, frantic to get it off as Harlan unfastened her shorts and tugged them over her hips, sliding her embarrassingly white granny panties off at the same time. As he stripped her bare, he followed the path of her shorts with searing kisses from her navel downwards, blazing a trail of rippling passion that seemed to burn right through her flesh.

She barely heard the sound of her shorts landing against the far wall as his mouth descended upon her core, showering kisses that made her body twist and writhe. His hands palmed her hips, holding her at his mercy while he bit, licked, and teased her. Intense desire rippled down her legs and up her spine, pooled in her belly, and burned in her veins. Her fingers tangled in his thick hair as she tugged at him, desperate for more. "Make love to me, Harlan."

He looked up, his whiskered face lit by the first rays of

dawn. His dark eyes were blazing with desire, with lust so intense that it made her tremble. There was no soft man looking at her. He was a warrior, a man borne of such primal instincts that her whole body clenched in response. "Oh, I will, sweetheart. I will." Then he slipped his finger inside her, and she gasped, her body almost melting down at the invasion. Everything he did felt so right, as if he knew her body intimately and had spent a lifetime memorizing her.

It had never been like that before. Not once. Never had her body come to life at a man's hands. Never had she wanted to surrender to anyone. But she did now. She wanted to be at Harlan's mercy, to have him show her what it was like to turn herself over to him and entrust him with everything.

His fingers still igniting new fires within her, he kissed his way back up her body, nibbling along her ribs, laving her nipples, kissing her collarbone, and then invading her mouth. His kiss was raw sex now, deep, pulsating ownership that exploded through her as he moved over her, his knee thrust between hers to make space for him.

"Now," he said against her mouth, his erection pressing against her body, the tip of it already demanding her body accommodate him. "Now, I will make love to my bride." Then he thrust, sliding deep inside her with one effortless move.

She gasped as he filled her, stunned by how right it felt, how easily they fit together. "It didn't hurt," she whispered, unable to keep the surprise out of her voice.

Harlan swore under his breath, as he broke the kiss, pulling back enough to look at her. "I wish I could have been your first," he said. "You don't deserve your past." Then he thrust again, holding her gaze as he slid into her.

Again and again he drove deep, binding them more closely with each stroke. She clung to him, riveted by the intensity of his stare, unwilling to close her eyes and cut herself off from him. She needed to see his face, to know the man she was with, that she had given herself to.

He seemed to feel the same, his eyes darkening as the intensity of their lovemaking rose, as their bodies bucked and twisted, screaming for completion as he drove them to the edge of pleasure and pain and need—

The orgasm exploded through her and she screamed as it took her. Harlan caught her scream with a kiss, his body bucking against hers as he gave himself over to her, their bodies arching and glistening as the climax thrust them over that precipice and tumbled them mercilessly into the roiling sea below.

EMMA AWOKE to the sound of a Jet Ski spraying past her cabin. Groaning, she pulled the pillow over her head, so exhausted she could barely surface from sleep. "Go away," she muttered, rolling onto her side. Something sharp jabbed her side, and she yelped, sitting up.

In her bed, tangled in the sheets, was a sprig from a rose bush, with three small buds on it. She recognized the pale yellow instantly. It was from the bush outside her bedroom. For a moment, she stared at it in confusion, trying to figure out how a rose got into her bed. Then, the memories of the night came back to her, and she turned around, scanning her room.

Harlan wasn't there. "Harlan?" She leapt out of bed and hurried out into the main part of the house. He wasn't in the living room and kitchen area. With a sinking feeling, she looked out her living room window and saw that her driveway was empty. His truck was gone.

The clock on her oven said it was ten fifteen. Harlan had left town more than two hours ago.

At first, the most agonizing sense of loss assailed her, so powerful that she sank down on the couch, her arms wrapped around her stomach. He was gone. She would never see him again. Ever.

Tears bit at her, and she lifted her chin, steeling herself against them. No tears. No tears. *No tears.* She didn't want to cry. She was tired of crying. The deal with Harlan wasn't supposed to bring tears. It was supposed to bring empowerment and liberation, right? But even as she thought it, Chloe's words echoed through her mind, that a heart could break only so many times before there was nothing left.

Caring hurt. Caring was dangerous.

Resolutely, she stood up, forcing her shoulders back as she walked across the old pine floors to her bedroom. But when she reached the door and saw the roses nestled in the off-white sheets, she almost wanted to cry again. Her roses were in full bloom, with plenty of beautiful blossoms to select. But he hadn't given her those roses. Instead, he'd chosen buds for her.

Rose buds, complete with thorns.

Emma padded softly across the beautiful hand-woven carpet she'd found at a garage sale and sank down on the bed. Propped up on the nightstand beside her birch tree lamp was their marriage certificate. Harlan Roger Shea and Emma Elizabeth Larson. She had herself a husband now.

She picked up the sprig of flowers, and as she did, a slow smile began to build in her heart. Preston had married her with a five hundred dollar bouquet. Harlan had married her with a dog-eaten veil, tissues in her bra, and a hair scrunchie around her leg. He'd given her rose buds, a night of unbelievable passion, and a husband. And then, he had left her so she could live her life.

Harlan had given her a chance for what she wanted most of all: safety. Now that she was married, no other man could touch her. He gave her protection at the same time he gave her space. And...he gave her the chance to fight for Mattie. Her heart resonating with hope for the first time in a very long while, Emma grabbed her phone off the nightstand and dialed. Chloe answered on the third ring. "Hi, Emma. What's up?"

"I got married."

There was silence. "What? To who?"

"A man from my hometown that I've known for years." Emma looked at the marriage certificate, and knew that she had to make it sound good enough for the court. The deception of true love and a solid marriage began with Chloe. "He's a good man. He accepts me as I am." She couldn't say he loved her, and she wouldn't even want to, but it felt good to know that he'd seen her crying and it hadn't fazed him.

More silence. "I thought you were never going to get married again."

"He's different." And he was. Darker. Haunted. And gone. "I've known him for a long time."

"You got divorced *two days ago*, Emma. First, you want to adopt Mattie, and then you get married? Aren't you at all worried that you're overreacting?"

"No." Emma gripped the phone. "You know how scared I am of marriage, men, and dating, all of it. The fact that I married him even though I'm terrified should tell you something about how I feel about him."

Chloe was quiet for another minute, and then she sighed. "Okay, Emma, you have a point, but I think it's a little weird that you're married to some guy I've never heard of. *Have* I heard of him? What's his name?"

"Harlan Shea. He's the brother of my friend Astrid."

"The one who has been gone for a year?"

"Yes."

Understanding filled Chloe's voice. "That's why he's safe.

Because he'd never be around. How long until he leaves for his next trip?"

Emma decided it was time to change the subject. Apparently, having a social worker for a friend meant it was too hard to keep secrets. "You said yesterday that I had no chance to adopt Mattie as a single woman. What about as a married couple?"

Chloe made a choking sound. "You got married to adopt Mattie? Tell me I'm wrong. For God's sake, Emma, tell me you didn't do something that foolish—"

"I got married to a man who makes me feel safe," she snapped. "I'm not afraid when I'm with him, and that is such a huge gift! Stop judging me! Marrying Harlan was the right thing for me to do, so can you try and be happy for me?"

There was a long silence. "You're right," Chloe said softly. "Sorry, Em. I just get protective of you. The first time I met you was the day you moved back to town when you had just left Preston. I'll never forget the dark circles under your eyes, or how thin you were. I don't want you to go back there."

Emma's anger faded, and she sagged back onto the bed. "I know, and I appreciate it. But Harlan is different. He has as much baggage as I do. We understand each other, but there's no pressure. It's good."

Chloe took a deep breath. "Okay, I accept that, but I want to meet him. Soon."

Yeah, that would happen... A tinge of fear echoed through her at the thought of Harlan on his way to the mission that he was so sure would kill him, but she pushed it aside. She hadn't agreed to love him, just to notice when he died. "I am serious, though, Chloe. I'm married now, and I want to adopt Mattie."

Chloe let out a small groan. "Emma—"

"What do I need to do to be considered?"

"You're not family—"

"Do *you* think she should be with me, or with one of her relatives?"

For a long moment, Chloe didn't speak, and Emma started to tense. She needed Chloe's support to have any chance at all of making it happen. After an agonizing delay, Chloe finally answered. "If you convince me that you really love Mattie and you're willing to commit to her for the rest of your life...well...I think you'd be a wonderful mom for her."

Emma's throat tightened. "Thank you."

"But I'll be honest. I'm not convinced of that, and the judge will be even tougher to win over. You're not exactly stable these days in terms of your personal situation."

Emma's fingers tightened around the stem of the roses. "Chloe—"

"But," Chloe interrupted. "I will make some phone calls and get back to you. Okay?"

Emma bit her lip, and she forced her hand to relax its death grip on her flower. "Okay. Thanks."

"You're welcome. And, Emma?"

She stared at the roses, a dull ache beginning to pulse in her chest as the enormity of last night began to settle upon her. What had she done?

"If you're really happy with Harlan, and it's the right choice, then congratulations."

"Thanks." But her words felt empty.

"I'll be in touch. Take it day by day. You'll get there."

"Get where?"

"Wherever it is you're going." Chloe disconnected without another word, and Emma sat on the bed for another minute, the rose sprig still clutched numbly in her hand. Chloe's reaction had been like a cold blanket dropping over her head and suffocating her. Last night, marrying Harlan had seemed like the perfect solution for both of them. Unconventional, yes, but conventional had already betrayed her.

By marrying Harlan, she'd get his protection, a husband who wouldn't be there to hurt her, and a chance to change Mattie's life. But in reality, what did she have? She was shackled to a man she didn't know, and maybe no closer to rescuing Mattie from a life that was too similar to her own...and if Harlan chose to come back and claim her, she could be in for another round of hell.

What had she done?

With a groan, she flopped back on the bed, staring at the rough wooden beams spanning her ceiling. The sheets were tousled beneath her, and his scent drifted up from the covers. Her cheeks burned at the memory of their lovemaking, how she'd given herself completely to him on every level. She hadn't even given herself to Preston that completely. Was Chloe right? Was she just losing her mind because of the divorce? No, she wasn't. Her heart ached for Mattie, and that wasn't only because she was finally liberated from Preston. She loved Mattie just because of who she was.

And Harlan...the lovemaking...the marriage...her fear of those things ran too deep. Loneliness would never have gotten her to trust him enough to do that if there wasn't a reason, if there wasn't something about him worth trusting, if there wasn't a connection between them that was deeper than fear.

Harlan Shea was almost a stranger, a man who had intrigued her for years, and yet he'd changed her life. The truth was, Harlan wouldn't be back. He'd made his decision, and he would continue his rescue missions until they took his life. She didn't need to worry about him returning. And it would make a difference with getting approval to adopt Mattie, regardless of Chloe's claims. She'd made the right choice, even if others wouldn't understand that.

And even aside from Mattie, it had been the right decision to give Harlan the gift of having someone care. She knew what it was like to not matter, just like she'd told Mattie, and she'd seen that same aching loneliness in Harlan's eyes. She, Harlan, and Mattie were the same. No one had been there to help her as a child, and it had been agonizingly lonely to be fighting all alone. But if she could help Harlan and Mattie avoid the same fate, then she would do it a thousand times over.

Harlan was gone physically, but she would remember him and honor him, just as he'd wanted. She raised the rose to her lips and pressed a kiss to the tender buds. *Harlan, I promise to cry for you, and I promise to notice when you don't come back.*

And she knew she would.

For one night, their lives had crossed paths, and they'd both gotten something they wanted, something they needed, something they burned for.

One night, and then two lives split again. Forever.

But as she stood up to retrieve a vase from her kitchen for the flowers, she couldn't help the brief wave of sadness for what might have been. Then she thought of Preston and a cold chill rippled through her. Never again would she make the mistake of entrusting her life to a man.

Never, ever again.

She would cry for Harlan. She would notice when he didn't come back. She would always remember the night of passion that they'd shared.

But she was glad, so glad, that he was never going to come back for her.

THE CIGARETTE SMOKE was swirling around Harlan as he sat at the bar. Despite the hot sun outside, it was dark and ominous inside. The heat was thick and oppressive, and the place was too crowded. Too many tourists in gaudy colors, and too many locals with shifty eyes, dangerous auras and guns strapped under their arms. It was a bad place to be, which was the reason he and Blue had been called down there. Lots of shit went down in this part of South America.

He glanced at the door, but Blue wasn't there yet. He still had time.

He pulled out his phone and typed a quick email to the woman he'd never met, the one who called the shots for him and Blue, and for all the others.

RENÉE. *I got married. Emma Larson. List her as my emergency contact and next of kin. Her contact info is below.*

HE JOTTED down Emma's info, satisfaction growing with each letter he typed. When he finished, he stared at the email for a long time, reading and rereading it. It felt good. Really good. He knew that she'd keep her end of the bargain. She would care. His father's past would not be repeated.

Finally, he hit send. The whoosh as his email was delivered was awesome, absolutely fucking awesome...but at the same time, he felt a slight wash of guilt. Was he a bastard for marrying her just so that someone would notice when he died? Then he thought of the determined gleam in her eyes. No, it hadn't been one-sided. She'd had a reason for getting married, too. Why had she done it? What had been so important to her that she'd been willing to overcome her fear of marriage to shackle herself to some guy who was going to come back to her only in a wooden box, if at all?

Restlessness itched at him, a desire to find out Emma's secrets. For a moment, he considered emailing her, using the address he'd poached from her phone while she'd been sleeping, but he immediately shut down the idea.

Ongoing contact wasn't part of the deal, and he wouldn't change the terms of their agreement. It had been one night, one connection, no ongoing chains holding them both back.

It was what it was.

"Miss me, gorgeous?"

Harlan looked up to see Blue standing beside him. He was wearing a loose khaki shirt, spiffy white pants, polished black shoes, and a Rolex. His blond hair was slicked back, and his blue eyes were hidden behind a pair of gold-rimmed sunglasses. He was ready to play his part. "You look like a pimp," Harlan observed.

"I'm a suave playboy. There's a difference—" Blue cut himself off, staring at Harlan's wrist. "A tat? You don't do tats. Ever. You'd shoot anyone who got within ten feet of you with a needle."

Harlan looked down at the mark he'd just finished getting inked on the underside of his wrist. "Yeah, well, I made an exception."

Whistling in taunting admiration, Blue raised his sunglasses to inspect it. "What is it?"

Harlan brushed his hand over the design. It was less than an inch big, but etched permanently into his flesh. "It's an 'E' with a yellow rose."

"No shit." Blue raised his brows. "Why?"

"So I don't forget." He pushed back from the bar and pulled his hat down over his head. "Come on, let's go. Time to get dirty."

CHAPTER SEVEN

EMMA WAS WHISTLING as she pulled into the driveway of the old Possum Farm later that morning. The huge wooden doors of the barn were flung wide open, and there was lots of activity inside as people worked on their floats for the festival's parade.

It was tradition for the Possum Farm barn to be used as a staging area, and the only people allowed inside were those actually working on the floats. Everyone else in town had to be surprised. Emma had not been in the mood to decorate when Clare had asked her to help update the float for Wright's, but Clare had begged her to paint the scenery to do justice to the store and Clare's cupcake business.

For the last few years, thrusting herself into the merriment of family time had been hard, and now that Clare and Astrid were being helped by their husbands, kids, and step kids, it was even more challenging to make herself participate. But today, it felt different. Not that she was going to tell them that she and Harlan had gotten married, of course, but she didn't need to declare it to the world in order for her to feel good. The private knowledge was enough to galvanize her. The knowledge that Chloe was making calls about Mattie, and the lovely memory of how Harlan had shown her she wasn't entirely dead as a woman were enough to make her feel like the world was a brighter place than it had been only the day before. She didn't need to announce it to everyone to make it real for herself.

And as for that good emotional place that Chloe had wished her luck reaching? Emma was already there. Everything was working out just right.

She loaded painting supplies into a wheelbarrow at the edge of the driveway, and cheerfully wheeled it into the barn. The Wright's float was at the back, and she could see Clare and Astrid arguing good naturedly with Clare's daughter, Katie, and her stepdaughter, Brooke, with animated hand gestures. Artistic differences no doubt, which Emma would raise to new heights as the only actual paint artist in the group. Clare's cupcakes were works of art, as were Astrid's jewelry pieces, but when it came to paintbrushes, Emma was the one with the goods. "Hi, guys," Emma called out. "What's going—"

"Hi Emma!" To her horror, from behind a massive cardboard structure of a pig walked Iris. "How's my newlywed? Did you and Harlan have a good night last evening after your wedding? Your love inspired us, and Ned and I had a lovely time as well—" She winked at Emma, then hurried on, shouting at someone not to break the plastic dandelion.

With a sinking feeling, Emma looked ahead, and to her horror, Astrid, Clare, and the two teen girls were staring at her with shocked looks on their faces. Had they heard? Maybe not. Maybe they were just surprised by the fact she was actually socializing with people. "Um... Hi?" She began wheeling the cart toward the float, trying to force her face into a casual grin as she walked past a stall occupied by a massive gray horse. "So, I brought all my stuff. I was thinking of painting a giant cupcake, a pink one, blended in with a drawing of Wright's—"

"Tell me I heard wrong," Astrid interrupted, her auburn hair cascading wildly around her shoulders, her eyes flashing. "Tell me I didn't hear what I think I heard."

Emma cleared her throat. "What—"

"You and Harlan got married?" Astrid still looked shocked.

Emma cleared her throat and peeked nervously at Clare, who was staring at her. "It was a convenience marriage," she said quickly, keeping her voice low, knowing that she had to keep up the pretense for the town. In order for her to have a chance with Mattie, a social worker would have to visit and interview people, and her marriage to Harlan had to sound legit. "He needed it for his work, and I—"

"You got married!" Clare shrieked. She threw aside the pot of pansies she'd been holding, sprinted across the barn, and lunged at Emma, sweeping her up in a huge hug. "I can't believe it. You and Harlan got married!"

Clare's shriek ricocheted through the barn, and suddenly Emma found herself the center of a thousand questions and jostling gossipers. The only one who hadn't joined them was Astrid, who was still standing back from the crowd staring at her. Emma managed to accept the boisterous congratulations, but her heart was sinking as she watched Astrid retreat. The assault of well-wishers was exhausting, as was the barrage of questions about a romance that no one else had known about—for obvious reasons. Once the rumor was confirmed, the discussion quickly shifted into self-congratulations for all the people who had apparently guessed that there was a hot romance brewing beneath the surface, and predicted that a marriage was on the way. A surprising number of people seemed to have been dead certain that Emma and Harlan had been dating secretly for two years, given that their first kiss had been a mere thirty six hours ago.

Emma felt her heart ache as she watched Astrid turn away and begin working on the float, but it took almost a half hour before the crowd finally retreated to their projects, still shouting congratulations. Cell phones were out, and Emma knew the whole town would know within the hour. It was what she'd wanted, but at the same time, she felt distinctly uncomfortable lying to the people she'd known her whole life, even if it was for Mattie.

Once she had space, Emma hurried up to Astrid, needing the support of both her friends. "Hey."

Astrid didn't look up from hammering two pieces of plywood together.

Emma touched her arm. "Astrid? Can we talk?"

Astrid finally looked up, and there was raw betrayal in her eyes. "I don't understand. What happened? Do you even love him? He deserves that, you know. He's a good man."

Her heart tightened at the question. "Oh, Astrid, it wasn't like that—"

"It wasn't like that? Really?" Astrid clenched the hammer in her fist. "He saved me from the hospital. He gave me a home. He was the only thing I had to keep me going when things were so bad. He might be a loner, but he's my brother, and he deserves someone who will love him. How dare you marry him if you don't love him?"

Emma felt her cheeks heat up. "He doesn't love me either—"

"Of course he does. Harlan would never get married unless there was no other choice for him, unless it was driving him so intensely that it would never let him go." Astrid stood up. "I understand you've been through hell, Emma. I really do. But that doesn't justify playing with my brother like this. I don't care what reason you had, or what reason you think he has, but it's absolute crap that you would marry him and not love him."

"But—"

"Isn't that what Preston did to you?" Astrid accused, her brown eyes flashing with anger. "Isn't that what broke you, because the man you loved didn't love you back?"

Emma stared at her, shocked by the comparison. How could Astrid compare what she'd done to what Preston had done? "That was different—"

"Not so different." Astrid threw down the hammer. "Where is Harlan? Did you move in with him? I need to talk to him."

Dread hit Emma. He hadn't told Astrid he was leaving? He'd left it to her? Resentment burned through her for the fact he'd left her in this position, that he'd forced her to defend herself against the woman who was one of her only friends. "He left."

Already halfway to the door, Astrid stopped and turned back. "Left where?"

"Birch Crossing. He's on another mi—" She stopped, realizing that Astrid didn't know he went on missions. Until last night, no one in Birch Crossing had known where Harlan went when he disappeared. And now, only she knew. "He left again. He isn't coming back...for a long time."

"What?" Astrid looked devastated now. "He married you and then left? What did you do to him?"

Emma stiffened. "I didn't do anything to him. He was already going to leave. He came back to tell you, but he didn't want to interfere with your happiness."

"My happiness?" Astrid strode over to her, her face furious. "My happiness is my family. Harlan is part of that. You know that. How could you not tell him to talk to me? How could you let him leave without saying good-bye? You knew that I would want to see him."

As Emma stared into Astrid's furious face, she realized with a sinking feeling that she *did* know that. Of course, Astrid could handle Harlan's life. Astrid had been through plenty of grueling things in her life, and she didn't hide from anything tough. But it hadn't even occurred to Emma to encourage Harlan to open up to Astrid. Had she really been thinking about herself the whole time, her need for how he made her feel, her desire to matter to someone, to him? Guilt churned in her belly, an aching emptiness. "I'm sorry."

"Sorry isn't enough," Astrid snapped. "What's his phone number? His old one got disconnected. I'm going to call him."

"His phone number?" Emma repeated, an ache settling numbly in her chest as she realized the truth. "He didn't give me his phone number."

Astrid raised her eyebrows. "How about an email address that he actually reads?"

Emma shook her head, wordlessly, her cheeks flaming. She felt like such an idiot, having to admit she had no way to contact her own husband.

Astrid walked over to her. "So, let me get this straight. In the middle of last night on some whim, you and Harlan got married. Then he took off in the morning without even telling his own sister, and he left you no way to get in touch with him? Not even in an emergency?"

Emma felt heat rise in her cheeks. "Yes, that describes it quite well," she said softly, a gruesome weight settling in her. What had seemed so brilliant this morning suddenly felt like a joke. She didn't know who had been the butt of the joke, her or Harlan. Or both of them?

"Wow. For a woman who had sworn off men, you really did a great job getting back into the game."

"Hey." Clare walked up, a streak of pink paint across her

forehead. "Astrid, come back to the float and help. I think we all need to talk about this—"

Astrid's eyes were blazing. "I don't think so. I need to find a way to get in touch with my brother." Then she turned and walked out, her shoulders stiff and her gait rigid as she ignored all the congratulations from the townspeople, wishing her brother good luck on his excellent marriage.

Emma bit her lip as she watched Astrid leave. "Should I go after her?"

"No." Clare put her arm around Emma's shoulder. "She needs space. Right now, she won't hear anything you say."

Dismay flooded Emma, and she turned back toward the float. Suddenly, the garish colors and bright glitter seemed obnoxious and rude, not cheerful and fun. "I think I'm going to skip out. I don't think I can do this—"

Clare put a paintbrush in her hand. "You have to. You just drove off one of my helpers, and I can only use certain paints." She patted her belly and winked at Emma.

Emma stared at her for a long moment as gradual understanding began to dawn. "Are you...pregnant?"

"Ssh!" Clare waved her into silence. "We're not telling anyone yet, but I wanted you to know. I'm only two months along."

The most amazing sense of wonder flooded her, chased ruthlessly by an envy and isolation so deep that she almost couldn't breathe. Emma was thrilled for her friend, she really was, but at the same time, it left an aching sense of loneliness inside her. "Congratulations." Emma hugged her, holding Clare so tightly, even as she felt her friend sliding out of her life. A new baby, a new husband, and a new business...what space would be left for Emma? She managed a smile, even though tears were burning in the back of her eyes. Tears of joy for her dear friend who had suffered so much, and tears of sadness for what it would mean for them, and for the way it made her look at her own, empty life. "I'm so happy for you guys. That is fantastic news."

Clare beamed at her. "Thanks." She nodded at her daughter, who was hitting up some teen boy to try to get him to climb the ladder and grab a couple of hay bales for her. "Katie is super excited to be a big sister. I was afraid she'd be jealous, but she's happy about it. Brooke's thrilled as well, which is wonderful."

"They're lucky to have a family," Emma said softly.

"I know they are." Clare sat beside her on an upturned tractor tire while Emma got out her paints. "So, tell me, why did you marry Harlan? I know how you feel about marriage."

Emma hesitated. "Because I love him?"

Clare laughed and shook her head. "Sweetie, I've known you since we were riding tricycles. You can't lie to me. Astrid might have known you for only two years, but I know you like I know myself. You don't love him, and I know you're still afraid of marriage and men. So why did you do it?"

Emma sighed as she pried open the can of light green paint. "He suggested it," she said. "But it made sense to me." She glanced around to make sure no one else was listening, and then lowered her voice. "You remember Mattie?"

Clare nodded. "The sweet little girl from your class? The one whose mother died?"

"Yes." Emma couldn't prevent the surge of anticipation that leapt through her. "I am hoping to adopt her."

"Oh, my God!" Clare screamed and jumped up to hug her. "That is so awesome! You'll be a great mother!"

"Wait." Emma peeled her arms off. "Her aunt and uncle want to adopt her, too, and so do her grandparents in South Carolina. Chloe, her social worker, said that I don't have a chance against them as a single woman."

Understanding flared on Clare's face. "So, you're now

married with an absentee husband." She cocked her head. "What's his job? Why does he travel all the time?"

Emma hesitated. "It's not my place to tell."

"Wow. It's *that* kind of job." Clare rubbed her chin. "Does Harlan know he's on the hook to become a dad if this works?"

Emma stared at her. "What? No, I'll adopt her myself—"

"What? Are you insane?" Clare gave her an incredulous look. "He's your husband. It'll be his deal as well, don't you think?"

Emma shoved the paint stirrer into the can and began to churn the paint, trying not to feel the weight of her words as she said them. "He's not coming back. Not ever." *He's not coming back. Not ever.* Words that had been a comfort to her last night, and even this morning, suddenly felt cruel.

"Oh." Clare looked sad for a moment. "He didn't want Astrid to know."

Emma shook her head.

"Men," Clare sighed as she absently ran a hand over her flat belly. "They just don't get women, do they? We're so much stronger than they think we are."

Emma didn't feel very strong at the moment. Wearily, she sank down on a hay bale across the aisle and looked imploringly at the woman who had been her best friend for more than two decades. "Will you help me?"

Clare raised her eyebrows. "With Mattie? You'll be a great mom, Emma. You won't need my help."

"No, not that." She shook her head, suddenly feeling so overwhelmed with the choice she had made, with all that was at stake. "With convincing the social worker that I'm really married to the love of my life."

Clare gave her a long, appraising look that wasn't entirely without censure. "You're going to adopt a child through lies?"

Emma swallowed, her head starting to throb. "It's not all

lies. I am married. I've known him for years. We have this...connection. It's real."

Sudden interest flared in Clare's eyes, and she leaned forward, swooping in on the nugget Emma had let slip. "What kind of connection?"

Emma's heart began to race again, and she inched closer to Clare, needing desperately to tell *someone* the truth. "I don't know what it is, but it's..." She didn't finish. She didn't know how to describe it. "I am absolutely terrified of marriage, Clare. More than words can express. When Harlan and I were about to do it, I started to get dizzy and I thought I was going to faint." She thought back to that moment when he'd wrapped his arms around her, how all the terror had seemed to fade in his embrace. "Then he held me, and the fear just...dissolved. I felt safe."

Clare's face softened, and she squeezed Emma's hand. "That's beautiful, Emma. You deserve to feel safe."

"It felt good," Emma admitted. "I'm not afraid of him. I don't know if it's because he was leaving or what it is." She managed a grin, trying to lighten the moment. "Maybe it's those blue eyes of his. Who could be afraid of a man with such incredible blue eyes? I mean, you should see them when he smiles, which isn't often, of course, but they get this little crinkle at the corners, like he's laughing in his heart, even though he can't hear it over all the noise in his head, you know?"

"Laughing in his heart? Harlan, the man who hasn't cracked a smile in five years?" A sudden gleam ignited in Clare's eyes. "Emma, did you sleep with him?"

Emma couldn't keep the smile off her face. "I did. And it was the best night of my life."

Clare clapped her hands, shrieking with delight. "Oh, my God, he broke through your walls! That's so incredible! I didn't think anyone ever would after Preston did so much damage. I'm so happy for you!"

"Ssh!" Emma grabbed her hands. "Stop!"

"Okay." Clare was beaming now. "Of course I will help you. Mattie deserves the two of you."

"Harlan's not in the picture. He's gone, remember? It's just me—"

"No, it's not just you," Clare scoffed, rolling her eyes. "Are you kidding? Harlan is not a drifter, and he's not a casual dater. The man has never even so much as looked at a single woman in the five years that he's lived here. Not once. The fact that he married you and took you to bed?" She grinned. "Sweetie, the man will be coming back for you, I can guarantee it."

THE MAN WILL BE COMING BACK for you.

Clare's words kept hammering at Emma, even as she stumbled through her week at the museum. Mattie only came to class on Mondays, so she wasn't in all week, and Chloe had no news to report on that situation. Between Harlan and Mattie, Emma couldn't even focus.

He wasn't coming back for her. He wasn't. He'd made it clear. She didn't want him to. That had been part of the deal. But even so, she found herself jumping each time she saw a black pickup truck drive past, or heard a motorboat slow down when passing her house. In the middle of the night last night, a boat had passed in the darkness, and she'd gotten out of bed so quickly that she'd tripped on her flip-flops and cracked her hand on her bedside table.

By the time she'd picked herself up, the boat was gone.

Of course it had been gone. Harlan wasn't at his house. She knew that, because she'd driven by it after her conversation with Clare. It had been locked down tight, with boards across the windows. But, true to his word, his boat was still docked, and the keys had been in the glove box. Had he really left it for her?

The thought made her want to cry, and she didn't know why.

By Friday afternoon, she was a head case. She leaned back in her creaky chair and stared out the dusty window of her office, trying to focus. He'd been gone a week, but it had felt like an eternity. The night of lovemaking seemed so distant. Could it really have been that good? Had the connection really been that intense?

A light knock sounded at her door, and she tried to pull on a smile as she sat back up. "Come in."

The door swung open and in walked Chloe. "I've been trying to call you all day," she said. "Is your phone off or something?"

Emma glanced at her phone and saw it was out of battery. "Sorry. I didn't even notice. I'll charge it when I get home. What's up?"

Chloe sat down across from her. "Good news."

"Really?" Hope surged through her, and she gripped the table "What is it?"

Chloe leaned forward. "Listen, Emma. The judge has agreed to table the decision about Mattie's placement and to consider you as an option."

Emma stared at her in disbelief, elation leaping through her. "No," she whispered. "No. No!" She screamed the last one.

"Yes!" Chloe laughed as Emma hugged her. "Don't get so excited. It's a long process and you're still the underdog. There's a lot of paperwork to file, and a home visit and all sorts of hoops to jump through. If you got approved, it would be a foster situation first and if that went okay, and her situation with her relatives didn't improve, only then would adoption be an option." She sighed. "I'll be honest, Emma, I don't like it. I really don't believe the judge will end up placing her with you, and if you foster her, it's going to create bonds that will crush her if they're broken. I don't think you should pursue foster. Just try for adoption and don't tell Mattie until and unless you are approved."

"And leave her in that house for months? The one where she was so unhappy that she crawled out the third floor window and almost got herself killed? You want me to back off and leave her there?" Emma couldn't keep the shock out of her voice. "You're kidding, right?"

Chloe grimaced. "I see your point, but I've also seen too many children get broken when enough people they trust abandon them."

Emma's mouth dropped open. "Abandon her? I would never—"

"Not on purpose, no, of course not. But to a child, it doesn't matter if it's intentional or not. In her heart, her mother abandoned her by dying. Her dad abandoned her by disappearing when she was born. Her aunt and uncle are abandoning her by being declared unfit. And if she falls in love with you and then gets sent to South Carolina to live, that will be the fourth abandonment for her. I think you should step aside and just pursue adoption."

Emma hesitated, her heart aching as she thought of Mattie sitting all alone in that huge house. How many hours every day had she done the same thing as a child? Just wanting someone to hug her once, just one time. One hug was all she'd wanted, and she'd never gotten it. "Sometimes," she said quietly, "it's better to have a friend for a little bit, even if you can't have them forever. If you are abandoned, at least that means someone loved you once, and that can carry you through a lot."

Chloe sighed. "I don't know that you're right, Em. Sometimes having the person you put your trust into walk away is worse than never having had them in the first place." She met her gaze. "I don't think you should do it."

Emma thought of Mattie sitting alone on the edge of that roof, and she knew that she would never forgive herself if she didn't try. Someone had to hold Mattie's hand during this tough time, and there was no one else doing it. "I'm going to petition to foster her."

Despite Chloe's grimace, there was no doubt in Emma's mind that she was doing the right thing. But as she grabbed her pen to take notes on the next steps, a little niggle of doubt nudged at the back of her mind.

Failed trust was brutal.

She knew that.

Which was worse, never having had anyone, or having them betray you?

They both sucked.

Dammit.

She didn't have the answers.

BY THE TIME Emma got home that night, she was exhausted, but feeling a little better than she had in days. With Chloe's help, she'd managed to talk to Mattie on the phone and reassure herself that the little girl was okay. Mattie's excitement about hearing from Emma had reinforced her decision to do all she could to get Mattie out of that foster home as soon as possible. She'd stayed at work filling out forms, not leaving her desk until she'd done everything she could.

So relieved to be home in her little cabin, she plugged her phone in and dropped onto her bed. Wearily, she studied her room, trying to evaluate it from the point of view of a social worker on a home visit. There were only three main rooms: her bedroom, the living-dining area, and a small room that she used as a studio for her painting. She'd have to change that to Mattie's room. Mattie's room. *Mattie's room.*

Emma kicked off her shoes and rolled onto her back, staring at the roughened boards of her wood ceiling. Was it really possible that she could give Mattie a home, and a family? That the next time Mattie cried, Emma would be there to hug her? She wasn't religious, but a little prayer slipped from her lips. "Please, God, let Mattie come home."

She could still remember the shock and then excitement in Mattie's voice when she'd heard Emma on the phone today. It was good. So good.

Her phone finally regained enough charge to catch service and beeped that she had a message. Probably Chloe. Her mind full of ideas about how to redo the house to make it a real home for Mattie, Emma rolled onto her side and picked up her phone. Five new messages?

She touched the voicemail screen and saw three from Chloe, one from Clare, and one from an unlisted number. Her heart jumped, and she stared at the blocked number for a moment. Harlan? Her hand trembling, she hit play. A woman's voice sent shards of disappointment through her. "Hello. This message is for Emma Larson. Please call me back immediately, no matter what the time. It's urgent." She then carefully recited a phone number.

A cold chill settled on Emma and she sat up abruptly, the phone slipping out of her hand. It couldn't be the call Harlan had warned her about, could it? Impossible. He'd been gone only a week. Her breath became tight in her chest and she swung her feet over the edge of the bed.

For a long moment, she stared at the phone, afraid to pick it up, afraid to touch it. *The man will be coming back for you,* Clare had assured her.

But what if he was dead?

She didn't want a husband who had the power to destroy her, but the thought of Harlan being dead was asphyxiating. Suddenly, she needed air.

Grabbing the phone with wooden fingers, Emma walked numbly out the door and onto her dock. The wood was hard and cool beneath her bare feet, and the water had the early evening stillness that made it feel like it was afraid to move, holding its breath in terrified anticipation.

Too restless to sit, she paced along the dock, a thousand possibilities running through her mind, all of them more terrible than the other. A boat sped by, startling her, and she spun around as it whipped past, spraying water just as Harlan's boat had done that night.

She knew she had to make the call. She'd promised him.

With trembling fingers, she dialed the number and held her phone to her ear. A woman answered before the first ring had even finished. "Emma Larson?"

She swallowed. "Yes, I'm Emma Larson."

The woman was business-like and direct. "Harlan Shea has you listed as his wife and next of kin."

Emma sank down onto the rough wood, suddenly unable to stand as she gripped the phone. "What happened?" she whispered.

"I am sorry to inform you that Harlan Shea is currently listed as missing-in-action."

"What?" She gripped the phone tighter, her breath coming in rough gasps. "What does that mean?"

The woman's voice softened ever so slightly. "I can't give you details, Ms. Larson. I'm sorry that there is no closure, but until we find his body, we can't officially declare him dead."

"His body?" Her own voice sounded distant and foreign, as if it wasn't even her speaking. "What? Dead? He can't be dead."

"I will contact you when we have more information. If you don't hear from me, nothing has changed. I'm very sorry." Then the woman disconnected.

The phone was cold in her hand. Her chest was tight. She couldn't breathe. Missing? What did that mean? Was he half-dead somewhere, waiting to die? Lying in the woods like his father had, unable to do anything but watch the ominous approach of death? That was what he'd feared, more than death itself. "Dammit!" She lurched to her feet, anger racing through her. How could that man, that vibrant, passionate man be out there somewhere, lost and dying?

He wasn't going to die alone. He wasn't! She grabbed her phone and dialed Astrid's number.

Her friend didn't answer.

"Astrid. It's Emma. I need Harlan's email address. Whatever you have. Now." She hung up, and called Clare. No answer there either. "Dammit!"

Why hadn't she gotten Harlan's email or phone number before? Why? Because she hadn't wanted to stay connected to him. But now, the thought of him trapped and dying out there, somewhere, alone...it was agonizing.

She knew what it was like to be alone, so alone that the very air itself was oppressive, crushing down until it became impossible to breathe. Almost frantic now, she scrolled through her phone, hoping against hope that maybe she had his contact information in there from the past. From before she *knew* him. But there was nothing listed for Harlan Shea.

Dammit!

She pressed the phone to her forehead, trying to think. Had he called her? She didn't think he had, but she scrolled through her recent calls, just to see. No missed calls from a number she didn't recognize...then she saw an outgoing call to a number she didn't know. A call that was made at six thirty-three on the morning Harlan had left, after spending the night with her. At six thirty-three, she'd still been asleep, and her phone had been by her bed. He'd used her phone!

Elation rushing through her, she hit "send" on the phone, but all she got was a weird buzzing and then a dial tone.

Dammit! She quickly checked her email. Incoming emails. Nothing. Sent emails—

The first sent email was one she hadn't sent. No subject line. No content. The email address was one she didn't recognize, a random assortment of letters and numbers that meant nothing.

But it had been sent at six thirty-four on that same morning, one minute after that phone call. For a long moment, she stared at it, hope rushing through her. Had Harlan sent it to himself so that he had her email address? Or had he emailed someone else?

She stared at the phone for a minute, then typed a couple letters into an email and sent it to that address. She waited, but received no error message in return. The email address was valid. Who was it? Was it his email address? Someone else's?

It didn't matter.

If there was any chance that it was Harlan's, she was going to use it.

She sat down cross-legged in the middle of the dock and started to type.

HARLAN. I just got the call that you're missing. Wherever you are, whatever is happening to you, I'm thinking of you. You aren't alone. I promise you're not. Emma.

SHE DIDN'T KNOW what else to write, so she just hit send and then set the phone down. Her hands were shaking. But she'd done it. He would have his phone with him. He would check his email. He would know—

Her phone buzzed that she had an email. Her heart leaping, she grabbed for it...and saw that both emails to that address had been returned as undeliverable.

CHAPTER EIGHT

HARLAN COULDN'T BREATHE.

The pain was too great. Cracked rib. Was his lung punctured? Not good.

He couldn't see. His eyes were burning.

He tried to crawl, but his body wouldn't work.

Rocks dug into his palms. Tore at his fingers. He dug into the wet dirt and tried to shove his hand into a crevice in the rock. Tried to pull himself a little farther. Just a little farther—

He lost his grip and fell, skidding farther down the rocky cliff. He hit the rocks below and couldn't move. His body was numb. His hip was screaming in agony. The rain was cold and relentless, like a thousand needles piercing his flesh. Mud washed beneath him, streaming down the side of the mountain.

He lay there, in the mud, in the pounding rain, unable to save his own damn ass.

Just like his father.

"Emma," he managed to whisper, his voice raw. He moved his left hand, trying to touch the tattoo on his wrist, but he couldn't reach it. Exhausted, he let his arms fall back into the mud. His thoughts went back to Emma, to the only thing he wanted to think about. He could see her blond hair spread over the pillow as he'd left her that morning. He could remember it so vividly that it still felt like it had been merely hours since he'd been with her. The curve of her bare shoulder. The scent of their lovemaking, combined with that barely-there fragrance of her hair. Some sort of flower that reminded him of spring. The innocence and sweetness of her face as she slept.

Walking away from her had been the hardest fucking thing he'd ever done. All he'd wanted to do was bury himself in her and cement himself into her soul until she lived and breathed for him. But he'd left, because that was their deal, and because he belonged out here, not in some life he couldn't deliver on.

But now, as he lay here rotting away, he realized it wasn't enough, what he'd gotten from her. The taste had been intoxicating and addictive, making him want to be the man he wasn't, the man he could never be, not for her, and not for anyone.

He'd walked away from her, knowing that he'd just gotten as close to heaven as he was ever going to get...and now...he was going to die out here in this fucking isolated stretch of hell.

Did she know? Did she care? What would she do when Renée called her?

But even as he thought about the fact that he had someone out there who would get the call, who would notice when he was gone, who would take care of his body after he died, there was no relief.

Emma was his wife, but in name only. She would honor his death, but not feel it in her heart.

Son of a bitch.

It wasn't enough.

He was going to die, and it wasn't fucking enough. He wanted to *matter*. Not to just anyone. He wanted to matter to *her*. And that made him the most selfish son of a bitch ever. He wanted to matter to her, so she would cry for him? He was a true bastard.

He was still the same as his father, and what he'd done with Emma wasn't going to change that fact, no matter how many damn times he replayed their lovemaking in his mind or called her his wife. He'd been a fool to think he could change who he was, to become a man other than the one he was destined to be.

His breath started to gurgle, and he knew he was out of time.

He was going to die alone, and he grimly realized that was the way it was supposed to be. "Emma," he said, his voice raw with the effort of speaking. "I release you from your promise."

It was done. This story was over.

THREE WEEKS HAD PASSED since the call.

Three excruciating weeks.

There had been no word about Harlan.

Astrid had been horrified when Emma had told her about the call from Harlan's business, and she'd sent repeated emails to Harlan, but received no answer. She'd even relented and given his email address to Emma, and she'd sent emails, too.

No replies.

In the last year, he'd never once replied to an email sent to that address, and Emma had a feeling he never checked it. The fact he hadn't responded didn't mean he was dead. He could be alive. Or not. The uncertainty haunted her night and day. Was he alive, dead, or suffering terribly somewhere? She couldn't shake the pulsating sense of fear that stalked her at every moment.

It was unnerving, how she was reacting to his disappearance. She didn't know him and had married him with the intention of never seeing him again. The situation was playing out exactly as he had predicted, so she should be fine, or even relieved. But instead, there was a dark cloud of uncertainty, fear, and raw grief following her around. She couldn't stop thinking of him dying somewhere. Alone.

She knew what alone was. Alone had haunted her for the first twenty-five years of her life, until marriage to Preston had finally showed her that going through life alone, which she'd always thought was hell, could actually be the greatest solace that existed. Alone meant no Preston, no one to rule her, no one to control her. She'd learned it too late, because her fear of being alone had been what had driven her into the arms of the man who had done his best to destroy her.

Alone was her safety now, but that didn't change the fact that there were days when it was no longer a relief, and instead plunged her into a darkness so penetrating that it seemed to suck the life from her soul, make her heart bleed, and strip her of the courage to take even one more step. Before she'd connected with Harlan, she'd been surviving in her shell, but now that she'd had her night with him, now that her name was etched beside his on a marriage certificate, now that she'd known what it was like to truly connect with someone, alone seemed to have retreated back to what it used to be. Too dark. Too haunting. Too agonizing. Was that the kind of alone that Harlan had faced before he died? Or that he was facing in that exact moment?

No one deserved that. Not Harlan. Not Mattie. No one.

Except maybe Preston, she thought with a small smile.

Not that she had time to dwell, she reminded herself as

she gripped her steering wheel, heading toward her cabin. The summer Shakespeare festival was only two days away, and the town was running on all cylinders trying to get everything in shape for the tourists who would descend for the week. The field at the rec center had been cleared of soccer nets to make room for the carnival. The town green was already decorated with dozens of tents for the local businesses. Emma, Clare, and Astrid usually shared a tent to sell Emma's art, Astrid's jewelry, and Clare's cupcakes, but this year, now that Clare's cupcake store was going strong, she had the tent next door to herself, and was paying Katie and Brooke, the teen queens, to help her run it.

Birch Crossing was alive with energy and fire, tearing Emma from her unsettling emotions about Harlan. Chloe had arranged for Emma to bring Mattie to the carnival on the last day, and Emma was excited about that. It wasn't a foster test or anything, just a field trip with a favorite teacher, but she knew it would make Mattie happy, and that was a start.

But Emma did have a home study scheduled in less than twenty-four hours, where a social worker would stop by and interview Emma and inspect her home. She had to pass the home study in order to get approved to adopt or even foster, and she was becoming increasingly nervous about it...especially the fact that she had a husband who had never lived there.

Just as the oppression seemed to settle in, however, she saw a stream of trucks driving toward her on the winding road. Her mood lifted immediately as she watched the caravan with the carnival rides pass by the town green, heading in the opposite direction than she was driving. Suddenly, she was flooded with years of memories about the carnival, all the wonderful times she and Clare had shared sneaking onto rides, begging for free cotton candy, and spying on all the actors while they were practicing their lines. The last truck had the painted horses of the carousel, and she grinned at the sight of it. She and Clare had ridden that merry-go-round a hundred times every summer until they were eighteen, the summer Clare had gotten married.

Maybe she would start a new tradition with Mattie.

Smiling to herself, she pulled up in front of her house, starting to think about what pictures she would display at the booth this year. There were none that she wanted to display. They all felt wrong for where she was right now.

She needed new ones. She hadn't painted much in the last weeks, so busy with the fair, but suddenly, she needed to. Desperately. She needed to sit out on her dock, and pour her emotions onto the canvas. Pour her feelings about Harlan into her art.

Grabbing her purse off the front seat, she ran up the steps to her cabin, the image she wanted to paint already forming in her mind. A carousel on a cloudy day. Empty, except for a half of a cupcake on the edge. The shadow of a man, just his shoulders, darkening the flank of a white horse—

A shadow moved on her couch, and she screamed, jumping backward.

As she stumbled back, Harlan sat up on her sofa, his broad shoulders hunched, his face ashen and hollow.

Shock rippled through her and she grabbed the door frame. "Harlan?" she whispered. Was she dreaming? There was no way that Harlan could be sitting on her couch in the middle of the afternoon. "You're alive?"

"Yeah." His voice was low and rough, and it sent chills tumbling through her. Chills of fear. Of relief. Of a thousand different emotions that threatened to overwhelm her. She wanted to burst into tears, race across the room, and throw herself into his arms. At the same time, her instincts were shouting at her to back out of the room, away from this man that she had bound herself to in one dangerous night, who had been haunting her since the day he'd walked out.

He lifted his head to look at her, and her heart seemed to shatter at the haunting shadows in his eyes. Suddenly, all the connection they had shared that night came flooding back, and her fear left. This man was not like Preston. He was not like all the others who had betrayed her. She had been right to trust him. "You came back," she whispered, putting her hand over her chest as if she could ease the hammering of her heart. He'd come back to her, just like Clare had predicted.

"Not for long," he said quietly. "Don't worry."

"You're leaving again?" Disappointment flooded her, anguish beyond what was reasonable. "Another mission?" She was going to have to wait for him to die again? Suddenly, it just felt like too much. She couldn't do that again—

"Not for a while." He shifted, and a flash of pain shot across his face. "I'm sidelined for a bit."

Her heart jumped, and she instinctively reached out to help him. "You're hurt."

"I'm fine. Just my hip. It's better now." He blocked her hand, redirecting it away from him, rejecting her touch.

Embarrassment flooded her, and Emma hugged herself. "Sorry."

"No, it's fine." Something flickered across his face. Not pain. Something else. But then he raised his gaze to hers, gripping her with the intensity of his stare. "Emma, I came back for one reason."

Her mouth went dry, and suddenly she couldn't speak as hope leapt through her. Hope and terror. Was this it? Was this when he said he wanted more than a paper marriage? That he wanted *her?* "Why?" she whispered. "Why did you come back?"

He met her gaze. "To get a divorce."

She was more than he'd remembered. More than he'd hoped. More than he could handle.

Harlan hadn't been prepared for the shock of seeing Emma again. He'd convinced himself that his memory of their deep, intense connection had been a fabrication, or at best, an aberration that was a result of a dark night, death, and a whole host of other shit.

He had not been prepared to feel like he'd been sucker-punched in the gut when she'd walked through that door, her hair up in an adorably innocent ponytail, her forehead scrunched in thought, her light blue tank top revealing skin so soft he wanted to trail his lips over it.

The moment he'd seen her, every thought had been swept from his head except for a raw, burning need for her. To touch her. To hold her. To kiss her. To claim her as his wife. He'd gone utterly still, like a predator, every fiber of his being screaming for her. It had taken every last ounce of willpower to speak the words he'd come there to say.

At his announcement, Emma's eyes widened in shock. The pain that flashed over her face was so brutal that he felt as if she'd jammed a knife into his chest. "What? You want a divorce?"

He had to close his eyes for a split second to cut himself off from the betrayal in her eyes. Why the hell was she looking at him like that? He was freeing her, not betraying her. "Yeah," he said, opening his eyes again, unable to cut himself off from the sight of her.

She had retreated to the far side of the room now, her arms folded over her chest, and her chin raised as she stood beside the picture window that looked out onto the lake. Gone was the look of vulnerability in her eyes, the stark anguish on her face. She was cool and collected, and he fucking hated seeing her like that. He liked her soft and vulnerable. He liked her raw and real, not throwing up shields against him.

"Why?" she asked, her voice trembling ever so slightly, her voice barely audible over the roar of a Jet Ski passing by the cottage.

Damned if he didn't like the shakiness of her voice. He didn't want her to let him go. He didn't want her to not care. Which made him an even bigger shit than he already knew he was. With a sigh, he ran his hand through his hair, trying to remember the arguments he'd been primed to make. "Because it was crap." Poetic? Not so much. He didn't know how to say it nicely, because he could barely grit out the words he didn't mean. Every thought he had of Emma and their night together was magical. Connection. A life worth living for. But he couldn't say that. He couldn't trap her like that. He had to set her free. He leveraged himself to his feet, but he had to grab the edge of the couch when his hip tried to buckle.

"Crap?" she echoed in disbelief. "Our marriage? Or the lovemaking? Or the promises? What was 'crap' exactly, Harlan, because I actually meant everything I said to you, including my promise to be married to you until death do us part."

He swore under his breath, searching for words. He owed her. This woman who had married him and agreed to cry for him when he died. She deserved the truth, not superficial sentiments that didn't matter. He was too old and too damn tired for superficiality anyway. "I was lying there in the rain," he said. "I thought I was going to die. I thought it was over." He grimaced, trying to articulate shit he had no words for.

"I wrote you emails," she said softly. "Every day."

He blinked, distracted by her words. "What?"

"Emails. To the address you left on my phone. To the

email address Astrid had. I started writing them after that woman called and said you were missing. I didn't forget you. You weren't alone. Did you see them?"

"No, I didn't. But...thank you for that." Weirdly, his throat tightened and he had to look away. He'd shut down that email address after he'd sent the information to himself, but it didn't matter. The thought that she'd actually been sending him emails while he'd been lying on that cliff. That she'd been thinking of him? It was too much to deal with. Almost overwhelming. She'd really been thinking of him?

He flexed his jaw, and looked back at her. She looked small again, vulnerable, not tough like the façade she'd put on a few minutes ago. "I'm a stranger to you, Emma, and I asked you to cry for me. What kind of bastard does that?"

She sighed, and her face softened. "The kind who doesn't want to die alone."

Shit. How was she not judging him for what he'd done? "No, Em." He walked over to her, needing her to understand. "The kind of supreme bastard who thinks it's okay to manipulate others just so he can get off."

Her eyes widened, and she started to laugh, a tension-relieving kind of laughter. "I had no idea you thought so highly of yourself, Harlan."

He was startled by her laughter. He didn't understand it. There was no humor in his life. In his choices. In their choices. "I need to free you," he said softly, barely resisting the urge to grasp one of the stray locks dangling around her face and slide it through his hand. He knew how soft her hair was, and he still wanted it as badly as he ever had. "I'm not a man that anyone should marry, especially you."

She cocked her head, and he had a sense that she was seeing right into his soul, stripping all his secrets bare and raw. It made him uncomfortable, but at the same time, it felt good. He liked it. He liked knowing that she wanted to learn the things about him that he didn't show to anyone. "Why me, especially?" she asked.

"Because you're specia—" He suddenly noticed a small scar on the corner of her mouth, and he tensed as he touched it with his fingers. "Did your ex do that to you?"

Emma brushed her finger over it. "Yes."

He ground his jaw and dropped his hand. Did he need more evidence that this life wasn't for him? That he had no business forcing Emma into his world? "I'm going to talk to Ned and see what we need to do—"

Emma grabbed his hand as he turned away. Electricity leapt through him, and he stopped, unable to pull himself out of her grasp. But he didn't look at her. "I need to go," he said softly. "If I don't go now, I'm not going to walk away ever, but I have to."

"Why?" It was a whisper, as if she didn't even want to say it, as if she were afraid to hear the answer.

He looked back at her, but didn't turn away from the door. He couldn't take his gaze off the scar on her lip. "Your ex hit you."

She frowned, her brow furrowing. "And that makes me tainted?" She released his hand, retreating. "Sorry about that," she bit out. "I didn't mean to bring you down."

"Tainted? Shit no, you're not the one who's tainted. You're...you're like..." Hell, he had no words, no poetry to describe what she brought into his life. He turned back to her, unable to stay away, knowing he had to say something to make them both realize that it had to stop between them, but somehow he had to do it without hurting her, without making her think that she was anything but the most beautiful treasure he could ever be offered. "I told you my father got injured and collapsed in the woods, and he lay out there until he died, right? Then rotted for a few more months after that?"

She grimaced, nodding slightly. "Yes, but—"

"I didn't tell you why he collapsed or how he got injured." Harlan ground his jaw, refusing to let his emotions revisit the memories of that night. He kept his mind rigidly focused, struggling not to relive that moment that he never allowed himself to think about.

She cocked her head, studying him. "What happened?"

He met her gaze and let her see the truth in his eyes. "I tried to kill him with a chair," he said neutrally. "I didn't completely succeed and he got away, only to die alone in the woods from the wounds I had inflicted upon him. I was fifteen."

Emma's mouth dropped open. "What?"

"My father was a bastard, Emma. He beat my step-mother. He did the same to me." He grimaced and told her the whole truth, needing her to understand who he was. "And I'm the same way. I'm his son in all ways. Getting married to you and then leaving was the only safe way for me to do it. I thought it would work." He shook his head, brushing his fingers over her cheek, needing to touch her, to feel the softness of her skin one last time. "But it was a lie," he said quietly. "A complete lie. I'm not that guy, and I can't do that. I can't be married to you and leave you alone. I dream about you every single night. I dream about our night together, and I wake up feeling your skin against mine, hearing your laughter, and craving you so much that it actually fucking hurts." He dropped his hand from her face. "As long as you're mine, it's not going to stop, and I'm not strong enough to fight it off forever. I need to go find Ned and free you, before I become the husband and father my old man was."

Her mouth was still open in wordless shock, and he didn't give her a chance to respond. He simply turned and walked out, almost hoping she would call him back and announce that he was wrong, that there was a chance for a guy like him...but she didn't.

Of course she didn't. Emma had seen darkness before, and she was too smart to go back there again.

Which was a relief.

She was not going to allow him to destroy one more life.

Victory.

A victory that felt like shit.

As Harlan walked out of her cabin, Emma's heart felt like it was being crushed. An icy cold terror crept down her arms like a slow, insidious poison. Fear so deep it seemed to freeze her very soul pulsed through her. Not just of Harlan, but of the fact that she hadn't seen that violent, dangerous side of him. Not even a tiny bit. She'd misjudged him, just like she'd misjudged Preston. Wrong again. *Wrong again.* So very, very wrong.

The screen door slammed shut and she slid down the wall, her entire body starting to tremble. Her mouth began to throb, the old wound from where Preston had struck her burning as if he'd just done it. The same fear rippled over her, that terror she'd felt as she'd scrambled back from him, not understanding who this man was coming at her, like she was in some alternate world. She'd never thought of Preston as a large man, not until he'd shoved her against the bookshelf with such force, not until the back of his hand had opened her lip, not until she'd been in that corner, with nowhere to go, with nowhere to hide as he approached her with such menace.

But Harlan *was* big. He was thick with corded muscles and broad shoulders. His whole being was physical, exuding such tremendous strength. It was his power that had attracted her to him, the sense of safety when she was with him. He was stronger than all the bad stuff in life. He made her feel like there was a great protective shield around her, like she could actually breathe deeply when he was holding her.

She didn't understand how that same strength that had drawn her to him, was actually something he would use against her? He used it to shield her from nightmares. He used it to rescue people who were kidnapped. He used it to do good things.

But what did he do to actually *free* those victims? She knew without words the world he inhabited. Of course he did violent, deadly things. No man could perform the job he did and be afraid to do what was necessary. She recalled too vividly his statement that he wanted to kill Preston. He wasn't lying about his violent side. It had been there all along. She'd just chosen not to see it. "Oh, God." She pressed her palms to her head. What had she done? Who had she married? She'd seen the absolute conviction in Harlan's eyes that he spoke the truth, that he was the man his father had been.

He'd married her so he wouldn't repeat his father's life by dying alone. But really, was a lonely death the part of his father he wanted to leave behind, or was it the other part? The part that had beaten his son and his wife? Was his father's violence actually the legacy that trapped him, not dying alone? "I can't do this," she whispered. "I just can't." But even as she said the words, cutting herself off from him, another part of her, a deeper part, cried for the loss of the man she'd believed he was.

CHAPTER NINE

HARLAN BRACED his palms on the warm hood of Emma's car, head down, fighting for control. He could still see the stark horror on Emma's face when he'd told her who he really was.

She'd trusted him, and he'd betrayed her. He could see it in every emotion on her face. The woman who had barely clawed her way back to life after a marriage from hell had put herself out there for him, believing him to be the good guy, and he'd ripped everything out from under her.

He'd broken his promise by coming back.

He'd taken the marriage away from her by declaring he was getting a divorce.

He'd cast filth on her dreams that she'd married a decent guy, telling her he was worse than the man who had nearly destroyed her. He'd made her realize that she'd married the very thing she feared most.

Why hadn't he been honest on the boat that night? Why hadn't he told her what he was really like? Why had he pretended that a midnight wedding and a quick departure would actually be a good idea?

Digging his fingers into the hood of her car, he raised his

head and looked back at the little cabin. She hadn't come after him. Of course she hadn't. He'd betrayed her. How many ways would he be like his father? More and more—

The sound of tires crunching on the dirt road caught his attention, and he swung around, instantly alert. Who was coming back into her private area? As he waited for the approaching car to emerge from the trees, he became grimly aware of how isolated her cabin was. What if her ex decided to come after her? Who would hear her cry for help? Who would come to her aid? Even as he thought it, a ski boat cruised by. On board were seven shirtless guys, shouting too loudly, with a few beer cans visible in their hands.

Harlan went still, watching them, his gut going cold. What if Emma was out on her dock one evening when they went by? There was nothing out here except for woods and lakefront. The lake was host to a bunch of rowdy summer residents, including testosterone junkies who might down a few too many beers and decide to cause trouble for a single woman living by herself.

A cold sweat broke out on his arms, and he whipped around as an antique Volkswagen lumbered into sight and parked in front of Emma's house. Harlan instinctively moved between the car and her front door as the driver's side opened and a young woman emerged. Maybe in her mid-twenties, she was wearing a loose white blouse and a pair of jeans. Her hair was tucked up in a loose bun. She looked casual, but there was an air to her that made Harlan think that a bullet would bounce right off her chest if someone tried to take her down. "Can I help you?" he said smoothly, intercepting her as she stepped out of the car.

She eyed him suspiciously. "You must be Harlan Shea."

He almost blinked in surprise. How in the hell did she know who he was? "I am," he said, not giving away anything. "And you are?"

"Dottie McPhee," she said. "Is your wife here?"

"My wife?" he echoed, an unfamiliar sensation rippling through him at the phrase. It felt good, but at the same time, dangerously wrong.

She peered at him. "You *are* married to Emma Larson, are you not?"

Harlan stared at her. "I am," he said slowly. "And who exactly are you?"

"Dottie McPhee," she repeated, her eyebrows going up when he didn't respond. "I'm here to conduct the home study. I'm a little early, but I was in the area so I thought I'd come by."

"Home study?" he echoed. "What are you talking about?"

Dottie's eyes narrowed. "You and your wife filed an application to become foster parents with intent to adopt, specifically of Mattie Williams." She drew her shoulders back. "Are you not aware of this petition?"

Harlan looked toward the house as understanding dawned over him. That was why Emma had been willing to get married. Because she had needed a husband. That was what she wanted him for. A child? Jesus. He was dangerous enough to her. A child? There was no way he could get involved in this situation. "I'm sorry, Ms. McPhee, but—"

The screen door slammed open, and Emma leapt into the doorway, her face stricken as she looked frantically back and forth between them. Her skin was ashen, so white that Harlan actually took a step toward her, reaching out to catch her if she passed out. "Dottie McPhee?" she croaked. "I thought the home study was tomorrow."

"No, it's today." The social worker eyed Emma, her mouth thinning out. "I was just speaking with your husband. He seems to be unaware of the petition you filed."

Emma's face paled even more, and her fingers gripped the door so tightly that her knuckles were white. Harlan had seen victims staring down death at the hands of their kidnappers, people so terrified that they could not even move, and yet never had he seen an expression of deeper, more heart-wrenching fear than the one on Emma's face. Not for her own life. For the life of some little girl named Mattie Williams, who was clearly a kid without a home or parents. "I —," she stammered. "He—"

Son of a bitch. He could not let this happen.

Harlan vaulted up the stairs and wrapped his arm around Emma, tucking her up against his side. She was shaking violently against him, and her skin was cold. "My apologies, Ms. McPhee," he said smoothly. "My job sends me into dangerous situations, and Emma was notified that I had gone missing in action. I was rescued two weeks ago, but I wasn't allowed to make contact until I was released. I was given permission last night, and I came straight home without even calling first. I knew that she needed to see me in person to believe I was still alive. I surprised her ten minutes ago, and we're both a little distracted." He pressed his lips to the top of her head. "I thought I was going to die without ever seeing her again, and she was afraid I was dead," he said softly, as he turned to Emma. "I'm here, Em. I really am."

Emma looked up at him, and he was shocked to see her eyes fill with tears. There was so much emotion in her eyes, so much fear, so much anguish, and a loneliness so deep that it seemed to reach inside him and tear open his chest. Unable to stop himself, he slid his hand behind her neck and lowered his head, brushing a soft kiss over her lips. "It's okay, sweet-heart," he said softly. "It's going to be okay." He didn't know what was going to be okay, or how, but he needed to say it. He needed to make it true. He had done so little right in his life, and he needed to change that, right now, right here, with the woman who had believed in him.

Emma's hand slid to his chest, and her fingers dug in, gripping the front of his shirt, as if trying to hang onto him and keep him from escaping. "Did you really almost die?" she whispered.

He put his hand over hers. "Nah," he said gently, unwilling to add more torment to the burden she was already carrying. "I was fine."

She searched his face. "You're lying," she said. "You really almost died, didn't you?"

He couldn't lie to her. Their relationship, what little of it there was, had been based on truths. "It was closer than I've been in a long time," he admitted. He managed a small smile. "But I kind of messed up my hip. I'm not doing anything more dangerous than limping to the fridge for a while, okay? No more missions."

Dottie cleared her throat, jerking Harlan's attention back to the present. Swearing under his breath, he tore his gaze off Emma and looked back toward the social worker, whose disapproving glare had been replaced by a misty-eyed romantic longing. "Well," she said, "I can answer one question already."

Harlan tucked Emma closer against him, and she wrapped her arms around his waist and rested her head against his shoulder, as if she was too exhausted to stand alone anymore. He didn't know why she was holding onto him, whether it was for show or because she wanted to, but all he knew was that it felt damned good. "What's that?" he asked.

"Whether you two actually love each other."

Emma's cheeks turned pink and she stiffened against him, but Harlan simply tightened his grip on her shoulders, pulling her even closer. Without a word, he held out his other arm, showing his wrist to Dottie.

She peered at his tattoo. "It's an 'E' with a rose bud."

Emma caught her breath as she looked at it as well. She touched his wrist, her fingers sliding over his skin so gently, a touch more delicate than he'd ever felt in his life. He wanted to savor it, to brand it in his memory, so he would never forget what it felt like.

"No matter how tough things get out in the field," he said, not taking his gaze off Emma, "my wife is always with me. The first flower I ever gave her was a sprig of yellow rose buds. She reminds me of sunshine and hope when I feel like the world is too dark, and the tattoo holds her to me even when we're apart."

He was aware of Emma's shocked intake of breath, and her gaze darted to his. Confusion and questions were etched on her face, but there was also a softness, as if it had somehow touched her. He hadn't meant to tell her, or anyone, about the tattoo, but somehow, it had seemed important that Dottie know. He didn't want her to doubt Emma's character, or question who she was. He might be dangerous for her in a thousand ways, but if he could protect her character and protect her dreams, then he would do it without hesitation.

He owed her that much. She'd married him. She'd sent him emails. She'd offered him her trust.

Dottie smiled and put her hand on her heart. "That is so beautiful," she said wistfully, and Harlan noticed that her left hand had no rings. No knight had ridden up to Dottie's front step. She smiled up at them. "Tell you what," she said. "It sounds like you two need a little time to adjust. Why don't I come back tomorrow? Maybe around noon?" She looked at Harlan for approval, but he turned to Emma. "Does that work for you, sweetheart?"

Emma nodded, and cleared her throat. "Yes, that would be great. Thank you for understanding."

"No problem." Dottie waved at them as she headed back toward her car. "I look forward to seeing you both tomorrow. Enjoy your afternoon."

They stood together and watched her go, Harlan's arm

still around Emma, who was still tucked up against his side, her hand still gripping his shirt.

Neither of them moved as Dottie started up her car.

Neither of them moved as she drove down the dirt road.

Neither of them moved as she disappeared from sight.

All alone they stood there, no longer needing to put on a show for Dottie, but neither of them made a move to pull away from the other.

It was Harlan who finally spoke, and the words struck fear deep into his own heart. Not fear for himself. Fear for the woman standing beside him. "So, I'm guessing divorce is no longer on the table right now."

Emma made a strangled noise and looked up at him. Her blond hair was tousled, making her look even younger and more vulnerable than usual. "We should talk."

"Yeah, I think that would be a good idea." He thought of the tiny cabin at his back, of the bed that held far too many memories of the woman he couldn't make himself let go of. "You have chairs on the dock?" He knew she did. He'd seen them that night.

She nodded, and finally, agonizingly, pulled herself away from him.

He let her go, and said nothing as she led the way around the cabin toward the water, toward the lake where it had all begun.

EMMA COULDN'T HELP IT. She really couldn't. She knew it was masochistic and pointless self-torture, but she couldn't stop herself from trying to get a better look at the tattoo on Harlan's wrist as he pulled two chairs together on the dock.

He suddenly stopped. "Just ask."

Emma straightened up, trying to put an innocent look on

her face, curling her bare toes into the worn-out wooden planks. "Ask what?"

One eyebrow quirked. "To see my tattoo."

"Tattoo?" she echoed, with feigned blankness, not quite willing to admit the insane curiosity burning through her to see it. "Do you have one?" Of course she knew he had something on his wrist. She'd seen it, and he knew it. But the quick glance hadn't been enough. She hadn't been able to see whether it really had been what he'd claimed. How could it be? He wouldn't really have gotten a tattoo for *her*, would he? She needed to know.

He studied her, then shrugged. "Fine with me if you don't want to see it." He sank down into the chair, sucking in his breath when his descent hitched, and he pressed his hand to his hip. He folded his arms over his chest and leaned back in his lawn chair that looked too white and girly for his bulk.

Emma cleared her throat and perched on the other seat. The late afternoon sun was casting a glow across the water, broken only by the occasional ripple of a passing boat. It was the ultimate serenity, but she felt as far from serene as it was possible to feel. She was jittery and on edge, so aware of Harlan's masculine presence in her space. He was as heavily muscled as he'd been before, but he looked more ragged and rough, like the mercenary he'd claimed to be. Had this man, this untamed crusader, actually inked her initial into his skin?

The way he had folded his arms made it clear that he was not going to reveal his tattoo unless she asked. "You're a jerk," she said lightly, all too aware that he knew exactly how much she wanted to see it.

He shrugged. "I think that gets me off easy, so thanks." He waited, watching her, his dark eyes so intense she felt like he was peeling away all her layers and exposing all her fears and insecurities to him.

Emma glanced at his wrist again. Had it really been an "E"

with a rose, or had he just claimed it was? Was it simply a close enough similarity that he could get away with the statement he'd made to Dottie? She needed to know what was really on his wrist. She needed to see for herself.

"You shouldn't care," he said softly.

She jerked her gaze to his, her pulse hammering. He was so close, only a few feet away, this man she'd married, and then thought she'd lost. She was so rattled by his presence, and at the same time, she couldn't stop thinking about how amazing it had felt to have him wrap his arm around her while they were on the steps a few minutes ago. Would it ever get old, the delicious feeling of warmth whenever he wrapped her in his arms? Even as the traitorous thoughts raced through her mind, she forced herself to lean back in her chair and look casually at the scenery behind him. "Care about what?"

"Whether some bastard like me actually got a tattoo honoring you," he said, his low voice rolling through her like a sensual caress. "You're more than that, Em. You shouldn't care what anyone else thinks or does."

Emma shifted in her seat, unable to keep her gaze off him. He was so intense, so sensual, so...there. "I know that." She did know that. But she wasn't a machine, and she couldn't turn off her emotions. "I want to see," she said. "I have to see it."

With a small grimace, Harlan unfolded his arms and leaned forward, holding out his wrist to her. She grabbed his hand to steady it. The feel of his hand in hers was electric, and for a brief moment, she froze, riveted by the sensation. He met her gaze, and neither of them moved. For a heartbeat, for two, for three, tension hung between them, a thousand unspoken words and emotions.

Oh, God, what was she doing? Embarrassed, she tore her gaze from him and peered at his arm. Her heart jumped when she saw the "E" inked on his skin, beautifully intertwined with a vine that had three yellow rose buds on it, exactly like the one he'd left on her bed. She looked up at him, but his face was stoic. "This is really for me?"

"Yeah. Yeah, it is."

"When...when did you get it?"

"The day I left." He looked at her. "The day I walked out on you. I couldn't get you out of my mind, the way you looked that morning. You were asleep on your back, with one arm above your head. Your hair was spread over the pillow, and there was a ray of sunshine across your cheek and one lock of your hair. The roses were next to your fingers, as if you knew they were there, even in your sleep." His voice became lower, a deep melody that seemed to vibrate in her belly. "I'd never experienced anything so perfect in my life. I didn't want to ever forget that moment."

"Oh. Wow. Um..." What did a woman say in response to that? This was the man who claimed he was so dangerous that he should never be near his own wife? "That's...beautiful. No one has ever said anything like that to me before."

"Then everyone you've met had his head up his ass."

A shocked laugh burst out of her, and she quickly released him. Too agitated to sit in the chair, she got up and paced the dock. Tied up next to it was Harlan's boat. For some reason, the tattoo and his reason for doing it were overwhelming for her. It was a permanent link to bind them, that he had designed to take into battle with him. A link that he couldn't lose, no matter what. They could get divorced a thousand times, and he would still have her initial and the roses on his arm. "I don't understand," she said finally, turning toward him, trying desperately to reconcile the heartfelt words he'd just spoken with the man he'd claimed to be just a short while ago. "Who *are* you?"

"I told you." His forearms were draped loosely over his

quads, his shoulders hunched, and his head low as he watched her through hooded eyes. She could easily see him as a predator in that position, and she shivered.

"Tell me about Mattie Williams," he said, changing the subject.

"Mattie?" This was a subject she felt comfortable with. Relieved at the new topic, Emma took a deep breath and walked to the edge of the dock, facing the mountains on the other side. "She's five. Her father left when she was a baby. Her mom died a few months ago. Her fourteen-year-old brother ran away three weeks ago and hasn't been found yet. Her aunt and uncle have been declared unfit, so the judge wants to send her to live with her grandparents in South Carolina, but she doesn't like them and doesn't want to move there." Her voice became tight with emotion, and she paused, trying to hold herself together. Too many emotional shocks were overwhelming her. Maybe Mattie wasn't the best topic right now. Maybe she should talk about the best way to skin a fish or something. Not that she knew it, but discussing fish dissection would be a good distraction, right?

Harlan swore under his breath. "How do you know her?"

"I teach her." Emma turned back to him, her mind filled with the memories his question had elicited. "I remember the first day she walked into my class. She had pink bows at the ends of her braids, and she was wearing a bright fuchsia shirt with sparkles. She looked like the sweetest, happiest little kid when she bounded in." Tears burned in her eyes as she recalled that first moment. "It was the first class, and I told them to draw whatever was in their heart. I believe that art comes from the soul, and I try to create that atmosphere for the kids."

Harlan was watching her intently. "What did she draw?"

"An angel floating in a blue sky smiling down at a girl who was standing in a field of pink flowers. She drew big tears on the little girl's face." Emma hugged herself, her throat tightening as she relived that moment, that terrible, heart-wrenching moment when she first understood the little girl standing before her. "When I asked her what it was, she said that her mommy was going to be an angel soon, and that she would smile down on her. She said she didn't want her mommy to go, and that heaven was not where mommies were supposed to be." She managed a smile. "I cried. And then we became friends."

Harlan swore under his breath and leaned back, running his hand through his hair. "And you want to adopt her."

"I want her to grow up feeling safe, knowing that someone loves her, no matter what." Emma turned to him, searching his face. "Do you know what it's like to be a child and to never feel safe?"

He met her gaze. "Yeah. I do."

Her heart tightened at his honesty, having some idea of what it might have been like to grow up with his father. "So do I." She actually lived that life every day still. She still didn't know how to feel safe.

Harlan bowed his head, bracing his forehead on his palm, muttering to himself. A motorboat went by, its roaring engine contaminating the afternoon silence. But long after the noise had faded, Harlan still hadn't moved.

Emma peered at him, trying to see his face. "Harlan?"

He looked up, and his face was strained. "That's why you wanted to get married. To make it easier for you to adopt her. Your need to save her was stronger than your fear of getting married."

Emma nodded.

He swore again, then shoved himself to his feet and strode over to her, a slight hitch in his gait that he tried to hide. But she noticed. He came to a stop in front of her and stared down at her.

She lifted her chin to face him.

Harlan traced his finger over her jaw. "My mom ditched me," he said. "My dad was a bastard. But my stepmom was a good woman, even if she was foolish enough to love my dad. She was the only good memory I had growing up."

Emma's heart tightened. "I'm sorry for—"

"It doesn't matter," he interrupted. "Life goes full circle, Emma. She bailed me out, and now you can help this kid. It's payback, and if you need me to help you get her, I'll do it."

Her heart started to beat again. "Really? You'll help?" She couldn't believe it. He was so anti-family, but he was willing to help her adopt Mattie? Unbidden, tears swelled in her eyes.

Harlan ran his thumb over her cheek, wiping away the tear that had sprung free. "I'll play the role, Em, but what I said earlier is true. I won't get involved. I can't." He hesitated, as if he were going to say something else, then dropped his hand, severing the contact between them.

Emma watched him as he turned away, remembering what he'd said about his past, his background, and the kind of man he was. A part of her shivered, but another part of her, the deeper part rebelled. She had seen nothing but kindness from him. Could he really be the violent, dangerous man he thought he was?

He got into his boat and started the engine.

She tensed. The last time she'd said good-bye to him he'd almost died. "Where are you going?"

He untied his boat from the pilings, moving with practiced efficiency. "Home. I gotta get some of my things. If you're going to pass this inspection tomorrow, I need to move in, and we need to figure out how to appear married. I'll be back soon." Then he shifted into reverse and began to pull away.

Move in? Fear rippled through her. She hadn't lived with anyone since Preston, and she didn't want to. It was too intimate, and it made her too vulnerable. She ran to the edge of the dock. "Harlan?"

He looked over at her as the engine rumbled softly, slowly taking him away from her. "Yeah?"

"Have you ever actually killed someone?" *Please say no. Please say no.* She didn't want him to be the man he thought he was. She wanted him to be the man he'd shown to her.

He met her gaze. "Many times, Emma. Many times. Don't lie to yourself about what I am. I'm not worth it." Then he gunned the engine and was gone.

CHAPTER TEN

THE DOOR to Wright's swung open so hard that the knob crashed into the wall with a crack that made everyone inside the store spin around to look at her. Emma's face heated up, but she managed a small wave as she hurried inside. "Where's Clare?" she asked the room at large, addressing no one in particular. Since Clare's husband now ran Wright's, and Clare had opened a cupcake shop adjacent to the store, usually someone in the place knew where she was.

The wooden shelves were overflowing with supplies now that the tourists were in town to buy things, and the long counter was filled with homemade desserts from local artisans. The air was filled with the delicious scent of home-brewed coffee, and the ten tables in the front of the store were packed to capacity with locals and summer folk enjoying a relaxing evening with the local ambiance.

Ophelia, who was running the deli, waved a spatula. "She's in the bathroom throwing up. It's the sixth time today. The girl's going to waste away to nothing before she makes it out of the first trimester."

Emma grimaced, looking toward the bathroom at the

back, realizing from Ophelia's comment that Clare must have told everyone about her pregnancy. Or maybe, she was just too sick to hide it any longer. How could she burden Clare with her own issues when she was ill? "Oh, well, I'll come back later."

"She looks stressed," Eppie shouted from the corner table. "Don't let her leave!"

"Clare?" Emma jerked her gaze toward the back room, where the bathroom was hidden behind the swinging white door that led to the back room. "Clare is stressed?" Her heart jumped. "Is she okay?"

"No, not Clare." Eppie stood up, tilting her tangerine-colored bonnet. "You. Grab her, Judith!"

Oh, crud. She did not have the energy for an intervention by Eppie. "No, that's okay." She started to back toward the door. "I need to go—"

A firm hand gripped her elbow, and she spun around to see Eppie's best friend, Judith Bittner, at her side. Judith was wearing a spiffy yellow tee shirt and a pair of hot pink slacks with lime green espadrilles. "Eppie and I were just going to go to bingo, but we can take a minute to help you out. Come sit, Emma."

Oh, man, she was so not up for this right now. "No, I—"

"I got beer for you all," Ophelia called out as the rest of the store continued to watch with great interest. Even the summer folk appeared to be fascinated, despite the fact they had no idea who any of them were.

"Come on, girl. It's time for a chat with the ladies." Judith's arthritic fingers were like steel claws digging into her arm.

Emma ground her teeth and gave up resisting, allowing herself to be led across the floor. Once seated, they would relax, and she could make a quick escape.

Les Mooney, one of the old timers from town, stood up as

she walked past. His gray hair was sparse now, and heavy wrinkles lined his face. "Don't be worrying about your fella," he said. "He'll be back for ya."

Emma managed a smile. "I know. I'm not worried—"

"Sure you are," Les said. "Every bride gets anxious when her man goes to war. When I was first married—"

"Later, Les," Eppie shouted from the corner where she was already kicking a well-dressed couple out of their seats. "This is girl talk."

Les chuckled and winked at her. "That Eppie sure is a hot ticket."

"You're too old for me, Les. I need a virile man in his twenties," Eppie bellowed across the room, triggering a combination of horrified gasps, and a few smatterings of applause from some of the older folk.

Emma allowed Judith to shove her into a chair across from Eppie, and she didn't even have time to settle before Ophelia plunked a four-pack of Birch's Best on the table and drew up a chair. "The burgers are cooking themselves," she declared. "I want some girl talk."

Emma looked around at the three wrinkled faces and bouffant silver hairdos staring at her with such eagerness. "I don't have anything juicy for you guys—"

"Sweetie," Eppie interrupted. "When you walked in the door, you looked like there was a murderer with a chainsaw on your tail. I've never seen someone look so spooked in my life. In this town, if there was a blood-letting murderer running around, we'd all know about it already and have him cornered at the gas station, so we know that's not what's bugging you." She leaned forward. "Man stuff, isn't it?"

Emma swallowed. "Listen, I—"

"Harlan came back this morning," Judith said. "I saw him taking the cover off his boat at two o'clock this afternoon. What time did he get to your place? Three?" She looked at her watch. "It's almost six now, so I'm guessing you maybe saw him around five o'clock, had some sort of high-octane confrontation, and now you're coming looking for Clare to get help, yes?"

Emma stared at her. She knew Eppie and her friends were dialed in to all the gossip in town, but seriously? How in heavens name had they figured all this out? "I—"

"You didn't expect him to come back, did you, girl?" Eppie leaned forward. "We're not fools, Emma. You and he never spoke a damn word in all these years. Just stared at each other across the room, practically oozing longing for each other. Then in one night you get hitched, and then he takes off again like he always does?" She nodded sagely at Emma's shocked look. "You thought you didn't have to be married, didn't you? You thought you could tie that knot and never have to play the role, eh?"

"Marriage is good," Ophelia said, popping the cap off her bottle on the edge of her table with a loud crack that made Emma jump.

The sound broke Emma's shock at having her life exposed. "Of course you think marriage is good, Ophelia," she protested. "You were married to the love of your life for fifty years." Everyone in town had been witness to the beautiful love affair between Ophelia and Norm. "But not everyone is that lucky—"

"I was married before Norm," Ophelia interrupted. "I know what a bad marriage can be like."

The entire table stared at Ophelia. "No, shit," Eppie said. "How in God's green earth did I not know that? I know everything in this town."

Ophelia smiled. "You don't know everything, Eppie. You just think you do." She turned to Emma. "Before I met Norm, I lived in a town on the coast. I married a fisherman when I was eighteen." She smiled. "I actually was only seventeen, but we lied on our marriage license. It didn't matter. As long as I had a man to take care of me, that was all that mattered. His name was Buck Masters. Never seen hands that big on a man before. The man had calluses so thick that he could bounce a butcher knife off his thumb and never cut it."

Eppie snorted. "That's just not sexy, Ophelia."

"I don't know," Judith said. "Strong hands are nice on a man."

"Harlan has strong hands," Eppie said, eying Emma. "And hardly any calluses."

"Shut up, Eppie," Ophelia said mildly. "I have a point to make." She turned to Emma. "Buck Masters was the best damn lobsterman on the island. I had married into the big time. But you know what?"

"No, what?" Eppie said.

"Yes, what?" Judith chimed in.

Emma just shook her head, willing the conversation to end so she could go back home and pace restlessly while she waited for Harlan to come back.

"Buck drank like a damn fish, and he was a right bastard when he drank." Ophelia nodded at Emma. "Not unlike that man you married."

"Preston?" She could barely get the words out, she was so startled by Ophelia's insight as to her ex-husband's true nature. "You know he drank?"

Ophelia rolled her eyes. "Honey, his family summered here for twenty years. His father crashed three boats as a drunken youth, and his boys were the same. There are no good genes in that family."

"This is true," Eppie said, nodding as she took a big gulp of her beer.

Emma sat back, a deep sense of betrayal burning through her. "If you all knew he drank, why didn't any of you say anything?" She felt her cheeks burn with embarrassment. Had the whole town been laughing at her while she'd been running around, giddy with joy, planning her wedding?

"Because, dear girl," Ophelia said quietly, "your eyes were glowing for the first time in your entire life. We all prayed that you were right, that you saw the gem in a sea of scum."

"I wasn't right," Emma said faintly. She'd known Preston for many summers as well, from a distance, just as she'd known Harlan from afar. She'd thought she'd known who Preston really was, beneath the flash and glam, and the money he threw around. She'd been wrong, so very wrong, and looking back, the signs were obvious. She'd been so desperate to believe he was someone he wasn't, to somehow be given a chance to matter to someone, to be rescued from her life, and her own shortcomings, that she'd ignored all the evidence to the contrary.

What was the truth about Harlan? Was she deceiving herself again, because she wanted Mattie, and because she loved how he made her feel when he looked at her with those haunted, yearning eyes?

"Anyway," Ophelia continued, interrupting her thoughts. "Even though Buck was a right bastard, he was considerate enough to die in a storm after less than a year. Nicest thing he ever did for anyone, I should think."

"You're a bloodthirsty wench," Eppie commented, raising her bottle to toast her. "I like it."

Ophelia tapped bottles with the other two women, as she continued her story. "I was thrilled to be free. I had enough money from his death that I didn't need to marry for money, and I swore on Buck's grave that I would never, ever, get married again." Then her forehead smoothed, and the most beautiful smile appeared on her face. "And then, one day as I was driving through Birch Crossing on my way to a writer's retreat in Vermont, I stopped at Wright & Son's for coffee.

Norm was just closing the door, but he let me in. He stayed open until six in the morning chatting with me." She grinned. "I never left this town again. He won my heart instantly."

Emma's throat tightened. "Norm was wonderful," she said softly. "I can see how you would have fallen in love with him."

"That's my point," Ophelia said. "I didn't fall in love with him. I refused to be so foolish. I was tired and cranky, and he just sat with me because I needed a friend. Men are scary. Friends aren't. To me, he was always my dearest friend, and never simply a man." She pointed her beer at Emma. "You need a friend, my dear. Not a man."

Tears filled Emma's eyes as the truth of Ophelia's words sank in. She did need a friend. Clare had Griffin now, and Astrid had Jason, which changed things for her, leaving her on the outside. She thought of Harlan's small cabin in the woods. There had never been a steady stream of people in his life either, at least not that she'd seen, unlike Preston, who had always surrounded himself with a retinue of admirers. For heaven's sake, Harlan had married her so he wouldn't die alone, which suggested he had no more connections than she did, not real ones at least. Maybe he needed a friend as well, and getting married was the only way he'd known how to do it.

Then again, the night they'd spent making love had not exactly been the honeymoon that platonic friends would have had.

"One's heart always sees more clearly with friends than with men," Eppie agreed. "Men cloud our vision with their five o'clock shadow, deadly kisses, and those looks that make you feel like you're all that matters to him in the world. They know that, and they use their manliness to make us forget our power as women. But with a friend, you can see all the ways that they suck, and yet love them anyway."

Ophelia laughed. "A charmer with words as always, Eppie."

Eppie shrugged. "I'm too old to be polite, Ophelia. And so are you."

"I was too old to be polite when I was seventeen," Ophelia said.

The three older women toasted again as Emma leaned back in her chair. Three women who had all once been married, who were all solo in their golden years, solid and secure in their friendships with each other, and their place within the town. Envy tightened in her chest, not simply for their friendship, but for the sparkle in all their faces. They'd all braved loss, death, and a callused lobsterman, and yet they all survived with spirit and ebullience. Wrinkles, empty beds, and age spots had made them more beautiful, not less.

Emma realized she wanted that. She wanted to laugh, to be silly, to stop being afraid to live, and she didn't want to wait until she was seventy to figure it out.

She didn't need to trust Harlan as a man, or as a husband. But as a friend? Yes, maybe, just maybe, that could be something. Maybe she could trust him as the friend she needed so badly. Resolution flooded her, and suddenly, she wanted to be home to greet him when he walked back into her house. Leaving her beer untouched, she stood up. "Thanks, ladies, but I need to go."

Eppie grinned at her. "There's a fire in her eye, isn't there, girls?"

Ophelia smiled as she took a swig of her beer. "I'd say there is." She pointed the mouth of the bottle at Emma. "Don't have sex with him, missy. It's hard to stay friends with a man when he's seen you naked repeatedly."

"She *is* married to him," Eppie pointed out. "Married couples do tend to get horizontal from time to time."

"Bullshit. They're married in name only," Ophelia said

with a perceptiveness that no longer amazed Emma. "Best to keep it that way."

"He is hot, though," Judith added.

"All the more reason to keep his pants zipped and his hands busy washing the dishes," Ophelia said, her face softening as she looked at Emma. "Keep the vision clear, my dear. Learn to laugh again. It's good medicine."

Emma smiled as she pushed her chair in. "Don't worry. I'm not having sex with him," she said, a personal confession so far outside her usual level of sharing that Eppie's mouth actually dropped open.

But as she hurried toward the door, she knew why she'd said it. Protecting herself against a romance with him was the only way she could handle what was coming tonight when he showed up at her door ready to move into her life.

Two hours after he'd left, Harlan was back at Emma's.

This time arriving by land, he parked his truck in front of her cabin, but he didn't get out. He just stared through the windshield at the tiny house with its faded gray shingles, red metal roof, and dark green shutters. Tall pine trees towered over it, but she'd still managed to nourish a small lawn and window boxes with brightly colored blossoms. He remembered the place from before she'd moved in, and recalled all too well how desolate and empty it had been. Now, it looked warm and welcoming, an actual home.

He couldn't remember the last time he'd lived in a place that anyone would actually classify as a *home*. Had he ever? The crumbling, battered house of his youth had been a bastion of hell, not a place where people sat around during family dinners laughing about the day's events.

But that damned hanging basket of flowers by the front

door wouldn't stop taunting him. It was so full that it was a good three feet wide, with more flowers than he'd ever seen in one pot. It looked like a house that someone cared about, it really did.

Grimly, he glanced at the pile on the seat beside him. Two faded black duffel bags, stuffed full of his crap, random items he'd grabbed from his shack that would take away the feminine feel of her home and turn it into a place that a man lived in. He looked at his bags, then back at the quaint cottage. Yeah, like there was a chance those two things could ever co-exist.

What the hell was he doing?

He leaned back in his seat, resting his wrists over the steering wheel, his mood becoming increasingly dark. He didn't like the idea of inserting himself into her life, or this little girl's. He'd have to manage it from a distance and keep them protected from him. He had to play a role, but not cross that line. He could do that, right? Just because his clothes were going to claim her house didn't mean he had to.

But then the front door opened and Emma appeared in the doorway, shading her eyes to inspect his truck.

Son of a bitch. Instantly, all his heroic keep-his-distance resolutions vanished, replaced by a dark, pulsating sense of raw need and protectiveness.

Whether he wanted it or not, it was *his wife* standing in that doorway in her short white cut-offs, a faded blue tank top showcasing arms that needed a little more meat on them, and breasts that barely filled his palm. There was nothing voluptuous about her, nothing bold, or overtly sexy. She was pure casual Maine girl, with a ponytail, flip flops, and a pair of large silver hoops he was guessing had been made by his sister. No make-up. No necklace. No glam.

Just a woman with no airs or pretense, almost as if she

wanted him to see her only as who she was. Ordinary. Plain. Simple.

Except she wasn't. She was raw emotion. She was burning sensuality. She was pure loyalty to those few who she trusted. She was hope in a dark night. She was light, *his* light, his anchor in a black ocean that was trying to drag him deeper and deeper into its depths. He wanted her again. He wanted to make love to her. He wanted to sleep with her. He wanted to wake up with her. He wanted to lose himself in her and never come back up for air. Ever. How the hell could he get out of his truck and walk into her life? It was dangerous as hell, for all of them.

Jesus. He leaned his head back, his fingers tightening around the wheel as she jogged down the steps toward him, the muscles in her long legs visible as she walked over to his truck. A lock of hair was trailing her jaw, and he had a burning urge to reach out and touch it, to wrap it around his fingers and tug gently, guiding her mouth toward his—

Shit. He couldn't do this.

Emma grabbed the driver's door and pulled it open. She shot him a smile so friendly that he actually had to catch his breath. "Hi, hubby," she said cheerfully. "Welcome home."

Hubby. *Hubby.* The words shot through him like a knife, tearing at his shields. Her endearment was a word he'd never thought he'd hear directed at him, never in his entire cursed life. And he'd never, *never* thought that it would make him want to be something he wasn't as badly as it did.

It was too much. He simply wasn't strong enough to play this role and walk away. "I can't do this. I'm sorry, but I can't." He was a shit, he knew he was, but he just couldn't do it. "I can't pretend to be your husband."

CHAPTER ELEVEN

His wife, apparently, did not care one bit what he could or couldn't do.

Undaunted by his croaked protest, she hooked her arms over the car door, leaning on her elbows as she swung the door back and forth. "So, I put some blankets on the couch for you," she said, completely ignoring his protest. Her voice was cheerful, but he saw the wariness in her eyes, the apprehension she was fighting hard to suppress.

The moment he saw her vulnerability, all his hesitation vanished, replaced by a need to protect her. That was his job. She was his wife. His role was to make sure she was okay. As his tension released, he finally registered the words she'd just said. "The couch?"

She nodded. "We'll get them put away before Dottie gets here, so she doesn't think we had a spat that left you on the futon. Is that cool?"

On the couch. She was putting him on the couch. Relief rushed through him, yet at the same time he felt a rising disappointment. Not that he'd expected or wanted to end up in her bed, but he couldn't help the flash of irritation. Fortunately, at least one of them was thinking clearly. "The couch sounds good," he lied. The couch sounded damned bad, actually, which was why he needed to plant his sorry ass on it all night long.

"I cleared out some space in my closet, but just enough for a couple shirts." She grinned, a sparkle in her eye. "She'll never believe we're actually married if you have as much closet space as I do. I think we should battle over that. Every time you go away, I encroach up on your closet space, and you find your stuff crammed into a smaller and smaller area."

He stared at her, not quite following her good mood. "What?"

Her smile faded, and the serious expression returned. "Here's the deal, Harlan. I need you, and Mattie needs you."

They needed him. He liked the sound of that. Liked it a hell of a lot. He felt like he hadn't brought a whole lot of good into his personal life, but he could deliver here. "I know. That's why I'm here."

She held up her finger to silence him. "But you also terrify me in a lot of ways."

He nodded. "That's good. You should be smart." But even as he said it, he couldn't keep the wave of bitterness from washing over him. He didn't want to be the guy who she had to run from or fear. He'd been around people who lived in fear, and he saw it in her. He didn't want her to be that way. He wanted her to walk with confidence, and to throw herself into life without looking over her shoulder.

She leaned forward, so close he caught a whiff of fresh soap, and he realized she'd just finished showering. Her hair was still damp around the nape of her neck. His groin clenched at the sudden image of her in the shower, and he tightened his grip on the steering wheel.

"You terrify me because I'm afraid of marriage, and relationships with men," she said with the candor he was getting used to expecting from her. "I don't trust my judgment when it comes to that. But I do trust my perceptiveness when it comes to friends, so if we keep our relationship platonic, then we're both good." She smiled. "I'll even keep my promise to cry for you if you die." She held out her hand. "Deal? Friends?"

He stared blankly at her extended hand. She wanted him to make an agreement to stay friends, and *only* friends, with her? He wanted to grab her, yank her into his lap, and show her how impossible that idea was. But at the same time, he knew she was right. It was the only safe path. Grimly, a part of him bellowing in protest while he did it, he reached out and wrapped her hand in his, intending to agree.

But the moment he enveloped her hand in his, all his good intentions vanished. There was no chance. "Sorry, Emma, but I can't promise that."

Apprehension flickered over her face. "What part? Letting me have more closet space?"

"No. Keeping it as friends only." He tightened his grip on her and pulled her close. "Each time I see you, each time I catch a whiff of your scent, each time I hear your voice, and each time I see that look of vulnerability on your face, every good intention I have disappears. All I can think about is you as a woman. There's not a single platonic thought in my head when I'm around you."

Her cheeks turned pink. "Well, Harlan, you're just going to have to do better than that."

"Better? That was my best line. It didn't work on you?" He knew what she meant, but he wasn't interested in being a good boy and playing along. He was not going to do better at thinking of her as only a friend. There was simply no way. ·

She pulled her hand free. "You're going to have to do better than that at restraining yourself," she clarified, as if he hadn't known exactly what she'd meant in the first place.

"You're the one running around saying how dangerous you are, right? So, why are you not stepping back? Or do you not believe your own claims?" she challenged. "Do you think that you're really a good guy who can be the husband every woman dreams of?"

A cold wave seemed to slam into him. "No," he said. "I don't. Point taken." He raised his right hand. "I swear to look at you and see only a telephone pole. Okay?"

She started to laugh. "A telephone pole?"

"It's the most asexual thing I could think of."

"I don't know," she teased. "It's actually sort of phallic—"

Heat rushed through him. "Oh, for hell's sake," he muttered, even as he laughed. "You're not helping." He grabbed his two duffel bags off the passenger seat. "Out of my way, woman. I need to take over your space."

Grinning, she stepped back, and the tension that had been so thick between them was gone. "How about a mud-covered pig? That's asexual."

"Mud? No way." He slammed the door of his truck shut. "Co-ed naked mud wrestling. You'd look sexy as hell in a string bikini caked in mud. Nope, won't work."

She led the way back to her cabin, her hips swaying far too seductively as she walked in front of him. "How about a moss-covered rock?"

He narrowed his eyes at her as she tossed a grin back at him. "Moss? The thick, green, felty kind?"

She held the door open for him. "Yes, sure—"

"No, sorry. It's soft. It'd make a great bed to throw you down on." He caught the door and stepped inside the building where he'd made love to her on their wedding night. Every memory of their night together was so vivid, it felt like it had been only hours since he'd made love to her.

She raised her brows. "How about a piece of cheese?"

"Cheese?" He eyed her. "That might work. The thought

of spraying canned cheese over your body and licking it off isn't all that appealing. Whipped cream would be better."

She set her hands on her hips. "Licking spray cheese off me? Seriously? Does your brain actually function in any normal pathways or do all thoughts lead to sex?"

"Normally, I'm pretty focused on catching bad guys and rescuing people." He walked past her into the bedroom and tossed his bag on her bed. Their bed. Because as long as he was faking the real husband bit, it was his bed, too. "But with you around, it's pretty much just sex."

She paused on the threshold, folding her arms over her chest as she propped her shoulder against the door frame. "Okay, then, how about mothballs? What if you just thought of mothballs whenever you looked at me?"

"Mothballs?" He couldn't wrap his mind around a single sensual connotation with the smelly, tan spheres. "Mothballs, it is. I promise to see you only as a giant mothball." He walked over to the closet and pulled it open. The small wardrobe was packed with more women's clothing than he thought could have fit in that space. "Where's my space?"

"On the floor."

He looked down and saw an empty shoebox in the left corner, surrounded by high heels, sandals, flip flops, sneakers and two pairs of hiking books. "The shoebox? That's what I get?"

"Yep." There was definite mirth in her voice.

Harlan looked over at her, and he couldn't suppress his own grin. "You're trouble, aren't you?"

"See, that's the difference," she said, her smile fading. "Knowing me, if we were really married, I'd probably yank all my clothes out of the closet so you could have the whole thing. Since we're not, you get a shoebox. I can claim my personal space from platonic friends, just not men that I—" Her voice faded.

"Men that you *what*?"

She cleared her throat. "Sorry, I was just thinking of mothballs for a second."

He grinned, allowing her the privacy. Hell knew, his own thoughts weren't appropriate for sharing when he looked at her. "You want us to live together as platonic friends?" Just saying the words made him cranky, but at the same time, he didn't like the image she'd presented of how she subordinated her own needs when in a relationship. When put that way, what the hell else could he say? "All I want from you is the shoebox," he said roughly. He unzipped his bag and tossed a pile of boxers and socks into the shoebox. "And if we were really married, you should still only give me the shoebox. Keep your space, Emma. Always."

Her shoulders seemed to relax, and a real smile lit her face. "How can you say you're such a bad guy when you say things like that and mean it?"

He held up his hand to cut her off. "Don't fool yourself, Em. You lied to yourself about Preston. Don't make the same mistake with me." He really didn't need her trying to make him into the good guy when being in her presence was tempting him almost beyond what he could endure.

He pulled open a dresser drawer as she fell silent. Staring at him was a pile of lace underwear and bras that made his entire body ignite. No thongs. Nothing risqué. Just classy and elegant, and nothing like the cotton underwear packed in beside it, which is what she'd been wearing the night they'd made love.

He hooked his finger around one of the lace numbers and held it up. "You don't wear these anymore?"

Her cheeks burned bright red, but she lifted her chin. "It's none of your business what I wear."

"You're right." Suddenly annoyed, he tossed the underwear back in the drawer, not sure whether he was more irritated at the idea that she'd worn that underwear for another man, or the fact that she had shut down her sexuality to the point where she tried to hide the fact that she was a woman. He braced his forearm in the middle of the drawer and shoved all the contents to the side, making enough room for the few tee shirts he'd brought with him.

It took him about three minutes to make space for the rest of his clothes. He tossed a couple pairs of his shoes in the corner, unloaded his shaving kit into the cramped space in the bathroom, and shoved a six-pack of beer and several frozen pizzas into the fridge. A couple sports magazines on the coffee table, a baseball hat and his denim jacket on a hook by the door, and he was done.

Emma was sitting on the couch by the time he stood back, surveying his claim to her home. "You unpack like a man used to being on the move all the time," she observed.

He glanced at her. "What does that mean?"

"You didn't care where anything went. You just unloaded it wherever you could fit it. Your stuff is here, but you could walk out the door without it and be gone forever." She cocked her head. "Is your own house like that? Transitional?"

"It's a place to crash," he said, leaning back against the kitchen counter.

Now that he was done unpacking, the smallness of her house seemed to close in. He became so aware of the bedroom only a couple feet away, of the fact that the kitchen counter he was leaning on was only ten feet from her. They were too damned close to each other, and there was nowhere to retreat.

Shifting restlessly, he looked around for a distraction, noticing for the first time all the artwork on the walls. Many nature scenes, all of it framed. Beautiful watercolors that seemed to bring the beauty and purity of nature into the room. "You did those?"

She glanced at them. "Yes. I rotate them in and out depending on my mood. The rest are in my studio." She nodded at the door on the other side of the living room. "That's where Mattie will live. I'm thinking of having Jackson Reed build me a studio off the kitchen instead. I always dreamed of having one with huge windows and lots of natural light."

Something inside Harlan shifted at the expression on Emma's face. She was sharing a dream with him, he realized. Something that made her truly happy and gave her peace. He'd never seen that expression before, not on anyone. It was pure tranquility and beauty, and he had to look away from it, feeling like he was intruding in a place he didn't belong. Invading her underwear drawer had not been a problem, but her dreams were different. They were beyond where he should tread.

Shit. How was he going to fake being married to her tomorrow? How was he going to look Dottie McPhee in the eye and say he was going to be around to take care of this woman, and that little girl? He couldn't make those promises. He just couldn't.

"I'm leaving," he reminded her. "As soon as my hip is good enough to deal with my job, I'm gone." He knew it wouldn't be long. It still locked up occasionally, but it was healing fast.

Emma's expression changed, growing harder. "I know."

"I need to be honest with Dottie about that. I can't promise to be around and raise that kid. I can't lie about that. My job takes me away."

She pressed her lips together. "I know." There was relief in her eyes. "That's the way it needs to be."

"Yeah."

Awkward silence fell. What did he say to her? He shifted restlessly, wanting to get away from the enclosed space, from implied promises, from the traps of domesticity—

"Emma!"

They both jumped as the front door swung open and Clare walked in, wearing jeans and a brightly colored blouse. The moment she saw Harlan, she stopped in her tracks, staring at him open-mouthed.

He shrugged. "Not dead."

"Oh, my God!" To his shock, Clare rushed at him, and threw her arms around him in a huge hug. "You're alive! We thought you were dead."

Harlan hugged her awkwardly, not sure how to handle her outburst. He didn't know her well enough to get that kind of greeting. "Yeah, well, I'm not."

She pulled back. "Does Astrid know?"

He grimaced. "No. I haven't been to see her." He actually had intended to slip in and out of town without anyone knowing. A quick divorce with Emma and then gone, which was clearly not happening.

"Oh, wow. She is going to kick your butt when you show up at the barbeque tonight," Clare announced cheerfully, clearly delighted by the idea.

Harlan blinked. "Barbeque?"

Emma sucked in her breath. "I forgot about that." She glanced at Harlan. "I think we'll skip it—"

"Skip it?" Clare set her hands on her hips. "You want to skip the opening night of the Shakespeare Festival? That's an outright crime, my friends."

Emma cleared her throat. "See, here's the thing, Clare. It turns out that the home study is tomorrow, and the social worker is expecting Harlan to be here. We have to figure out how to act like we're madly in love and solidly married by tomorrow at noon."

Harlan raised his brows, realizing that Emma must have

confided the truth in Clare. He liked that she'd had someone to talk to while he was gone. "I need to find out all her secrets," he added, "you know, the kinds of things only a husband would know."

Clare rolled her eyes, giving them both an exasperated sigh. "And you think you're going to figure that out sitting here like two geeky teenagers on their first date? The tension between you two is ridiculous, and no social worker is going to buy it."

Harlan swore under his breath. He had no damned idea how to be married, or even in a real relationship. He'd been very careful not to get attached, and he'd been completely successful. Until now.

"What better way to get more relaxed with each other than to go out and socialize like normal people? Try winning Emma a stuffed animal at one of the booths. Share a hot pretzel. Drink beer. Watch fireworks. Deal with gossipy people from the town." Clare eyed them both. "Isn't the social worker going to need references from friends and family? How are you going to get people to swear that you two are a great couple if you don't go out there and mingle?"

Mingle. *Mingle?* "I don't mingle—" Then he saw the expression on Emma's face. Pure, unmitigated yearning to go to the barbeque. She was like a little girl, so excited for a night out with her friends. And Clare was right. They did need the town to buy into it. For Emma, and for a little girl who needed a chance. Knowing he was probably going to regret it, he shrugged. "All right. We'll go."

Clare grinned, but when Emma's face lit up, he knew he'd socialize all damn night to see that look on her face again. And that, he figured, was kind of a major problem. Getting addicted to Emma's smiles could lead only to trouble.

But after seeing her grin, it was trouble he was willing to risk. At least, for tonight.

EMMA BIT her lip nervously as Harlan pulled his truck in between two pine trees beside the town fields that had been converted into the fairgrounds for the next ten days. A small Ferris wheel topped the skyline, plus an assortment of other rides. At the far end of the field were the carnival booths with silly games and cheap food, but at the near end of the field were the booths manned by the locals: crafts, food, beer, and everything else created and designed by people who cared. Those booths were draped in velvet cloths with real geraniums, and the vendors knew the names of half the people attending. Beside the entrance was the same antique carousel that had been set up by the farmer from Surrey who had been bringing it for fifty years, since the time when it was the only ride at the entire fair.

She'd had her first kiss on that carousel, and many afterwards. Seeing it made her a little bit nostalgic for the days when all that mattered was whether her socks matched her belt and the right guy thought she was cute.

Nowadays, if a guy thought she was cute, she was more likely to run away screaming than fix her lipstick and flutter her eyelashes at him. Glancing over at Harlan, she added a third option to her cute guy response: marry him. Oy.

The beautiful weather had resulted in the place being packed both with lots of summer folk and a healthy share of locals as well. Everywhere she looked, she saw people who had known her for her entire life. People who had watched her go on her first date, cry when her parents left town, and drive off with a summer guy to get married and start her new life. People who knew her well. Too well. She would never be able to fool them.

She sighed and leaned back against the seat, suddenly not feeling quite so eager to leap out and join the crowds that had called to her since childhood. "How on earth am I going to convince them that we're madly in love and the perfect parents for Mattie? They know me better than that."

Harlan eased the truck to a stop and shifted into park. "You mean, they know you'd be a rotten mother?"

She glanced at him with a small smile. "No, I mean they will be able to tell that we barely know each other. They've seen us in town for the last few years. Everyone knows we've hardly spoken to each other until this marriage thing. How are they going to believe we suddenly fell in love?"

Harlan leaned toward her. "Sweetheart, even total strangers can fall madly in love with each other within moments." He traced his finger over her jaw. "You don't need to know the name of someone's fifth grade homeroom teacher to know whether your souls connect."

Her heart started to pound at the intimacy. "Don't say romantic things like that, or I *will* fall in love with you."

He laughed. "Never. I'm the most unlovable guy there is." He dropped his hand. "But, I do think that we can pull this off. If we don't, Mattie goes to South Carolina, right?"

Emma nodded. "Yes—"

"Then you, my dear, must instantly fall head over heels in love with a man that you have worshipped from afar for years, and who instantly fell into your lap like a lost dog who finally found his home."

She giggled at his goofy expression. "You're the dog?"

"I'm the dog," he agreed. "But a really cute one. Floppy ears and stuff. Instant love. No one will blame you for falling victim to my charms." He winked at her, giving her a look so ridiculously innocent she laughed out loud.

She grinned, relaxing. Any man who could put on that goofy of a look was simply not to be feared. "My heart is melting," she teased. "I have this weird urge to feed you dog bones."

"Awesome. I love dog bones." He looked past her, and a thoughtful expression creased his brow. "We've been spotted."

Emma twisted around and saw a group of locals she'd known for years pointing at his truck. Her stomach tightened. "Oh—"

"Let's make this convincing, sweetheart." Harlan touched her arm and turned her back toward him. "I'm madly in love with you, babe. Come to papa."

She started to laugh. "Come to papa? You're kidding."

"Never." He locked his hand around the back of her neck. "Time for a show."

She had a split second to realize he was going to kiss her, and then his mouth closed down on hers.

It wasn't a sweet, gentle kiss. It wasn't the dark, desperate need of a forbidden night like they'd had before. It was the raw, untamed passion of a man who was thinking about *nothing* except how long it was going to be until he could get his woman's clothes off.

She knew the kiss was for show, but that didn't lessen its impact on her. Heat exploded within her, wildfire that seemed to burn all the way through her body. His kiss was deep, a sensual seduction designed to shred all her defenses and turn her into helpless mush in his arms. His hand was on her jaw, holding her where he wanted her, staking his claim to her on all levels.

It was dangerous, decadent, intensely sexual, and she loved every second of it. Since it was for show, since they were about to get out of the truck and mingle, and since there was no future in the kiss, it was a safe kiss, one that she could simply lose herself in and bask in every glorious sensation cascading through her body.

Harlan made a low growl in the back of his throat, and then he pulled her closer. The kiss grew deeper, more intense, and she couldn't keep herself back from him. Her arms went around his neck, holding him close. Suddenly, her breasts were against his chest, her nipples tingling where they felt the heat of his body igniting them. His hand moved to her lower back, and when she felt the brush of his palm against her bare skin, electricity seemed to leap between them—

A loud banging on the window made them both jump. "Helloooo!!! You're in public, remember?"

Emma started to laugh even as her cheeks flamed with embarrassment. Harlan pulled back, and he was grinning, too. Neither of them bothered to look at the window to see who was knocking. They both knew. "Well, if there's a place for the rumors to start, I think we hit the jackpot," he said.

A knock sounded again. "Get out of the truck, newly-weds," Eppie's voice rang out. "Everyone's waiting for you! No one believes that either of you would actually marry anyone, so they're all waiting to see for themselves whether you really did it."

Nervousness rippled through Emma as she looked at Harlan. "Okay, you ready for this?"

He cocked an eyebrow. "To deceive an entire town who wants nothing more than your eternal happiness? Yeah, I'm on it. You good? Can you stand to stare into my eyes and do a little love-sick sighing?"

She giggled at his goofiness. "No one would believe any love-sick sighing from me. When I was with Preston—"

"No." He covered her lips with one finger. "You weren't in love with him. Not the way you are with me. It's different this time. Once you realize that, so will they. You didn't sigh with him. You do with me. That's what real love is, sweetheart. I'm the one for you, and everyone will know it the minute they see how you look at me."

Her mouth dropped open in surprise at his speech. He sounded deadly serious. "I'm not in love with you—"

He cut off her protest with a kiss, a kiss that left no room for coherent thought or rational response. Just like before, emotions and sensations flooded her, and the world around them seemed to vanish. Even Eppie's amused cackle barely registered under Harlan's assault. Finally, after what felt like an eternity, but one that was far too short, he broke the kiss, but kept his lips against hers. "Never, *ever* again say you don't love me," he said quietly. "From now on, until I leave town, there is no space for any thought in your mind except for how madly in love with me you are."

She swallowed. "I have to remember the truth—"

He kissed her again until she thought her body was going to explode. "You can't afford to remember the truth," he whispered into her mouth. "You were betrayed once, and the town is going to be looking hard for any sign that I'm going to betray you again. Any doubt, any flicker of fear in your eyes, any withdrawal at all by either of us, and they are going to be all over it. And then, when Dottie shows up and starts asking questions, this town is going to take it upon themselves to ensure your future is the one they think you should have. They need to be absolutely convinced that I will protect your heart and keep you safe for the rest of your life or they will not let this happen."

At his words, Emma closed her eyes, her soul aching with yearning for the image he had painted. As terrified as she was of marriage, as resistant as she was to putting herself in another man's control, the idea of having a man who would protect her heart and keep her safe for the rest of her life made her want to cry with longing. The truth was, she didn't want to be alone and brave. She wanted to have someone she could trust. She'd been lying to herself thinking that life alone was what she wanted. "I hate you," she whispered. "Don't make me want things that I can't have."

"You can hate me," he said softly, "as long as you still love me unconditionally. The town has to believe it, and they will be searching for some reason to kick me out of your life onto my ass. You know they will." His breath was warm against her mouth, whispers meant only for her.

"You're right. I know you're right." She'd seen the way the town had tried to protect Clare from Griffin. She'd seen it with Astrid. Even Harlan had tried to stop Jason and Astrid from being together until he was convinced Jason would be good to her. "Okay."

"Good." He smiled, smoothing her hair back from her face. "Which means—" He kissed one corner of her mouth.

"—that you—" He kissed the other corner.

"—are madly—" He kissed her nose.

"—and passionately—" He kissed her forehead.

"—committed to me in your heart—" He placed his hand on her chest.

"—and in your soul." He kissed her full on the mouth, a kiss so tender and beautiful that tears sprang to her eyes.

It was the kiss she'd wanted her whole life. Tender. Gentle. Passionate. Kind. Sensual. Except that it wasn't real. It was acting. It was a lie.

"This is real, Emma. Believe it, or no one else will." Then he threaded his fingers through hers and kissed her until she finally, reluctantly, and wholeheartedly kissed him back.

CHAPTER TWELVE

A DEEP SENSE of satisfaction pulsed through Harlan when he felt Emma accept his kiss. It felt so right to feel her relax and lean into him, exactly how it was meant to be. He cupped her throat, loving the feel of her pulse hammering so fast from his kisses. It was incredible the level of satisfaction that thrummed through him as her hand tentatively went to his shoulder, her fingers digging in ever so slightly. She was so tiny in his arms, too delicate, too vulnerable. Instinctively, he palmed her lower back with his hand, needing to support her and hold her as he kissed her.

Her mouth tasted of mint toothpaste with a splash of strawberry. Her lips were decadently soft, her kiss so vulnerable that he wanted to erect a shield to protect her from any more of the crap that life was going to throw at her...including himself.

Instinct made him want to pull back, to cut off the kiss, to distance himself from her, but he knew he couldn't, for all the same reasons he'd outlined to her. Because there was a little girl who needed a break, and she was depending on the two of them to make it happen.

It wasn't until there was more hooting from Eppie that he finally broke the kiss.

Emma stared at him, her cheeks flushed, breathing a little hard. "You are way too good at that," she said.

He grinned. "I practiced on my teddy bear a lot when I was a kid. It's an important life skill for a man to have."

"Well, remind me to come back in my next life as your teddy bear."

He burst out laughing. "I'll remind you."

She smiled, but her cheeks were still flushed. "Thanks."

"Anytime." Harlan saw movement behind Emma, but before he could warn her, Eppie yanked the passenger door open. "Showtime," he whispered to her, just before he glowered at Eppie, who had stuck her head in the front seat with them. "I wasn't finished with her yet," he said.

Eppie beamed at him, her face barely visible beneath all the crystal teardrops hanging off the brim of her yellow straw hat. "Well, you have to share her now." She grabbed Emma's arm. "Come on, girlie. Show off this husband of yours. We all want to see."

Emma shot Harlan a resigned look, and he grinned as she scooted off the seat and out the door. Eppie slammed the door in his face, and he let out his breath as he opened his own door. It had been one thing to boost up Emma and to be focused on her, but as he stepped out of the truck and saw the number of eyes on him, he suddenly wondered whether he really could pull this off.

It wasn't a matter of convincing anyone he was in love with her. That was easy. Emma was one of the most interesting and appealing women he'd ever met. The question was whether he was going to convince anyone that he was the man Emma deserved to marry, especially when he didn't believe it himself.

Then he saw Jackson Reed, one of his few real friends

from town, walking toward him, and he stiffened. Jackson knew him well. They'd shared many beers over the years, and he would know Harlan was lying. The small crowd parted as Jackson walked up, his stride easy and relaxed as he headed toward Harlan. Everyone knew that Jackson was the man who knew him best, and they were deferring.

Shit.

Harlan drew his shoulders back as Jackson neared. The other man stopped in front of Harlan, his dark eyes studying him carefully, his Red Sox cap pushed back on his forehead. In typical Jackson fashion, he was wearing jeans, work boots, and a collared plaid shirt, clearly dressing up for the event. "You really did this? Married her?"

Harlan nodded. "Yeah."

Jackson glanced past him at Emma, who was being interviewed by Eppie and a few other women. "She's a nice girl."

"I know."

Jackson looked at him. "She's been through hell."

"I know."

"You're a self-proclaimed bastard."

Harlan didn't look away. "I know."

Jackson narrowed his eyes. "So, what changed?"

Harlan knew his friend would smell a lie a thousand miles away, so he gave the truth. "Sunshine."

Jackson raised his brows. "Sunshine? What are you talking about?"

"If I asked you whether Trish was your sunshine, what would you say?"

"Trish, my wife?" Jackson frowned at Harlan's nod. "Hell, yeah, she's my sunshine. She's the light that saves my ass every damn day of my life."

Harlan smiled. "Exactly." He held out his wrist and showed Jackson his tattoo. "I take Emma with me. She gives me hope that my life is worth more than I think it is." Which was the absolute truth. "I never had sunshine before her. Ever."

Jackson stared at the tattoo, then looked at Harlan. "So, this is about you? Not her? You want her because of what she can do for you?"

Harlan had expected the resistance, and he had an answer. "If something made your heart beat, would you do everything in your power to protect it, treasure it, and keep it safe? Would you swear on your own bastard father's grave that you would never, ever, destroy that light or make the flame die?" As he spoke the words, he couldn't help his gaze from wandering over to Emma.

She was laughing now, her eyes sparkling with merriment that made his heart tighten. It was the truth, what he'd said to Jackson. She was his angel, and he would do whatever it took to protect her, including haul his sorry ass out of her life before he could do any damage. "I would do anything for her," he said softly. And for that little girl somewhere, who needed Emma in her life. He couldn't offer the world the kind of sunshine that Emma brought into it, but he could help her and Mattie. He could stop the cycle of hell that was spinning around them both.

Jackson stared at him, and then a broad grin broke out over his face. "Son of a bitch, man. I can't even believe it." He slammed his hand down on Harlan's shoulder, then yanked him forward for a massive bear hug.

Harlan grinned, laughing when Jackson ruffled his hair. "Lay off the hair, man. I worked hard on that." He shoved Jackson's hand aside. "Go away. I need to rescue my woman."

"Beer later?" Jackson called as Harlan headed over to the women.

"You got it." As Jackson headed back into the fairgrounds,

Harlan felt a strange sensation settle over him, almost disappointment that Jackson hadn't seen the truth. He realized that a part of him had wanted to be called out, to be hauled away from Emma before he could screw it up and hurt her.

The truth was, he still had the opportunity to walk away. He could do it. He didn't need Jackson to free him.

But when Emma's face lit up as he approached, he knew there was no chance. He hadn't been lying when he'd said Emma was his sunshine. She was, and he needed to drink in every last ounce of it to sustain him when he had to leave it behind.

"Good afternoon, ladies," he said as he held out his hand to Emma. "Do you mind if I borrow my wife?"

Emma glanced at his hand, and for a split second, he thought she wasn't going to take it. His entire body seemed to go numb and the world seemed to careen to a dead halt, every level of his being suspended in tense anticipation, waiting for her to accept him.

Then she set her hand in his, and the world surged back to life.

～

Emma had to admit it.

Harlan was dangerously handsome.

There was simply no way to deny it.

As he guided her through the stone pillars at the entrance to the park, there was no mistaking the number of appreciative female gazes sent his way, and she didn't like it. Women had appreciated Preston's expensive car and custom suits, and he had appreciated their appreciation of him. She didn't want a man that other women coveted—

She stiffened as a pair of twenty-somethings in skimpy bikini tops and cut-offs that had been cut a little too short sidled up toward them, their eyes latched onto Harlan so tightly she was sure they hadn't even noticed she was beside him.

Carefully, Emma watched Harlan scan the crowd, and she saw the moment that he noticed the two women approaching him. Emma instinctively slowed down, distancing herself from Harlan, refusing to insert herself into a battle for his attention.

The two women got closer, and Harlan glanced backward at Emma, that same gesture she was all too used to seeing from Preston, that double-check to make sure he wasn't going to get caught. She turned her head away, giving him the freedom to do what he wanted to do—

"Hey." A heavy arm settled around her shoulders, and she glanced up in surprise as Harlan tucked her against his side. "You okay?"

She was too surprised to answer, and stole a quick look at the two women. They had stopped a few feet away, annoyed disappointment on their faces.

"Em?"

She looked back up at him, and the strangest feeling of warmth began to spread through her. The smile she gave him was real, and she felt it all the way to her heart. "I'm good," she said. "Thank you."

He raised his eyebrow. "For what?"

"For honoring me." She stood on her tiptoes and pressed a quick kiss to his mouth.

He didn't pull away. Even though they were in the middle of a crowded area, a few feet from two women who clearly wanted to get some action from him, he didn't shrug her off with some muttered excuse. In fact, he actually locked his arm around her lower back, hauled her against him, and upped the heat on the kiss by about a thousandfold.

He broke the kiss quickly, but there was a satisfied grin on his face as he drew away. "You're putty in my hands," he observed.

Emma's cheeks heated up. "I think it's the other way around."

He grinned at her as he slung his arm over her shoulder again. "Oh, my darling, there is no doubt about that." He kissed the top of her head affectionately, leading her past the two younger women without even glancing their way.

Emma couldn't quite keep herself from grinning broadly at them as she leaned into Harlan. Yes, it was a little childish, but it just felt good to know that the man she was with didn't want anyone else. She was still grinning as Jackson came up to them, handed Harlan a beer, and tipped his hat to Emma. "Congratulations, my dear," he said. "I hope you know what you're doing." There were questions in his eyes, just as Harlan had predicted.

She smiled, casting about in her mind for a response that would sound legitimate and innocent. "I'm happy," she said simply, but even as she said it, guilt flickered through her. Could she really lie to all these people? Not that he didn't make her happy, but not in the forever-and-ever way that she needed to present to everyone.

Harlan squeezed her hand, and she managed a smile.

Jackson grinned, but there was still concern in his face. "If you're happy, that's what matters." He kissed her cheek, and a flicker of fear drifted through Emma.

Jackson was Harlan's best friend. If he was worried about her being with him...what did he know? Did he see the same things in Harlan that her husband saw in himself?

They hadn't even made it ten more yards, when the owner of the town's hardware store, Link Nelson, strode up. Although he was only in his late thirties, his dark hair was flecked with gray, but he had the same powerful build he'd

always had. He was another Birch Crossing original, gradu-
ating from the regional high school, and then disappearing
for almost ten years before he'd bought the hardware store
five years ago. Emma didn't know him well, but he'd always
been a nice enough guy.

"Harlan!" Link grinned at him. "It's good to see you back.
The real estate market in town is tanking without you. No
one wants to list their houses with anyone else. You need to
get things moving again. People are hanging onto homes, and
they need to sell them to new folks who will remodel. The
lumber business has gone to hell without you to keep the
market going."

Harlan blinked. "I'm not starting up my business
again, Link—"

"Of course you are. We need you." Link nodded at Jackson. "You with me, Jackson?"

"Hell, yeah. We need you back, man." The two men
started in on Harlan, working on him to hang up his travels
and settle down in Birch Crossing.

"Hey!" Griffin Friesé, Clare's husband, slammed his hand
down on Jackson's shoulder. "Volleyball court just opened up.
Let's get it started. Me and Harlan against you two." Link and
Jackson were all over it, and before Harlan could finish
explaining about his hip, they'd abducted him toward the
south end of the field.

As other people joined them, Harlan relaxed visibly,
shaking hands and accepting congratulations. Emma heard
his laugh echo across the grass as he met up with other
townspeople welcoming him back, a man who belonged in
Birch Crossing even though he'd been away for over a year.

Emma smiled as she watched him. He was charming and
personable, even when taking the hits about keeping his relationship with his new wife a secret. He glanced back at her

once, and raised his eyebrows, as if to ask whether he was doing all right.

She grinned and gave him a thumbs up, laughing as he was redirected toward the beer tent. This was the man who wanted to leave this town? The people loved him and had welcomed him back with open arms. As she watched more and more people cluster around him, thumping him on the back in congratulations, she felt the genuineness of the town's reception of him.

"He looks good," Clare said, appearing at her elbow.

"People like him," Emma said quietly.

"Of course they do. He's a nice guy."

Emma bit her lip, thinking back to the fair when she'd started dating Preston, the man she'd had a crush on from afar for years. She didn't remember the people from the town approaching him. She and Preston had spent all their time with his friends, with the summer folk. That experience was so different from even these few minutes with Harlan. "Can I ask you a question?"

"Of course."

She looked at her friend. "Did you like Preston?"

Clare cleared her throat. "The truth? No, not really, but we didn't know him very well. He'd been summering here for years, but his family wasn't one of those who really socialized with us. But we all had hoped that whatever you saw in him was real."

"So, everyone in town saw Preston for what he was, everyone except me." She'd been such a fool, so desperate for a family and to be loved that she'd seen only what she wanted to see. Sighing, she watched Harlan get swept into a rowdy discussion about whether to open the town boat ramp to non-residents, and smiled when she saw people listening to his opinion. "Harlan's different, don't you think? He's a good man." Despite what he thought. Despite what Jackson thought.

Clare raised her brows. "That doesn't sound like the kind of question you'd ask about a man who you were only pretending to be happily married to. That sounds like the kind of question you'd ask if you were actually falling for him."

Emma clenched her fists. "No," she said firmly. "I'm not."

Clare gave her a skeptical look. "No?"

"Absolutely not." Emma bit her lower lip and glanced at her friend, needing an answer to the question she'd already asked. "You *do* think he's a good guy, right?"

"Hey." Clare touched her arm, her face softening with understanding. "It doesn't matter what people think. No one believed in Griffin, but he's a wonderful man. People all thought my first husband was a great guy, and most of them still do, but he wasn't. Only you know the truth about Harlan. What works for you may not work for anyone else, but it doesn't have to. It's only about you and him."

Emma grimaced. "That doesn't help. I don't have a good track record for making good judgments about men."

"Sometimes you just have to trust your instincts." Clare looked across at Griffin, who had given up on the volleyball and was now back at the Wright's food stand he was running, where the sign simply said to pay what you could pay, and take the food for free if you needed to. "I had a bad marriage, Emma, and fifteen challenging years afterwards, until I met Griffin. It's better to be alone than with the wrong person, but if you find your way to the right person, then nothing will ever shake you again." She looked at her. "It's your life. It's your call. No one else's. Don't worry about what other people think. Just focus on what your heart is telling you." She touched Emma's arm. "You care about him, don't you?"

Emma sighed, restlessly fiddling with her bracelets.

"There's something about him that calls to me, but I don't know if it's enough. He has issues."

"Don't we all have issues, sweetie?"

Emma managed to laugh at that one. "Okay, good point."

"You'll figure it out. Just be patient. You don't need all the answers now." Clare winked. "Besides, you've already had sex with him, and you already married him, so it's not like you have any big decisions left to make, right? Just enjoy the night. Fool the crowd. Kiss a hot guy. It's all good."

"Yeah, okay." Emma took a deep breath, trying to clear her head. "You're right. Thanks for the advice."

"Anytime." Clare nodded at Griffin, who was beckoning to her. "I need to rescue my man. Dinner, later?"

"Yes, of course." Emma hugged Clare good-bye, then stiffened when she saw Astrid across the field, chatting with Jason and his parents, who had come to town for the festival. Jason was holding their baby, and Astrid was smiling, but her smile didn't reach her eyes. She looked drained and exhausted, and Emma suddenly realized that Harlan might not have talked to Astrid yet. Did she still think he was missing?

Astrid looked across the field and caught Emma's eyes, and her face grew more shuttered, as if she blamed Emma for Harlan's disappearance. Emma realized her assumption was correct, that Astrid didn't know he was back. How had he not approached Astrid yet? What kind of man would torment his sister like that? Sudden anger surged through her, and she pointed at Harlan, directing Astrid's attention toward her brother.

Astrid turned her head to look, and then her face went stark white, and her mouth dropped open. And then she was running, running, running across the field, shouting his name. He spun around, his face shocked as he saw Astrid nearing. He barely had time to open his arms before his sister flung

172

herself into them. Astrid buried her face in his neck, clinging to him as if she was afraid he would vanish right out of her arms.

Tears filled Emma's eyes as she watched Harlan's awkward response and his hesitation, until he finally returned the hug. It was so apparent that Astrid loved him dearly, her wayward brother who thought he had nothing to offer her.

As Emma watched Astrid pull back, tears rolling down her cheeks as she framed Harlan's face with her hands, Emma realized that Astrid saw in him the same things that Emma did. Maybe he had a tough background. Maybe he lived a dark life. But somewhere in the depths of his soul, there was something good. Something honorable. Something worth holding onto.

She wasn't going to keep him. She wasn't going to fall in love with him. And she wasn't going to turn her life over to him. But one thing was for absolute certain: she'd chosen the right man to marry so she could bring Mattie home.

He wouldn't let them down. He wouldn't betray them. He wouldn't hurt them. The realization was a rush, a sense of freedom as she began to walk across the field, to her man, her husband, to claim him in front of everyone else. He looked up and saw her coming. Astrid turned in his arms, a tight-knit brother-sister unit, the kind of family bond Emma had craved her whole life, but never found.

Even now, she felt herself slow down, not wanting to intrude—

Then Harlan held out his hand to her. "Come," he said.

But still Emma hesitated, unsure about Astrid's reception. Then Astrid held out her hand to Emma, too. "I'm still mad at you both," she said, a teary smile still on her face, "but I'm so happy to see my brother that all I want to do is hug both of you. Come on, Em." Her smile broadened. "Sis," she added.

"Sis?" Emma echoed, unable to keep her voice from cracking.

"Of course." Astrid grabbed her hand and yanked her close, and then Emma found herself sandwiched between them, hugged tightly as if that was exactly where she belonged.

CHAPTER THIRTEEN

"I CAN'T BELIEVE I'm doing this." Almost five hours later, Harlan watched Emma tie a strip of burlap cloth around their ankles, binding them together, not quite able to believe he was standing in a field, barefoot, about to do a three-legged race.

The sun had set, and most of the families had gone from the fair, turning it into a more adult evening. Hot dogs, burgers, and Birch's Best beer had created a festive atmosphere in which plastic knives tapping on beer bottles had commanded that Harlan kiss Emma seventeen times during dinner.

Not that he'd been counting, but Eppie had. Loudly. Threatening the crowd each time too long had passed since he'd last kissed his wife. Weirdly, he hadn't minded it. It had been...fun, in a surreal sort of way. It felt like he was visiting someone else's life, and finding it not as foreign or difficult as he'd expected it to be.

"Oh come on. It's a Birch Crossing tradition. Everyone who has been married less than a year has to do the three-legged race." Emma grinned up at him, her eyes glowing. "I didn't get to do this with Preston because we didn't come to the fair the year after we got married. Now's my chance, and you're not going to bail on me."

"Did I mention that I blew out my hip when I almost died?" Harlan glanced around as the rowdy crowd cheered them on. There were twenty people getting tied together, ten sets of newlyweds. Two of the couples had more gray hair and wrinkles than Eppie, but they were all grinning. "You're going to cripple me."

"It's your other hip, and we'll go slow," she said as she tied his right knee to her left knee. "I promise to take care of you," she teased, looking up at him with a mischievous glint in her eye.

Harlan pretended to scowl at her, but he couldn't quite help being amused by her sassy expression. He liked it. He liked seeing her happy and carefree. "Do you realize what an insult that is to my male ego for you to even suggest you have to take care of me?"

She grinned up at him, but suddenly, he forgot about everything they were talking about. Her tank top had slipped down, and he could see the swell of her breasts, and the plunging crevice between them. He went hard, rock hard, almost instantly.

Emma's smile vanished, and her breath caught as her fingers stilled on the knot. "Oh, my," she whispered, her cheeks turning red. "No one has ever looked at me like that."

"Like what?" His voice was raspy, croaking as he fought down the desire that had suddenly surged through him, despite the ridiculously inappropriate surroundings.

"Like *that*."

He cleared his throat, jerking his gaze off her breasts and back to her face. "Sorry."

"No," she said. "It's fantastic. I love it."

"Oh, well, in that case..." He broke out into a grin then, and she beamed up at him, intensifying the battle he was waging not to jump her right then and there. "How is it that I married the hottest girl in town?"

"You're just a lucky guy, I guess." She picked up a third piece of burlap and slid it around his inner thigh.

He sucked in his breath as she stood, leaning her thigh against his as she looped it around her leg. "No woman has ever tied me up before," he said, unable to keep the heated desire from his voice.

"I've never tied anyone up before," she said as she bound them together, a wicked gleam in her eye that did nothing to help him regain control of the lower half of his body. "I guess that's why this race is for newlyweds. It's too spicy for old married folks."

"Is that why?" He couldn't take his gaze off her, couldn't stop from sliding his hand over the soft flesh of her bare shoulder as she straightened up, so close to him that he could have kissed her without even bending over.

"Maybe." She slid her arm around his waist. "Put your arm around me."

"It's about time you gave me that order," he grunted as he locked his arm around her shoulders, tucking her up against him. Her body fit perfectly, and he had a sudden, beautiful memory of exactly how well they fit together.

Then the starting bell went off. They took one step, and immediately went down in a pile of tangled limbs. Instantly, all thoughts of sex were swallowed up by the sight of Emma laughing so hard that she had to hold her sides.

He was riveted by the sheer joy shining on her face. He'd never seen her so happy, so relaxed, so *beautiful*.

"Come on," she laughed, as she tugged at his arm. "Get up, you big oaf."

He became aware of people hooting their names, urging them to keep going. He surged to his feet, making sure to take his weight on his good leg, and then pulled Emma up. A gray-haired couple who were in their seventies was already ten feet ahead. "Come on, babe, we're not getting beaten by them." He locked her against him, took a step, and they both face-planted back into the grass again.

Laughter roared around them, and Emma was cracking up. This time, even he had to laugh as he tried to untangle himself from his wife. As it turned out, the mere act of standing up when one of his legs was firmly attached to Emma's wasn't that easy.

"You have to time your steps with mine," she ordered him, still laughing as they fought to stand up again. "We'll never have a successful marriage if you don't learn to notice me."

Enduring a chorus of friendly jeers from the crowd, Harlan and Emma managed to right themselves this time. Even Harlan was chuckling as Emma held up her fingers. "On three," she said, "take a step with your right leg! One, two, three!"

This time, he followed her orders, and they hobbled along after the others, gaining speed, catching up to the old couple. They were almost there, almost in the lead. Yeah, they were going to win!

"Slow down," Emma shouted, pinching his waist. "I can't keep up—"

Harlan slowed instantly, too fast, and then they were down again, in a tangled heap on the grass as the gray-haired speedsters shot across the finish line to resounding applause. Emma was giggling as Harlan flopped beside her, propping himself up on his elbow. Her hair was spread over the grass, the smile on her face riveting as she laughed. He realized he was laughing as hard as she was.

Shit. Who the hell knew that being married was so much damned fun?

"So, why the rush?" Eppie asked, as they were sitting around one of the tables an hour later. The band had started, the dance floor was open, and the Christmas lights had been turned on so they cast a cheerful light on the sheets of plywood that Link had donated from his hardware store for the dance floor.

Emma was sitting in one of the end chairs leaning against Harlan, and the table was full. Astrid and Jason, Griffin and Clare, plus Astrid's stepfather, who everyone was pretty sure was having a fling with Eppie, and some of the others from the town.

"What rush?" Emma said as she yawned. It had been an amazing evening. She'd always loved the opening night of the festival, but it was a completely different experience enjoying it with Harlan. It was amazing to have someone to laugh with, to partner with, and to root for. Someone who was there only for her. She knew that the night had been a gift she would remember for a long time.

"On the marriage. You could have waited until at least daybreak." Eppie raised her brows. "You aren't going to convince me it was for the sex, because the morals at this table don't ride that high."

Emma grinned, too tired to be horrified by Eppie's sex comments, or the fact the rest of the table had gone quiet to hear her answer. "Mattie," she said sleepily, sagging wearily into Harlan's side as he put his arm around her and pulled her close. "Mattie Williams."

"Mattie? Who's Mattie?" Eppie asked, raising her voice to be heard over the music, while Clare smiled knowingly.

Emma reached into her pocket and pulled out her phone. She flipped to a picture of Mattie, the one that showed her with her beautiful brown skin, pink ribbons on her braids, and her big smile. "I teach her. She lost her parents, and I want to adopt her—"

"*We*," Harlan interrupted. "We want to adopt her." He took the phone from Emma and looked at it. His brow furrowed, and his face grew serious as he studied it.

Emma realized that she'd never shown him a picture of Mattie before. Suddenly, uncertainty rippled through her. What would he think of her? Would he change his mind? Would he—

Then a smile softened his face, a genuine smile, and he brushed his index finger over the screen of her phone. "Mattie Williams," he said softly. "She needs a family."

Emma's heart tightened as he handed the phone to Eppie, grinning as he answered the sudden barrage of questions about this little girl. As he talked about Mattie, repeating the things she'd told him, he leaned forward. His voice was urgent, and he was making eye contact with everyone. Emma realized that he cared about this little girl he'd never met, and he was making sure that everyone knew it. She could see his genuine concern in every line of his body, in the tone of his voice, in the way his gaze kept flipping to the picture still on her phone.

Tears filled her eyes, and she bit her lip as true understanding filled her.

She wasn't alone anymore.

Harlan was her partner in this, and he would see it through to the end. She looked across the table and saw Astrid watching her. Quickly, she wiped away the tears, but it was too late. Silently, Astrid handed her a tissue. "Harlan," she said. "I think Emma needs to dance."

Harlan glanced down at her, then his arm tightened around her shoulder. "Dance with me?" he whispered. Without waiting for an answer, he stood up, took her hand, and led her onto the dance floor.

The music wasn't slow, but he took her right into his arms, pulling her close as he moved them across the floor. Emma wrapped her arms around his neck and hid her face in his chest, trying to regain her composure.

"Em?" Harlan's whisper tickled her neck. "What's wrong?"

"Nothing," she muttered into his chest.

"Emma." He lightly bit the side of her neck, tickling her. "Talk to me."

"I'm fine."

He feathered a kiss over her earlobe, making her shiver. "I know that we don't have a real marriage," he said quietly, "but I thought that the one thing we had was honesty. You're not fine. Talk to me."

She couldn't help the small smile as she finally lifted her face to look at him. "Aren't husbands supposed to be insensitive boors who never notice when their wives are upset?"

He grinned. "I think I made it pretty clear I wasn't going to be a good husband." He flattened his hand on her lower back and pulled her closer, until her breasts were flat against his chest. "So, talk to me, wench."

She laughed then. "I wasn't upset. I was actually happy. I —" She hesitated. "You seemed to really care what happens to Mattie, and..." She shrugged apologetically. "I'm a girl. I get weepy at things like that."

Harlan spun her around in time to the music. "Of course I care. I told you that."

"I know, but I could see it." She touched his face. "You're a good man, Harlan."

Something flickered in his eyes, something dark that seemed to take the lightness out of his expression. "No, Emma, I'm not. Don't let today fool you. I can play the game very well, just like my father could."

The ominous tone in his voice was like a cold wind on the back of her neck, and suddenly she didn't want to have that conversation. Not tonight. Tonight had been too perfect. She wanted to pretend right now that this night was going to last forever. "You look like you're mad at me," she managed to tease. "I think you better kiss me or people are going to think we're heading for divorce already."

Harlan didn't look away from her, but his eyes seemed to gleam with sudden heat. "I don't think I should kiss you," he said.

She couldn't fight the stab of disappointment. "Why not?"

His grip tightened on her. "Because I've spent all day kissing you and holding you. The night's almost over. It's dark. We're going to be home in a few minutes where your bed is. If I kiss you now, I'm going to unleash something that isn't going to stop when we get home."

Her heart started to pound, and excitement leapt through her. "Then you shouldn't kiss me," she said.

"I know." But his hand slid up her spine, a slow, decadent caress that seemed to curl right into her belly. His fingers cupped the back of her neck in that little move she was beginning to recognize as his trademark when he wanted to really kiss her. "But I think I'm going to do it anyway."

She swallowed. "Okay," she whispered.

"Okay?" He bent his head until his mouth was hovering over hers, like a great promise.

Her throat too tight to speak, she could manage only a nod, but that was apparently enough. His lips closed on hers instantly, a kiss of ownership, a kiss that was pure seduction and desperate need, the explosion of tension that had been building for hours.

She clung to him, kissing him back, losing herself in the very essence of who he was, in the strength of his body, the scent of soap and man, and the taste of his kisses. She knew him, this man, his kisses, his touch, and he seemed to ignite a fire within her.

There was no fear lurking within her, no anxiety, and no worry, just an unreserved need for Harlan and for what he gave her. The kiss grew more intense, more dangerous, more—

"Okay," Griffin's hands came down on both their shoulders. "I think you two are excused for the night."

Harlan broke the kiss, but didn't release his grip on Emma. He simply grinned at Griffin, the highly satisfied gleam of a man who liked what he had in his arms. "Yeah, I think you're right. Emma? You ready?"

She knew she should be embarrassed to leave early after such a searing kiss, but she didn't care. To the world, they were newly married, so what else would they want to do but be alone? "Let me just grab my purse."

She hurried over to the table, which was empty now. There were lots of summer folk still roaming around, but most people were on the dance floor. Her purse was on the floor by her chair, and she bent down to pick it up. As her fingers closed around it, a polished dress shoe appeared next to her foot, and a hand settled on her shoulder. "Emma?"

She went ice cold at the familiar voice, and her breath seemed to clog in her throat. She couldn't move. Couldn't stand. Couldn't tear her gaze away from the white wingtip next to her sandal.

"Emma? Did you hear me?" The hand tightened on her shoulder, and Emma stumbled to her feet, twisting out of his reach as she stood.

His hand fell from her shoulder, but there he was, as glitteringly handsome as he always was. The man she'd given her heart to. Preston Edward Jones, the third. Her ex-husband of barely one month.

$\sim$

EMMA'S THROAT went dry and her heart was hammering so hard it was like a drum thundering in her head. Instinctively, she took a step back. Her foot caught on a chair rung and she tripped.

Preston reached out to catch her—

"No," she hissed, twisting out of his reach again, only to wrench her ankle violently, where it was still caught on the chair. She yelped in pain and sat down hard on the floor, grabbing her ankle.

Preston crouched in front of her, his eyes gleaming as they roamed over her. "I thought I might see you here," he said.

Emma felt exposed and raw with him staring at her like that. Pain was spiraling through her leg, and she pressed her palm to her injury, biting back a sob. "You don't belong here," she snapped. "Go back to Florida." She glanced toward Harlan, and was horrified to discover that the table was blocking her view of the dance floor. She couldn't see Harlan, and he wouldn't be able to see her. With both her and Preston on the floor, no one would see they were there.

Frantic, she grabbed the chair seat to pull herself up, but Preston blocked her hand, leaning in closer. "We need to talk."

"What is wrong with you? We're divorced. It's over. You can go be with all your other women—"

"I don't want them." He leaned closer. "See, here's the thing, Emma. Once I lost you, I realized that it had all been a mistake. I want you back. I want to marry you and give you all the things I didn't give you before."

She closed her eyes against the promise that she'd heard so many times. Each time she'd tried to leave him, he'd talked her into giving it another try by promising the things she craved so deeply in her heart. Promises that she had believed every time because she'd wanted so desperately to believe someone could love her like that, to matter. "Stop it," she hissed. "Just stop it."

"No, I won't stop it. I love you." His hands were on either side of her hips now, crowding her. "I won't give up. I made a mistake when I let you go, and I won't stop until I fix it."

She stared at him, into those blue eyes that had once made her believe in love, the ones that had once made her believe in fairytales and prince charming. Those same blue eyes that had once made her heart heal. Those same blue eyes that she had trusted so completely.

God, she was such an idiot. Even now, when she knew what a bastard he was, a little part of her still responded to him, wishing that he meant what he said, that there really was a chance for her to be treasured the way she so desperately craved. As she tried to shield herself against her stupid yearnings for his words to be true, for the first time in her life, true hopelessness spiraled through her, a realization that she simply could not, *ever*, trust her judgment when it came to men, not if she was actually sitting there, her instincts searching for a chance that he might actually mean it this time. "Get away from me."

"You don't mean that. I can see the conflict in your eyes." Satisfaction gleamed on Preston's smug face. "You still love me, I know you do. Listen, I fucked up. I never meant to hurt you—" He suddenly went flying backward, crashing into a table and upending the contents across the floor.

Harlan stepped in front of Emma, and she realized that he'd grabbed Preston by the back of the shirt and tossed him across the floor. "You stupid bastard." His voice was a low, deadly whisper that made chills run down Emma's spine.

She stared in shock at the expression on Harlan's face. It was such raw fury, such visceral hate that she froze.

Preston shot to his feet, evidently unharmed, his fists balled as he faced Harlan. "What's it to you?" Preston's blond hair and white dinner jacket were like glaring perfection against Harlan's black tee shirt and blue jeans. Both men were large and well-muscled. She knew exactly how hard Preston could hit, and how many hours he put in at the gym with his trainer working on kickboxing, but it was Harlan who scared her the most. The anger and fury were gone from his face. His features were schooled into a cold, lethal expression of pure destruction. The face of a warrior intending to kill. He looked like a man who could kill without remorse, the one he had claimed to be all along.

She froze, stunned at the change in Harlan. "Harlan?" she whispered, as if she could call him back from the place he'd gone.

"You were dancing with my wife," Preston snapped, his hands bunched into fists.

"Your ex-wife," Harlan said, his voice still edged with lethal chill. "She's my wife now."

"Your wife?" For a split second, Preston's face paled, and Emma felt a surge of triumph at his panic.

"What? You never considered that anyone else could want me?" Emma leaned on a nearby chair, taking the weight off her injured foot.

"She's mine," Harlan snarled, still not taking his gaze off Preston.

"Is she?" Preston shot a glance at her left hand, then gave Harlan a triumphant smile. "She's not wearing a wedding ring," he said.

Emma looked down at her hand, even though she already knew she'd see bare skin. No ring. Of course no ring. Suddenly, the absence of it felt hauntingly empty, a statement to the world that she didn't really belong to Harlan, or anywhere, that her life was simply a lie.

"She always wore mine," Preston sneered. "I guess you're just the rebound guy." His condescending gaze took in

Harlan's attire, and disgust twisted on his face. "I give you a month," he said, "until she realizes that she likes the life I can give her better. When was the last time you bought a woman a new car? Or a pair of shoes? Or even a package of gum?"

"Stop it!" Emma began to shake with anger. How many times had she heard that derisive tone directed at her? By Preston. By her parents. By his parents. Memories slashed at her, ugly memories that seemed to cascade through her mind, one on top of the other.

"Push me," Harlan said evenly. "Just push me a little further, you piece of shit." A new wave of coldness seemed to settle over Harlan. His hands were loose, not fisted like Preston's, but there was far more danger emanating from Harlan. She could see now the killer he claimed to be, the man who killed to save those he had vowed to protect. "You hurt her," Harlan snarled. "You stripped the light from her spirit. You made promises to her, and then you betrayed her."

Oh, God. It was too much. Was he going to kill Preston right there in the middle of the fair? "Stop." Emma grabbed Harlan's arm, shocked at how tense his muscles were. "Harlan, let's go—"

"You don't deserve to breathe the same air as she does." Harlan didn't take his eyes off Preston, who was starting to circle him, his fists ready.

"Hey, hey, hey!" Griffin jumped between them, followed quickly by Jackson and Jason, as well as the bartender that Clare had tried to set Emma up with. "Stand down, guys. Jason, get Preston out of here. Harlan, take off."

Jackson grabbed Harlan's arm, but Harlan didn't even seem to notice. He was just staring at Preston, with that same deadly expression on his face.

"Come on, big guy," Jackson said to Harlan. "Stand down. He's not worth it."

"No, he isn't worth it," Harlan said, not moving. "But Emma is."

Emma's throat tightened at those words, and suddenly it all felt like too much. She wanted to fall into Harlan's arms for defending her, and at the same time, he scared her to death the way he was bleeding violence. Seeing Preston again was overwhelming. How many tears had she shed over him? Seeing him, hearing his voice...it was like reliving everything he'd ever done to her. Numbly, she stumbled backward, clutching her purse. She just needed to get out. Get away. From Preston. From Harlan. From all of them.

Eppie came racing over. She yanked her hat off her head and smacked Harlan with it, and then Preston. "Stop it!" she shouted. "You boys are acting like toads! Pull it together! Harlan, for God's sake, didn't you even notice your wife is hurt? She needs you to help her, not be an ass!"

At Eppie's words, Harlan jerked his gaze off Preston for the first time, whirling around to face Emma. "You're hurt?"

She shook her head, hugging her handbag to her chest as she fought back tears, still inching away from everyone. "I just twisted my ankle. I just have to go. I need to go—"

His gaze shot to the foot she was favoring. Anguished guilt flooded his features, turning him back into the man she knew. Swearing violently, he strode toward her and scooped her off the ground, not even noticing when Preston started shouting at him, daring him to come back and finish. Harlan's entire focus was on her, his arms so tight around her. "I didn't even notice," he said, his face tormented. "How bad is it?"

"It's fine." She pushed at his chest, frantic, needing space. "Let me down."

"No. I'll take you to the hospital." He didn't even turn back to look at the crowd. He just strode across the field toward his truck, not even hearing her protests.

"Harlan!" She hit his chest in frustration just as he

reached the truck. "Let me go!" Tears were streaming down her face now, and she couldn't stop them.

He looked down at her, and his face went ashen. "Am I hurting you?"

"Just leave me alone," she whispered, too exhausted to fight. "I just want to go home."

He yanked open the door to the truck and eased her onto the seat. "I'll take you to the hospital—"

"No!" She grabbed his shirt. "For God's sake, just once, just this one time, will someone *please* listen to what I want? I just want to go *home*."

He stared at her for a long moment, and then he nodded. "Home, it is."

She leaned back against the seat and closed her eyes, relief cascading through her. "Thank you," she whispered.

He said nothing, but she heard the gentle click of him closing her door softly. She didn't open her eyes when he got in the truck. She simply wanted it all to go away. And by "all" she meant all the men who she'd ever married for any reason.

They just needed to go away. Forever.

CHAPTER FOURTEEN

HARLAN FELT LIKE SHIT, which was appropriate, because that was all he was worth.

There was no mistaking the way Emma tensed in resistance when he carried her up the steps to her cabin and across the living room to her bed. She hadn't spoken the whole ride home. She hadn't even made eye contact with him.

He deserved it. He knew he did. But hell, after having seen Emma smile at him earlier in the night, losing that affection felt like someone had taken a sharp dagger and carved out his damned heart. Her silence felt like hell.

Harlan set her down on the bed. For a moment, he hesitated, unsure what to do, but then quickly stepped back when she groaned and rolled onto her side, burying herself under the blankets. The faded quilt wrapped around her, its colored patterns mocking the blackness pulsing through him.

He should leave her. Go sleep on the couch. Give her privacy.

But he couldn't.

She was hurting. He'd seen her face. He couldn't walk away from her. "Em?"

No response.

"Emma."

No response.

Harlan ran his hand through his hair. "Did I hurt your ankle?" he finally asked. "When I grabbed Preston? Did I somehow hurt you?" The thought made him sick, literally sick, and he sat down in the middle of the floor, pressing his palms to his forehead. He'd been mad, so unbelievably angry when he'd seen Preston with his hands on Emma. The sight of Emma's stricken face had undone him, and he'd snapped, just completely fucking snapped. Jesus. *Jesus.* He dug his hand into his hair. What the fuck had he done? What—

"No." Emma's soft voice broke through his torment, and he jerked his head up.

She was on her side, the pillow tucked under her head as she looked at him. Her face looked pale and vulnerable against the faded yellow of her sheets, her blond hair strewn carelessly across the cotton. Her knees were pulled up to her chest, and the blanket was tucked up to her chin, but her head was uncovered now. Her cheeks were streaked with tears, and her eyes were rimmed with red.

"No, what?" he asked. He had no idea what she was responding to. All he could do was look at her, and fight the desperate, unforgivable urge to crawl under those covers and pull her into his arms, to hold her until nothing could ever hurt her again. But he was the danger to her. *Him.* So how could holding her protect her from him?

"No, you didn't hurt my ankle," she said quietly. "I hurt it trying to get away from Preston."

The air seemed to stand still inside his chest, as if oxygen were circling so close, almost close enough to breathe again. "You mean it? I didn't hurt you?"

The smallest furrow appeared between her eyebrows. "How would you have hurt me? You didn't even touch me."

"I didn't?" He tried to remember, to replay the scene, but all he could think of was how much he'd wanted to attack Preston, how he'd thought of nothing else but getting over there and stopping him from touching Emma. "I can't remember what happened."

She frowned at him. "What do you mean?"

"I don't know." He pressed his fingers to his head, trying to ease the pounding inside his brain. "When my father would go into a rage, no one around him was safe. He broke my stepmother's nose twice, and he threw me into a glass door when I was ten."

Emma's face blanched. "Harlan," she whispered. "How could you live like that? I'm so sorry for you."

"No, don't feel sorry for me. It was fine. I survived it." He couldn't take his eyes off her face, off the beautiful delicate visage of this woman who was allowing him into the sanctity of her bedroom, even after she had seen a flash of the beast within him. "But he taught me how to react to situations. My instinct is to do what he did, and to react first and think later. I lost my shit when I saw Preston touching you, when I saw the look of fear on your face." He met her gaze, not hiding from her anymore. "I don't know what I did in that moment. All I remember is the fury, and then charging at him."

Her face paled slightly in the moonlight, but she shook her head. "You didn't hit anyone, Harlan."

"I didn't?" When she shook her head, there was a moment of raw, stark relief ripping through him, stripping away his strength, but then it was quickly replaced by the grim truth. "But I wanted to." Swearing, he stood up, lacing his hands on top of his head as he paced the room. "I wanted to kill him, just like I told you that night in the boat. I was so pissed. I—" He broke off as he swung to face her. "I've never hated anyone like I did in that moment, when I saw the look of terror that he'd put on your face. I lost it, Em. I absolutely fucking lost it, just like my father."

Slowly, she held out her hand. It was steady now, not shaking, an invitation so beautiful he wanted to fall to his knees in disbelief that she could offer him her trust again. "Come here."

"No." He backed up, fighting off the instincts howling through him to reach out to her, to touch her, to bury himself in all that she was. "No, I'm not getting close to you—"

"I need you to come here," she said softly. "Please."

Please. There was no chance for him to resist that. Reluctantly, he walked over to the bed and crouched beside her, so his face was level with hers. "What?"

She held out her hand again in silent appeal.

Gritting his jaw, he shook his head. "I can't hold your hand and give you comfort. I'm not that guy, Emma. We both saw it tonight."

"You didn't hit him. You were angry, but you didn't hit him, or me, or anyone else."

"You saw my anger. I know you did. I scared you." And as God was his witness, that had nearly broken him when he'd seen the fear in her eyes when she'd looked at him. Not at Preston. At *him.* He'd seen his stepmother terrified of his father. He'd seen kidnap victims recoiling in horror from even their rescuers. He'd always known he had the capacity to put that look on a woman's face, but he'd always, *always* promised himself he'd never get close enough to actually do it.

He'd broken his promise.

Silently, he took her hand and pressed his forehead to the back of it. Her hand was cool and soft, a respite from the emotions pouring through him. "Forgive me, Emma, for thinking that I could be someone that I'm not," he whispered, his throat aching with the words. "I don't belong here, in this house, with someone like you. With a child."

"Harlan—"

"No." He raised his head to look at her. "I do my job easily," he said. "I go in, I do what I need to do, and I get out. It's business to me, so when I see kidnap victims who have been mistreated, I can keep my focus and do what I need to do. Tonight was different. Tonight, I couldn't think. All I could do was feel. Hate for him. Terror for your safety. Fear that I'd lose you, that somehow he'd win you over again and you'd walk away from me forever, back into hell." He tightened his grip on her hand, willing her to understand. "I can't afford to feel," he said. "Don't you understand? I can't control it when I feel. It makes me dangerous. And you make me feel. I can't look at you and stay emotionally detached. I'm so far past that, Emma. So far."

She smiled faintly and curled her fingers around his, holding on. "Have you ever hit anyone in anger?"

"Yeah." He thought back to the incident that had prompted him to leave town almost a year ago. "When I heard that Jason had gotten my sister pregnant, I walked over to his store, and the minute he opened the door, I laid him out." He rubbed his knuckles, as if he could still feel Jason's jaw against them.

Emma laughed softly. "Any good brother would do that, Harlan. As far as we knew, Jason had abandoned her. Clare and I were actually debating ways to sabotage the opening of his store, and Eppie actually did it. None of us are saints, Harlan. We will all protect those we care about."

"It's not the same thing." He looked at her. "When I lost it with Jason, I realized I was caring too much about Astrid. I got scared of what I might do to keep her safe, and I left before I could turn into my dad." He met her gaze. "And you," he said softly, almost desperate to touch her cheek, to feel her beneath his tainted hand. "You already suffered with

Preston. You don't need the shit that I bring, and I won't do it to you."

But still, the stubborn woman would not look away, and would not accept his refusal. "Have you ever hurt a woman? Even by accident? Even on all those rescue missions?"

Harlan's answer was instant. "No, but that was business. I wasn't invested emotionally. It's different with Astrid." He met her gaze. "And with you. When I saw Preston's hand on your shoulder, and the expression on your face, I finally understood the power of emotions, how they could drive my father to such extremes. I truly believe he loved my step-mother, but his love for her is what made him so dangerous. I'm like him, Emma. I'm exactly like him. I'm not the good guy."

"No?" Emma's eyes were glistening, and the damn woman actually looked happy, like he'd said something beautiful. "Do you realize that good men don't always come in perfectly wrapped packages with beautiful bows? Sometimes, they are dirty and rough, and unable to survive polite company unscathed, while the beautiful, polished packages are the scum who really hurt people."

He swore under his breath, hating that she wouldn't believe his true nature, but at the same time, he clung to her every word, desperately needing the way she looked at him like he wasn't a monster. "Emma—"

"When I was ten years old, my parents took me to the town beach," she said quietly, absently stroking the back of his hand with her thumb. "They brought their wine and cock-tails, and I went off with my friends. My friends went home at dinner, but my parents kept on with their drinking. I played by myself, and then I went swimming too far out. I couldn't make it back to shore, and I started to drown. It was so fast, so sudden, the way I went down. I didn't even have time to scream. I just started sinking down. I tried to get air, but sucked in water. I couldn't keep my head up. I knew I was drowning, but I couldn't even call for help. My parents didn't notice, but a fifteen-year-old summer boy saw me. He swam out and got me just as I went under for the last time. An ambulance came, and the whole beach converged. My parents were the last ones down to the shore. They hadn't even bothered to find out who had almost drowned until someone told them it was me. When we finally got home that night, my parents told me that I was rude and selfish to try to get their attention by pretending to drown, and that I was banned from the lake for the rest of the summer."

Harlan stared at her, trying to fathom a parent being angry at a child who had almost drowned. "Were they serious?"

"They didn't want me," she said. "They liked their life the way it was, and having me dragged them down. I did everything I could to get them to notice they had a daughter, and they never cared. When I was drowning, I remember thinking, 'well, at least I don't have to try to impress them anymore.'"

Harlan stared at her, stunned. A ten year old being relieved to die? His life had been shit with his father, but he'd never thought about giving up. He'd just wanted out. Dark anger swirled inside him, a fierce protectiveness for this woman before him, a need to keep her safe. She deserved to be honored and loved, to have someone who would walk ahead of her with a machete and kick the shit out of anything life tried to throw at her to hurt her.

"All I wanted, Harlan," she said, drawing his attention back to her, "the *only* thing that I wanted was to have someone actually notice me. I wanted someone to care when I drowned. To love me. I used to be so jealous of Clare and her mom, doing their stuff together, that it would actually make my chest hurt." She met his gaze. "Tonight, I was scared when Preston had me cornered. It was like I was drowning again, only this time, someone was there for me. *You*. When you went after Preston, I mattered to you. I saw it in your eyes. *I mattered*."

Harlan's throat tightened. "Sweet Emma," he said softly, brushing the hair out of her eyes. "Of course you matter to me, but that's not enough. You need to raise your standards higher than what you got from me tonight. I saw your face when I went over the edge. You were terrified of me, and you were right to be scared. Your instincts know who I am." He thumbed the corner of her mouth, the tiny scar. "He hit you."

Emma made a noise of irritation. "On purpose, Harlan. He hit me *on purpose*. For God's sake, can't you understand the difference? Are you so determined to hate yourself that you can't even register basic facts?"

"He hit you." Harlan gritted his teeth as that same anger rose within him, that same need to destroy that bastard.

"Yes, he did, but you—" Her voice softened, and her fingers drifted gently across his skin. "You would never hurt me on purpose, would you?"

"Fuck no." He couldn't keep the shock out of his voice. "Jesus, Emma, *never*."

"See?" Triumph gleamed in her eyes. "You're different than he is."

"I'm not—"

"Stop it." She put her fingers over his lips. "I need you to be different." Her voice was strong, but her eyes were haunted with shadows. "I was so wrong about him, Harlan. I believed in love and magic and fairytales, but he was so evil. I see goodness in you, and I need to be right this time. I am well aware that you're not perfect. You did scare me for a minute, but I also know you would do everything in your power to protect me, even from yourself. That's the sign of a good man. I need you to let me see that side of you. I need to be right, that there is one person in this world with a good heart who cares." She gripped his hand. "I tried everything to win my parents over, and in the end, I meant nothing to them. They're in Italy and I haven't spoken to them in eleven years. I keep choosing the wrong people to believe in, and I have to be right for once. I need you to be the man I think you are."

Harlan's heart seemed to crack for her. "Your soul is so beautiful," he whispered. "Never stop believing that there is goodness in the world. It's a beautiful trait."

"Let me be right about you," she said again, ignoring his compliment.

Harlan closed his eyes against the urge to draw her into his arms and to bury himself in the fantasy that Emma held about him. He'd never cared that he was his father's son, not until this moment. Not until tonight. With Emma snuggled in her bed, her hand clenched in his, he suddenly wanted to be the guy who didn't sleep alone anymore. "Emma," he said in a strangled voice. "I'll hurt you."

"I already know you're going to leave me."

He opened his eyes. "Not that kind of hurt—"

She met his gaze, and there was a shrewd gleam in her eyes. "What if I told you that when Preston said he still loved me, I knew that on some naïve, foolish, desperate level, I still loved him? What if when he told me that he had changed and wanted another chance, that a part of me wanted to give it to him?"

Harlan felt like a hunting knife had been jammed into his chest. His breath seemed to slice through his chest, and his body went cold. He couldn't breathe, and his fingers seemed to go numb, slipping out of her grasp. "You...want...him?"

She met his gaze, a challenge in her voice. "What if I told you I would go back to him if he agreed to counseling, and I could make sure it was safe for me to go back to him?"

Harlan lurched to his feet, stumbling backwards, his mind reeling. A thousand thoughts were rushing through his mind, and the one most vivid, most clear was an image of Preston rearing back to hit her. "You'll get hurt," he managed to say. "Don't take me, but don't go to him. He'll hurt you." Searing pains seemed to cascade through his chest, as he went back on his knees before her. He grabbed her hand, barely able to find the words for his urgency. "Don't do it, Em. Just don't."

Through his desperate haze, a smile filled Emma's face, the most beautiful, most genuine smile he'd ever seen. She scooted over to the edge of the bed and kissed him lightly.

Stunned, Harlan pulled back. "What are you doing?"

"Jealousy is a terrible thing for a man," she said. "That was why Preston hit me, because one of his friends made a move on me. And yet, when I presented you with a reason to be jealous, your only thought was for my safety." She locked her arms behind his neck, smiling broadly.

He still didn't understand. "You aren't going back to him?"

"No." She ran her fingers through his hair, a touch so gentle and tender that it shook him right down to his core. "I just wanted to know who you really were. I offered you the worst scenario I could think of to expose the darkest side of you, and it simply wasn't there. I was right." She locked her fingers behind his neck, a satisfied look on her face. "Kiss me, Harlan. Kiss me as if you were going to stay with me forever."

He wasn't a good enough man to walk away from what Emma offered him. Not just the kiss, but her belief in who he was. She was wrong, he knew that, but right now, in that moment, he couldn't tear himself away from the feeling of having someone believe in him.

Maybe she needed to be right about him, but he was beginning to think that he needed her to be right about him even more.

"I'm still going to leave," he said gruffly as he slid his hand behind her neck.

She met his gaze. "I know you are. That's why tonight is okay, because it will just be for tonight. Kiss me, Harlan. Please."

He had no willpower left to resist. None at all. He did as she asked, and kissed her.

CHAPTER FIFTEEN

THE MOMENT he tasted Emma's lips, Harlan knew he was lost. There was no chance he could be the hero tonight and ride off alone to leave the fair maiden untouched. He wanted to be the good guy, the one who rose above temptation, but with Emma's mouth responding to his, and her fingers tangling in his hair, there was simply no way to pretend to be the man he wasn't.

He needed her tonight, on levels he couldn't even understand, and there was no chance he was walking away from his wife.

Not breaking the kiss, he rose from the floor and slid onto the bed, even as Emma's hands tightened around his neck, keeping him close, preventing him from leaving her. He chuckled as he settled on top of her, the softness of her body a precious treasure beneath his. "You don't know what's good for you, do you?"

"I know exactly what is good for me," she said as she tugged his shirt up.

"I married a crazy woman," he said, even as he helped her pull his shirt off. The minute his shirt was out of the way, she splayed her hands over his chest in a possessive move that made dark, dangerous desire begin to build inside him.

"Of course you did," she said. "I never claimed to be otherwise." She propped herself up on her elbows, and pressed a kiss to his left nipple.

He leaned his head back, bracing his hands on her headboard as she kissed her way across him, lightly nipping. His body tightened, and raw need pulsed through him. She was different than she'd been the first night they'd made love. That night, she had been desperate and vulnerable, but tonight was different. It was as if seeing Preston had changed her, given her strength. She wasn't afraid of him tonight...even after the flash of his true nature that she'd seen at the carnival.

Her fingers found the button on his jeans, and his stomach contracted as she unbuttoned them, the brush of her fingertips a decadent tease on his flesh. With a low growl of desire, he grasped her shirt and tugged it upward, breaking her grip on his jeans. She looked up at him as she raised her arms over her head, letting him slide the soft cotton over her wrists and off her hands. Her face was upturned toward his, her green eyes burning with desire...and trust, making something shift inside him.

"I don't get it." He leaned over her, using his body to direct her back down. "How can you look at me like you want me?"

She put a finger on his lips. "Stop," she said. "I don't want to hear any more arguments. I just want to be with you tonight."

And there it was in her voice, that same vulnerability that had been there before. She might be strong and tough, but there was a softness about her that broke through the shield he'd worked so hard to erect around himself. With a low groan, he kissed her again, deeper this time, unable to hold back. "I need you," he whispered between kisses.

"I need you, too." Her hands were roaming his back, his neck, his hair. She was touching him everywhere, as if trying to memorize his body, or to stake her claim to it. He didn't know why she welcomed him the way she did, but it felt incredible to be touched like that, in softness, in seduction, with honest desire.

He owed her. He had to be the man she wanted him to be. He had to find a way. She'd decided to trust him, and he couldn't let her be wrong. Protectiveness surged over him as he unhooked her bra and slid it down her arms, never breaking the kiss. This incredible woman had offered him such a gift by giving him her trust, and he wanted to cradle it in his palms, guarding it with his life.

He softened his kisses, turned them into a languorous seduction of sensual desire, kisses that took a lifetime to finish. Her body softened beneath his, and her hips shifted restlessly.

Yes, yes, yes, he thought as she responded to him. This was right. This was how it should be. She deserved kisses that would last a lifetime, not the quick seduction of a one-night stand. He trailed his kisses down the side of her neck as he unfastened her jeans, laving her breasts with a teasing seduction that was raw torment to endure, at least for him. The need to make love to her, to connect them intimately was pounding in his ears, hammering at him, but he fought it off, refusing to succumb to his base needs, determined to give her what she deserved.

He pressed his mouth to her navel as he slid the jeans down her hips, and she gasped, her belly quivering beneath his assault as he slid her jeans over her legs. Her eyes met his as he ran his hand down her calf, kissing her leg. The intensity of her gaze took his breath away, and he suddenly couldn't wait anymore.

His jeans hit the floor within a heartbeat, and then he moved over her, his own body trembling in anticipation as if he were a schoolboy who was in over his head. And in a way, he was. In Emma's arms, he felt different than he'd ever been before, struggling to find his footing before he drowned in her softness. She wrapped her legs around his hips, pulling him against her, again a statement of such trust that he swore under his breath. "I swear I will never hurt you," he said fiercely.

She smiled. "I know that. I've always known that."

The words were so simple, and yet so beautiful that it made something inside him simply snap. He couldn't be the gentleman anymore. He needed to consume her and all that she offered him. With one swift move, he sat up, pulling her onto his lap, her legs around his hips, her breasts against his chest. He slid his hand through her hair, anchoring her as he kissed her, kissing her so deeply that he poured his soul into the kiss.

Emma locked her arms around his neck, holding him even more tightly as she kissed him back. Their tongues danced, their breath hot and mingled, heart rates hammering as the intensity built between them. He was right at her core, pulsing against her, and she moved against him, closer, increasing the pressure, teasing him, inviting him, a sensual invitation that raged through him.

"Make love to me, Harlan," she whispered. "Make love to your wife."

His wife. By some miracle of heaven, this woman was *his wife.* "You're mine," he growled as he grabbed her hips and lifted her. "All mine." Then he pulled her onto him, and she gasped as he filled her, a moment of such sheer perfection that he went utterly still, holding her against him, just breathing in the sensation of being inside her. "Perfection," he said softly.

Emma raised her face to his, and a smile filled those beautiful eyes. "You have no idea how you make me feel, Harlan. Thank you."

"Thank you?" He ran his hands down her spine and then grasped her hips. "I'm far from finished with you, sweetheart." Then he shifted inside her, and they both gasped. She took control, moving her hips, working them both into a frenzy as he kissed her, the kisses rising in intensity with each move, each touch, each caress—

He slid his fingers into her hair again, and then suddenly remembered her fear. Quickly, he released his grip. But she grabbed his hand and put it back. "It's okay," she whispered. "I like it."

I like it. The enormity of that statement, that she now liked him to do the very thing that used to scare her seemed to plunge right into his gut. "*Emma.*" He rolled her onto her back with sudden fierceness, and drove into her, deeply, so deeply, burying himself inside her as he braced himself above her, trying not to crush her with his weight. She gasped and threw her head back in a position of complete vulnerability as he thrust again, and again, until both of them were drenched in the sweat of passion, lust, and raw need.

Tension coiled inside him, building more and more, and he crushed his mouth to hers, a kiss that seemed to explode within him. She gasped his name and grabbed his shoulders as she convulsed beneath him. With a roar of desperate need, he surrendered to the orgasm. Fire whipped through him, searing every cell in his body as he shouted her name over and over and over again, until her name was all he could hear, until Emma was all that would ever, ever matter to him again.

∼

HARLAN SAT on the edge of the bed, his forearms resting on his knees, as he watched Emma sleep. Her hair was tousled over the pillow, the moon's rays making it shine like silver-spun silk. She looked vulnerable and beautiful, pure innocence.

She shifted restlessly, her forehead puckering. "No," she whispered in her sleep. "Leave me alone."

He stiffened. Was she talking about him? But he didn't even have time to worry before she spoke again, whispering the name of her ex-husband, her voice taut with tension.

Defiance flared through him, and he bent over her, brushing his palm over her forehead. "I'm here, Emma," he said softly. "I'm watching over you. He can't get you. I'll keep you safe."

The lines on her forehead smoothed. "Harlan," she mumbled.

"Yeah, it's me." He kept stroking her forehead. "You're safe, sweetheart, always safe now."

Her angst subsided, and she fell back into a heavy sleep, her breath deepening into an even rhythm. He traced his finger over the curve of her shoulder, over her collarbone that was too prominent. She was too thin, maybe even thinner than when he'd last been with her.

She needed someone to take care of her. To make sure she ate enough. To hold her while she slept. He ground his jaw, staring out the open window at the lake. A light breeze rippled through the curtains, and the moon was bright across the water. It reminded him of the night when he'd taken her for a boat ride, the night they'd gotten married.

It was pure simplicity out on the water, a place where the world faded and reality was left behind. No baggage. No rescue victims. No ex-husbands. No bastard fathers. Just quiet. He took a breath, inhaling the scent of the night. It always felt good to be on the lake. He never longed for the missions when he was on the water. He looked back down at Emma, who had turned toward him. Still asleep, she tugged at his hand, tucking it beneath her chin. What if she was right to believe in him? What if there was a part of him that wasn't like his father? What if being married to her and caring about her didn't have to bring out the worst in him?

But even as he thought it, his cell phone buzzed.

He stared at it for a long minute, not wanting to answer it. It buzzed again.

Finally, he lifted it off the nightstand and looked at the text. It was from Blue, simple and direct. Just a place, a time, and a date. Their next mission. Shit.

Then came one more text. A question mark. Asking if he was coming.

Blue never asked. He always assumed...until now. Did Blue think he was going to be tempted by the life Emma represented?

But there it was, a question mark. Was Harlan going to show up?

And then came another question mark, making Harlan laugh. He typed a quick reply. *Impatient bastard.*

Blue's reply was a third question mark.

Harlan looked down at Emma. Her left hand was curled over his, and his gaze fell upon her fourth finger, the one that wasn't wearing a wedding band. Preston's words echoed in his mind, the challenge, the insult when he'd noticed Emma's bare hand.

Harlan thumbed the tiny scar at the corner of her mouth, knowing what he had to do. He typed a one word reply to Blue, and then got dressed and walked out the door.

HARLAN EASED along the front porch, testing each board

before he stepped on it. Not a creak sounded as he approached the door, carefully stepping around the toys strewn across it. A skateboard. A red, plastic bat. Two Frisbees. Several large tubs of water, which appeared to be croaking, suggesting that some bullfrogs had been invited to spend the night in them. He leaned against the door frame and lightly dropped one knuckle on the front door, not wanting to have to face the rest of the inhabitants. He hoped Astrid had managed to sneak downstairs alone.

The door opened instantly and Astrid stuck her head out, giving him an annoyed look. "It's three in the morning," she whispered, her hair twisted up in a tangled ponytail. "Never wake the mother of an infant at three in the morning. If she's actually asleep, she'll shoot you for waking her up."

Harlan grinned. "It's good to see you too, sis."

Astrid rolled her eyes and stepped back. "Come on in, but be quiet. Rosie just went to sleep, and Noah is snoozing on the couch. He heard me with Rosie and wanted to be with us." She smiled fondly in the direction of the living room. "He still has nights where he can't sleep, and we keep each other company while I'm feeding Rosie."

"Noah?" Harlan stepped inside the darkened foyer of his sister's new home, the one that Jason had provided for her.

"My son," she explained as she led the way through the living room, nodding at the couch. "Our son."

"Your son," he repeated, finally figuring out she was talking about Jason's son. He realized she hadn't called him her stepson. Just son. Harlan's stepmother had never even made it as far as calling him her stepson, let alone son. Astrid's words seemed to tighten his chest, almost painfully.

Trying to shrug it off, Harlan stopped and studied the boy asleep on the couch. He had a knitted afghan pulled up under his chin but he'd kicked his feet free. Harlan vaguely remembered hearing that Jason had a kid, but it had never registered that the boy would become Astrid's stepson. Son, rather.

"Yes, and he's your nephew now. It would be nice if you'd actually stay around long enough to meet him." Astrid sat down on an oversized denim couch at Noah's feet, tucking them onto her lap, apparently not concerned about waking the youth up by having a conversation right next to him. She nodded at a small cloth bag on the wooden coffee table. "I got out an assortment of different styles when I got your text. I didn't know what type you wanted." As she spoke, she ran her hand affectionately over Noah's back in a gesture that was so nurturing and domestic that he almost didn't believe his own sister had done it.

He sank down into a leather armchair next to her end of the sofa. "You're like a real mom."

She smiled. "I'm not 'like' a mom, Harlan. I *am* a mom. It's amazing." She rubbed Noah's back as the boy muttered in his sleep. "I'll be honest, I didn't know if I could figure out how to be a good mother, after our role model, but I'm doing okay." Her face softened. "Jason is wonderful. He doesn't expect me to be any way other than what I am."

Harlan felt a twinge of guilt. "Sorry I hit him."

Astrid shrugged. "He says he owes you a thank you. He needed it." She waggled a finger at him. "But don't do it again, okay?"

He managed a half smile. "That's why I'm leaving town."

Astrid's smile faded. "Again? For how long?"

He shrugged noncommittally as he picked up the bag. "A while." He undid the draw string and poured the contents out onto the table. A pile of rings glittered up at him. Gold ones. Silver ones. Plain ones. Rings with engravings.

"They're all in Emma's size," Astrid said. "They'll all fit her."

Harlan picked up a gold one that had a pale green stone in

it. "It's like her eyes," he said, "but a little lighter." He picked up another, a simple silver band with beautiful etchings. "This is like the painting she has over her bed. There's a border on it of trees that's similar to this design." He set it down, not sure. "I don't know."

Astrid was staring at him. "What are you doing, Harlan?"

He looked at her. "I told you. I want her to have a wedding ring for our home study interview tomorrow."

"No, not that." Astrid scooted forward on the couch. "You're being thoughtful about the ring. You're trying to pick something that will be meaningful to her."

Harlan frowned as he picked up another one. It was gold, with silver inlay surrounding tiny chips of diamonds that made it sparkle just like the night sky when they'd been out on the lake that night. "So? Isn't that what a husband is supposed to do?"

"But you're leaving."

He looked up at the accusation in her voice. "Yeah, she knows that. It was part of the deal."

"Part of the deal?" Astrid echoed, her voice rising. "She's in love with you, Harlan. Was that part of the deal?"

He stared at her as a sudden heat seemed to consume him. "What? She's not—"

"Of course she is. I was watching her tonight at the fair." Astrid shook her head reproachfully. "Do you have any idea how broken she was after her marriage? There were days that Clare and I thought she was literally going to simply fade away before our eyes. Preston betrayed her—"

"I know that," he said sharply as he put down the ring and picked up a plain gold band. A ring that had no personality or emotion. Just hard metal.

"Well, you may know it, but have you *thought* about it?" She didn't give him time to answer. "Do you know what I go through every time you leave?"

Surprised by her question, he let the plain ring fall back to the table. "What do you mean?"

Her brown eyes were blazing now. "Women can't shut off their emotions, Harlan. Before Jason, you were *all* I had. That's it. One lifeline. You rescued me from the hospital, but then you never gave me any more than that. I've been waiting for my brother to come back to me, but you keep pushing me further away."

He gave his sister his full attention. "Astrid. I can't—"

"No!" She held up her hand to stop him. "There are no excuses, Harlan. You either commit to family, or you don't. I love you regardless, but when I thought you were dead, I was shattered. You could have sent me a note that you were okay, you know. It was horrible, wondering if you were dead, only to find that you were actually *in town* and hadn't bothered to tell me you were okay!"

"I didn't mean to hurt you." He grimaced, guilt coursing through him. "You aren't supposed to care about me that much—"

"You don't get to choose how people feel about you," she snapped.

His head started to pound again, like there was pressure hammering at him from all sides. "That's why I'm leaving. So that no one cares—"

"It's too late, Harlan." She leaned forward. "I care. Emma cares. Eppie cares. Jackson cares. People care about you."

He ground his jaw as he picked up another ring. This one was all gold with twelve roses engraved on the band. Roses. Like the ones he'd given her on their wedding night.

"Every time Jason goes out of town, I get scared," she said softly.

He looked over at her. "You think he's not coming back?"

"Intellectually, I know he is, but I still get scared that he might not. Old fears take a long time to die." She tucked her hair behind her ear, suddenly looking like the little sister he'd met for the first time when he was seventeen, and she was twelve. "We all carry our baggage with us our whole lives. Emma has terrible ones, and you're messing with her."

He set down the rose ring. "I'm not. We both know what's going on. It's so she can adopt Mattie. You know that, right?"

"I know that, but what are you doing to Mattie?" She gestured at the sleeping boy. "Noah still has nightmares about his mother dying. He sleeps in my bed with me when Jason's not home. He's afraid of losing me, because he already lost one mother. Parents aren't supposed to abandon you, and we both know how much it sucks when that happens." Her eyes were glistening. "You never forgave Mom for letting your dad take you away. If you're part of the adoption for Mattie and you're not there when she moves in, you're breaking a promise to her."

Harlan scowled at Astrid as emotions hammered at him, emotions he didn't recognize, but that left a cold void cascading through him. "I'm not making a promise. I haven't even met her—"

"What about when she asks Emma where you are? She's almost five, Harlan, old enough to understand that she was adopted by a couple, and one of them is not there. You're not just messing with Emma, you're messing with Mattie, too."

Harlan ran his hand through his hair, shifting uncomfortably. "I'm not messing with them. I'm protecting them. I'm helping them have more than they can have on their own—"

"No. You're abandoning them."

"I'm not." He swore. "I just—"

"When we thought you were dead, Emma told me why you guys had gotten married. She told me you didn't want to die without anyone caring. When you married her, you bought yourself a future widow, Harlan. Are you buying yourself a child, too? Someone else to cry when you die?"

He stared at her. "I'm not even going to meet her—"

"It's not about protecting them, is it? No, it's not. It's about making yourself feel better." Astrid shook her head in disgust. "It's like when you rescued me, and then you disappeared. You run in, save the day, and then move on. You can't do that in real life. You can't do that to me, and you can't do it to Emma, or Mattie." She looked at him, and there were tears glistening in her eyes. "It's not fair, Harlan. Not to any of us."

He swore again. "I know it's not," he tried to explain. "That's why I'm leaving—"

"Seriously?" She gaped at him in obvious disbelief. "Oh, so *after* you marry Emma and get her to fall in love with you, and *after* you make promises to a little girl you've never met, *then* you're going to spare everyone and leave? Really? That actually makes sense in your head?"

"Astrid?" Jason's sleepy voice interrupted the conversation, and Harlan turned to see the man standing in the doorway.

Jason was wearing a pair of striped pajama bottoms. Pajamas. Who the hell wore pajamas? Harlan had a sudden feeling that he'd stepped into some surreal world of pajamas, children, and domesticity. He didn't belong here, and he needed to get out.

"Harlan stopped by," Astrid said. "He needed help with something."

Jason yawned and nodded a greeting at Harlan. "You couldn't wait until morning?" His voice was friendly, though, as he ambled across the living room and dropped a gentle kiss on Astrid's mouth. He brushed a thumb across her cheek, then looked at Harlan, his face a little less friendly. "You made her cry again?"

Harlan looked at the threesome: the sleeping child, his sister, and Jason. They fit together, and he felt like an intruder. He quickly grabbed his choice from the pile of rings and stood up. "Sorry. I wasn't thinking. I'll go."

"No, it's fine." Jason eyed him. "Stay for breakfast. I'd like to get to know the man who rescued Astrid from the hospital. She talks about you a lot."

He glanced at Astrid, who stood up and put her hand in Jason's. "You do?"

"Of course I do," she said wearily. "Stop being surprised by human nature. It really shouldn't be that unexpected that you matter to me." Challenge flickered in her eyes. "I don't think you should stay for breakfast," she said. "Go back to Emma. Be there when she wakes up, and stay there. For good. It's too late to back out now."

Jason's eyes narrowed. "Back out of what? Your marriage to Emma? You're going to walk out on her?"

"No," Harlan started to say, but when Astrid's face darkened, he cut it off. "What, Astrid? What would you have me do?"

She met his gaze. "Just stop lying to yourself. That's it. That would be enough to get you started." She paused. "And put me on the call list if you die. Believe it or not, I care enough about you to be willing to be burdened by your death." Then she turned to her husband and touched his arm. "I'm tired."

Jason ran his hand over her shoulder, squeezing gently. "Then go to bed, my dear. I'll grab Noah and follow."

Astrid didn't even look back as she walked out of the room and headed up the stairs. Jason glanced at Harlan, but said nothing to him as he scooped up Noah, cradling the boy to his chest. He paused for a moment, and silence hovered between the two men.

"Sorry I hit you," Harlan said finally, voicing the apology that had been haunting him for almost a year.

Jason shrugged. "You hit like a wimp, so it was no biggie." He tucked Noah tighter against his chest and lowered his voice. "But you should know, that if you break my wife's heart or Emma's, I *will* hit you back, and I won't pull my punch like you did. Have a nice night and see yourself out."

CHAPTER SIXTEEN

LIKE THE LAST time they'd made love, Emma awoke to an empty bed and an empty house. She bolted upright in bed, her heart hammering in her chest as she looked around. "Harlan?"

The only sound was that of a Jet Ski racing by the house.

He was gone. Again.

The urge to race to the living room to look for him was like a desperate scream of need, but she didn't move. She forced herself to sink back into the bedding, and she took a shaky breath, trying to slow the hammering of her heart. "He won't let Mattie down," she said aloud. No matter what he did after today, he would be there for the home study.

But she couldn't help but look at the nightstand for a good-bye note...and what she saw made her breath catch. On the nightstand was a bouquet of pink roses cut from her garden. He'd included some of the buds, like before, but this time there were also three blossoms in full bloom, their fragile scent decorating the air. Three? One for her, him, and Mattie? Her heart seemed to leap, and then she saw a note taped to the vase.

She quickly sat up and pulled it off. It was written on notepaper that she'd designed and printed. His scrawl was bold and brief on the outside, just her name. She opened the note, and then her breath caught when she saw he had taped a ring to the paper. "Oh, Harlan," she whispered, her heart leaping...until she read his message. *This might help convince Dottie.*

It might help convince Dottie? He'd given her a wedding ring, and that was how he'd phrased it? Her heart sank at the terse note. Yes, she knew he still planned to leave, but last night's lovemaking had been incredible. The passion had been intense, but there had been more than that. Tenderness. Laughter. Telling stories about their childhood. It had been a night of bonding. Not that she'd expected everything to change long-term, but...well...maybe a little. Maybe she hadn't been able to kill all hope for how he made her feel, for him.

Pressing her lips together, she peeled the ring off the paper and studied it.

It was a plain silver band, and she recognized the imprint on the inside as one of Astrid's. With all the beautiful rings that Astrid made, he'd chosen the plainest one for her, one that was utterly devoid of any personality. In private, Astrid called them her no-love-rings, because she firmly believed that anyone who would choose that ring didn't have enough passion in their souls to make a marriage work. She sold a surprising number of them, much to her dismay.

Emma leaned back against the pillows, and stared out the window at the lake. It was a beautiful sunny day, with the water sparkling, but she barely noticed it, unable to think of anything but the man who'd given her the ring. Between the fact Harlan hadn't been there again when she'd woken up, the impersonal note, and the plain ring, he had made certain that she understood exactly how it was between them.

Sighing, she turned the ring over in her fingers, the

smoothly polished silver like a mirror. What did it reflect? A marriage based on nothing. She'd been a fool, hadn't she? She'd thought she was protecting herself, but it had been a lie. She'd opened herself to him on every level.

She'd told herself she'd married him for Mattie, but the truth was, she'd married him because, during that night on the lake, he'd made her believe again. In life. In hope. In humanity. In love. It hadn't been a desire to help Mattie that had overruled her haunting fear of men and marriage. It had been the fact that Harlan had awakened her soul again, and she had been so desperate to feel alive that she'd clung to that moment, to him, thinking that he would bring her back to life.

After all her talk about how she didn't want or need a man, the reality of how vulnerable she was to Harlan was a terrifying shock. She'd been lying to herself that she was fine being alone. She hadn't been fine. In truth, she'd simply been letting her soul die until a man could revive it for her.

Well, screw that. She was tired of being the pathetic female.

Emma kicked her blanket off and padded across the floor to her dresser. She pulled out her top drawer and fished around in the back of it until she came across the velvet box she'd hidden in there. She pulled it out and opened the lid. Sitting in the plush velvet was her wedding ring from Preston. It was a plain platinum band that looked almost exactly like the one Harlan had selected, except it was obscenely more expensive. Her engagement ring had been an enormous diamond. He'd demanded it back as part of the divorce, but he hadn't cared about the wedding ring.

She had. It represented a time when she had hope, and she'd also kept it as a reminder that a wedding band didn't solve her problems.

She tightened her fist around both wedding bands, and then slipped out her back door onto the dock. She walked all the way to the end, and then looked at Preston's ring. "No more," she whispered. "I release you from my life." Then she hurled it into the water. It landed with a small splash much too close to the dock, sinking slowly down into the clear water until it settled in the grasses at the bottom, blinking out of sight.

Relief rushed through her, a sense of accomplishment, and she realized how tightly she'd still been holding onto her old life and her old dreams. It felt unbelievably good to finally let him go.

Feeling triumphant, she looked down at Harlan's band, still clutched in her hand, her intention to cast it into the water fading as she looked at the gleaming metal. "Damn you," she whispered. "Why did you have to leave me the roses, too?" Because she couldn't stop thinking about the roses. Why had he left them? He'd even taken the time to put them in a vase.

The plain ring was the man he claimed to be.

The roses were the man he couldn't help being.

If she didn't believe in him, who would? No one, and certainly not him.

She had a feeling he wouldn't appear until noon, right when Dottie was scheduled to arrive, trying to be the plain-ring man. He'd tried to put distance between them, but he hadn't been able to walk away without picking flowers for her. She had to decide who she believed, her or him.

With a deep breath, she set the ring at the tip of her fourth finger on her left hand, but her hands were shaking too much to get it on. "You couldn't have picked one that was different from Preston's?" she muttered.

She took a deep breath and let her hands fall to her sides.

"Okay, Emma, you can do this. You're already married to him. You already believe in him. The ring isn't a trap." Putting the ring on wasn't for Mattie. Dottie had already seen her without a ring. Dottie wasn't the one who needed convincing. It was Harlan. And her.

Emma looked down at the ring again, then knelt at the edge of the dock. She dragged the ring through the water, through the lake that gave her peace and a home, letting the warm water coat the ring and her hand. Finally, she took it out, and with hands that were still shaking, she slipped it onto her ring finger.

It fit perfectly, settling onto her hand as if it had been meant for her all along. A part of her wanted to tear it off and hurl it into the lake before it could hurt her, but at the same time, something seemed to settle inside her, something that had been running for so long.

Closing her fist to protect the ring, as if it might fall off on its own, Emma turned back toward the house. She had less than four hours to make the house into a home fit for a five year old, and to make herself look like the perfect mother for Mattie.

Less than four hours until her husband would walk in that door.

THE SILENCE WAS OVERWHELMING. The tension brittle. The laughter gone. Even the sun had disappeared behind dark storm clouds that were encroaching upon the afternoon.

Emma squeezed her fists in her lap, fighting back the most incredible sense of desolation and betrayal.

"It's almost four o'clock," Dottie said, closing her notebook, watching Emma carefully. "I have only one more question for you."

Emma managed a smile. "What is it?"

The social worker's eyes were thoughtful, and far too astute. "In your opinion, why is it that your husband failed to make it to the home study today?"

He hadn't appeared. In four hours, Harlan had not called, texted, or walked in the door. He had simply blown it off. "This happens sometimes," Emma said, almost choking on the words. "As I said, sometimes he gets called to an emergency and he can't let me know until he's done."

"Not even a text?" Dottie leaned forward. "Not even for something as important as this?"

Emma bit her lip, fighting to keep her composure, when all she wanted to do was leap up and scream at him, at the world. "He has a sensitive job."

"Indeed." Dottie set her notebook in her briefcase. "It seems to me that a man whose job requires him to abandon his wife in critical moments without so much as a text might not be the best father for a child who has already suffered a great deal of loss."

"No!" Emma felt like her heart was going to crack. "It's not like that. He's a good man. And I love Mattie. She doesn't want to go to South Carolina. She'll be happy and loved here—"

"And abandoned regularly?"

"I would never abandon her—"

"Just you? Shouldn't you have said 'we' will never abandon her?" Dottie's eyes glittered sharply.

Tears stung her eyes, but she fought to control them. "Dottie, I know what it's like to be a child that no one cares about. I would never let Mattie feel that way—"

"I don't doubt that." Dottie shook her head. "But you aren't the only one in this house." She stood up, signaling the end of the interview.

"No." Emma lurched to her feet. "Please don't. It's not

like that—" And suddenly the entire story came tumbling out, every bit of it, including why Harlan had married her and why she'd married him. "It's all just because I want to do what's right for Mattie—"

"You faked a marriage to get approved? Really?" Dottie shook her head. "I'll be honest. I like you, Emma. And I even liked Harlan when I met him." Sympathy flashed in her eyes. "And I even understand, on some level, what drove the two of you to get married. But neither of you, alone or individually, is in a place where you're ready to focus on Mattie, or any other child in need." She shut her briefcase, locking it down. "She may not like her grandparents, but based on my conversations with the social worker from South Carolina, they can provide a stable home for her, and they want to."

Emma's heart felt like it was breaking. "No, please—"

"There are always children who need to be fostered," Dottie said. "In a year or two, when you're in a better place, give me a call. I think you could be good for kids when the time is right, but for now, I am not going to be able to approve you as a foster parent, or recommend you to adopt her or anyone else."

"Dottie." Emma followed her to the door, desperately trying to think of what to say. All she could think of was Mattie's desperate face when she'd said that she didn't want to go to her grandparents. "But Mattie needs me—" Dottie paused with her hand on the doorknob. "Mattie will survive. Children always do."

"Do they?" Emma challenged, no longer able to contain her frustration and anger with Harlan, with a system that erected barriers between families that were supposed to be together, like she and Mattie. "What about Mattie's brother, who ran away? Has anyone found him yet? How well did he do without a home?"

Dottie raised her brows. "They did find him."

Emma blanched. "What? When?"

"In California. The police arrested him, but by the time we found out, they'd already released him. Actually, he escaped from the hospital."

Emma stared at her, a vice tightening in her chest for the boy she'd never met, the one Mattie had told her so much about. "The hospital? What was wrong with him?"

"He'd been stabbed in some sort of street fight."

Emma's stomach turned, and she clutched the doorframe. "Is he okay?"

Dottie's gaze flicked to Emma's fingers, where they were clenched around the wood. "They don't know. He escaped before he could be evaluated."

Emma felt sick. "So, he's out there somewhere, injured? He's only fourteen!"

"Yes, he is." Dottie studied her. "There's one more question I have for you, Ms. Larson."

Hope leapt through Emma. Was all not lost? "What is it?"

"If you were to adopt Mattie and her brother was subsequently located, are you willing to also adopt him? A fourteen year old boy who was recently arrested for drug possession and fighting?"

Emma blinked, startled by the question. "I hadn't thought—"

"Of him. Of the fact that maybe you alone aren't enough for Mattie, and she would want her brother with her? Her grandparents want them both. Family matters, Ms. Larson, and we try to keep them together whenever possible." Sympathy flickered in Dottie's eyes. "I know you tried, but children aren't a game. Good day."

Then she was gone, leaving Emma standing in her empty cabin, the world seeming to crash in around her. She couldn't breathe. She'd failed Mattie. *Failed her.* "Oh, God." Numbly, she sank down onto the couch, her hands starting to shake violently. Tears started to pour down her cheeks, and they wouldn't stop. Anger roared through her, fury at Harlan for not showing up. She grabbed her phone and scrolled down to her recently made calls. She found the one she wanted.

It rang twice and then the voicemail came on for Renée, the woman who had called her to report Harlan had gone missing. Emma fought back sobs as she waited for the beep, then spoke into the phone. "This is Emma Larson, Harlan Shea's wife." She swallowed, trying to catch her breath. "Tell him that we failed the home study because of his complete failure to appear, and—" A fresh sob caught her, and she pressed the phone to her forehead, needing a desperate minute to compose herself before she could even speak. "Mattie's going to South Carolina," she finally said. "Tell him I will no longer cry for him. I take back my promise, just like he took back his."

Words then failed her, and she hung up the phone, throwing it on the carpet as sobs caught her.

"Come on!" Harlan shouted at the inert figure in his arms, rain pouring off them both as he fell to his knees, clutching the woman he'd just rescued from a cement hellhole that had made his stomach turn.

"Stay here," Blue commanded him as he jerked his chin toward Harlan's left. "There's another cabin over there. I want to check it out before everyone gets back." They'd timed their retrieval for the time of day when no one bothered to be on duty. The kidnappers had had the victims for long enough that they'd gotten too relaxed, a mistake they would pay for.

"You've got one minute." Harlan couldn't take his gaze off the woman. She was young, maybe twenty, and so thin, hidden away in a hellhole for two months until his team had been called in. "Don't die," he growled to her, not sure what to say. Blue was the one who'd always done the pretty talk with the victims, but the bastard was already sprinting away. "We're here for you. Don't give up."

Her eyes flickered open, hopeless pits of weariness. Her eyes were pale green, almost the same color as Emma's, making his stomach clench. "Too late," she said quietly. "It's too late."

"It's not too late." He held her closer to his chest, using his body to protect her from the driving rain. "We're on our way out. All you have to do is hang on for a few more minutes."

"No." Her eyes fluttered closed. "He's gone. I have to go with him."

"Who's gone?"

"Ricardo. My husband. They took him. They killed him." Her body went limp. "There's no point."

Shit. She was giving up. He could feel her despair, like a thick coat of anguish on his flesh. "Come on," he urged. "You can't give up. Ricardo wouldn't have wanted you to." But even as he said it, it felt like a lie. Who the hell knew what Ricardo would have wanted her to do?

"I got another one!" Blue shouted, tearing across the clearing with a man tossed over his shoulder. "But I can hear their trucks returning. We gotta go!"

Harlan lurched to his feet, holding the woman in his arms. "Don't give up," he ordered her. "There's a lot to live for." She didn't answer, her breath becoming even shallower. "Shit!"

Blue caught up to him. "Let's go—"

"Maria?" A raspy hoarse voice seemed to grind out of the

chest of the man Blue was carrying. His thin hand reached for the woman in Harlan's arms as Blue raced past.

Harlan swore. "Blue! Stop!"

"We don't have time—"

"Stop!"

Blue whirled around, his face streaked with dirt and mud, his eyes hollow from their three-day stakeout without enough food or sleep "What?"

Harlan sprinted over to Blue and positioned the woman so she could see the man on Blue's shoulder. Tears filled the man's bloodshot eyes, and he rested a hand on hers. "Maria," he croaked.

Her eyes fluttered open. She saw him through half-mast eyes. "Ricardo?"

"You're alive," he whispered, tears streaming down his cheeks. "They told me you were dead, but I knew you weren't. I stayed alive because I knew you needed me. I'm here, Maria. I'm here for you." He grabbed her hand, and Maria's thin hand clutched his.

"They said you died," she whispered. "I thought you were dead."

"No, no, no," Ricardo said. "I would never die on you." His body was bruised and bleeding. He was so thin that the bones on his wrists seemed to strain his skin, but his voice was fierce. "I never gave up."

"Ricardo," Maria whispered, a single tear sliding down her parched cheek.

"We gotta go," Blue said. "Now!"

Harlan directed his command to the two people holding hands. "We're going to get you both out of here. Do you understand?"

This time, the woman in his arms nodded, keeping her gaze fixed on Ricardo. "Hurry," she whispered.

Hurry. The woman who had been surrendering to death

was now ordering him to hurry? Shit, yeah. Harlan broke into a dead sprint for their truck, hidden almost a hundred yards away, keeping pace with Blue.

They reached it quickly. Harlan grabbed the wheel, and Blue took care of the victims, as was their tradition. A split second later, they were on the road, hauling ass to the helicopter waiting for them. Harlan had just pulled off the road beside it when he heard the howl of agony explode from the backseat.

Blue swore as Harlan slammed the truck to a stop beside their ride. He shoved the door open and leapt out, shouting for the medic. But when he opened the rear door to extract the victims, he froze. Ricardo was holding his wife, but her head was lolled back, her eyes closed. The man was sobbing, his face pressed to his wife's chest, his arms holding her so tightly.

Blue looked at him grimly. "She didn't make it."

"No!" Harlan tore Maria out of Ricardo's grasp. "We have a medic on board. Come on!" He sprinted across the grass and almost threw her into the medic's arms, shouting at him to help her. The next few minutes were a frenzied whirlwind of agonizing sobs from Ricardo, quick and desperate action by their medic, and the roar of the helicopter as they got airborne.

But when Harlan saw the medic shake his head, he knew it was too late. Ricardo let out a keening wail of agony, pulling his wife into his arms as he broke down. All the dirt, all the bruises, all the hell he had suffered...had all been for naught. He'd survived for his wife, and she had not survived for him. The depth of loss wracking his body was devastating.

Son of a bitch. They'd failed. They'd been too late.

Blue looked at Harlan, his face grim and exhausted, then turned away, staring out at the treetops.

But Harlan couldn't look away as he watched Ricardo

rock back and forth, holding his wife in his arms, howling with grief for the woman he loved. The woman who had loved him enough to try to come back from the edge of death for him, but couldn't, because she had given up too soon.

Son of a bitch.

He'd never hated his job before, until now. Until it hurt.

CHAPTER SEVENTEEN

HARLAN SPRINTED up the stairs to his hotel room, his boots thudding on the cracked cement stairs. He was still filthy, covered in mud and Maria's blood. He couldn't get the sound of Ricardo's grief out of his mind, couldn't stop seeing the image of him holding his wife as if he could somehow bring her back to life by the sheer strength of his love.

He shoved open the door to his hotel room and grabbed his phone. His hands still filthy and grimy, he wasted no time. He just hit send on his favorites. The phone went right into Emma's voice mail, and Harlan tightened his grip as he listened to her voice. Ricardo would never hear his wife's voice again. Never. They had been too late.

He sat down heavily on the lumpy bed, resting his head on his palm as he waited for the message to end. He didn't even know what to say. He just had to say something. The recording ended. "Emma," he started, but his phone beeped.

He quickly took the phone away from his ear to look at who was calling, hoping it was Emma. It wasn't. It was Renée. Shit. She would want to know about the mission. Swearing, he switched over. "Hey—"

It was a recording that she had forwarded a voicemail to him. He ground his jaw and let the forwarded message play, but for the first time in his life, he didn't really give a shit about work. He didn't want to know about the next person in crisis. He just wanted to talk to Emma.

Then Emma's voice came on the line, and he froze, gripping the phone tighter. "This is Emma Larson, Harlan Shea's wife." Harlan's chest tightened. *His wife.* There was a pause, a sound almost as if she was breathing heavily.

His adrenaline spiked, and he shot to his feet. Was she okay?

"Tell him that we failed the home study because of his complete failure to appear, and—" *Son of a bitch.* He closed his eyes as he heard another intake of breath, and this time, it was clearer. She was crying. Crying. *He'd made her cry.* "Mattie's going to South Carolina," she said, her voice broken with pain. "Tell him I will no longer cry for him. I take back my promise, just like he took back his." Then she hung up.

Stunned, Harlan sank back onto the bed. Jesus. What had he done? The ring hadn't been enough? His text hadn't worked? Complete failure to appear? He'd explained. That wasn't enough? He couldn't even remember what he'd written in his text. Something about how he'd been called away to an emergency. He'd made it sound good enough for Dottie, hadn't he? He opened his text messages, and then froze when he saw the message sitting there...*unsent.* Jesus. He hadn't sent it.

Numb, he stared at his phone, a rising sense of failure consuming him. Maria's death. Ricardo's grief. And now Mattie. *Mattie.* He quickly dialed Emma again, pacing across the room as it rang. A thousand words raced through his mind of what message he was going to leave for her—

"Hello?"

He froze, going utterly still at the sound of her voice. "Emma?"

Silence, then... "Harlan?"

"Shit, Emma, I'm so sorry. I wrote a text but it didn't send—"

"A text. You wrote a text? Really? That's all you have to say? You wrote a text, but forgot to send it?"

"I swear I did—"

"I don't care if you did," she interrupted, tears thickening her voice. "It's not enough. I don't want what you have to offer anymore."

He gripped the phone. "I never lied to you—"

"No, I lied to myself. I was too scared of marriage to admit that I wanted it, so I took your offer and tried to pretend it was perfect for me. But you know what? I don't want that. I'm tired of falling in love with people who can't even understand love, let alone return it. I'm tired of hiding from life. Go do your job, Harlan. I'll take care of the divorce, and I'm going to go live my life."

His mind was spinning. "You fell in love with me?" He hadn't heard anything past that statement. The words were hammering in his mind, and he felt numb.

"You don't deserve the answer to that question."

"I know, but I don't care. Answer it anyway."

She said nothing for a minute, then she said, "Harlan, I can't play this game anymore. Good-bye." Then she hung up.

Harlan swore and immediately called her back.

This time, she didn't answer, but he was prepared to leave a message. "Emma, a woman died in my arms today. I didn't get there in time, and she died. But all I could think of was you dying, and what it would be like if I wasn't there, if I hadn't told you how I felt." He gripped the phone tighter. "Dammit, Emma, I don't know how to love anybody. I don't know how to be a part of anyone's life. But today all I could think of was you. I'm—" He leaned the phone against his forehead. What was he doing? Begging her to take him back? She was the one who was right. A fucking text? That was what he was capable of? Shit. He didn't belong in her world, but suddenly he didn't feel like he belonged in his world either. He was completely fucking lost. "Never mind." Then he hung up.

He knew that she would check the message right away, and he waited, a part of him desperately hoping that she would call him back, that there would be one more time when she said that she believed in him.

He sat by his phone for two hours, and she never called back. Then, he did something he hadn't done. Ever. He called his sister.

Astrid answered on the first ring, and he gave her no time to speak. "It's Harlan. I fucked up. How do I make it right?"

There was a long silence. "You can't make it right, Harlan. You cost Emma the only thing that mattered to her: a family. You, Mattie, and her. She opened her heart to you, and you took everything away from her. You can't make it right."

Sweat began to bead on his brow. "I have to."

"Well, it's too late."

"Is Mattie already in South Carolina?" In his business, too late meant dead. Unless someone was dead, it was never too late.

"No, they're waiting on her brother first. They want to give him more time."

"Her brother?" Harlan frowned, trying to fit the pieces together in his mind. "She has a brother?"

"Yes, he's gone missing in California." Astrid quickly filled him in on what little she knew of Mattie's brother, and Harlan went cold when he heard that the teen had been stabbed in a fight and was now missing. Suddenly, he was brutally hurtled into his own past, to his own little sister, who had been torn from him when they were both young, forcing them to grow up as strangers. Now there was another little girl living in hell while the brother who was supposed to protect her got his ass kicked out in the world? No more. *No more.* This had to fucking stop *now.* "What's his name?"

Astrid paused. "Why?"

His adrenaline kicked in, that same razor sharp focus he always got when he was at work. "What's his name?"

"Robbie. Robbie Williams. Why?" She repeated the question with more force.

"I'll explain later." He hung up and then made two more phone calls. Then he packed a small bag, strode out into the hall and pounded on the door of his partner. "Blue," he yelled. "We gotta go."

EMMA SAT in her car outside Mattie's foster home, her fingers clenched around the steering wheel. "I don't think I can do this," she whispered.

It was the day that had been arranged for her to pick up Mattie for a visit to the fair, a day that had seemed so triumphant and exciting when it had first been arranged a month ago, but now it seemed like broken promises and fresh pain. She could still hear Harlan's message, his voice hammering at her mind as she recalled every word he'd spoken. A text he'd forgotten to send. Even now, as she thought of that moment, both grief and hope plunged through her. Hope that he'd meant it. Grief that even if he had, it wasn't enough. She deserved more than to be grateful for a text from a man who walked out on her.

But how many times had she held her phone in trembling fingers, desperate to call him back, to give him one more chance. But she hadn't, and he hadn't called again. The nights had loomed dark and lonely. No Harlan. No Mattie. No future with either of them.

And yet, she hadn't filed for divorce yet. His ring still sat on her dresser for her to look at every day. Damn him for making her unable to let him go or condemn him. It had been a week since his phone call. A week since he'd no-showed for the home study. A week since all her hopes had crashed down around her.

Spending the day with Mattie, pretending that everything was all right, felt like too much. How could she fake it, when every minute just made her think of all that had slipped through her fingers? Not calling him back was the right choice. Despite his belief to the contrary, he was a good man, but she simply needed and deserved more than he could give her. As long as she clung to the half-life he offered, she could never be free to move forward and claim the life she deserved.

But it was so hard. She simply couldn't stop thinking about him. Did that make her weak? Pathetic? Or simply a woman who had finally opened her heart? Because she knew that he cared. Their connection was real, deep, and beautiful. She would never forget their last night together, their conversations, their lovemaking. Harlan might have walked out, but she knew he cared. Deeply. How could that not be enough? But it wasn't. She sighed, feeling depleted and weak as sadness and grief washed over her—

Then the front door opened, and Mattie appeared, wearing her favorite pink sneakers, a pair of white leggings, and a hot pink short-sleeved shirt. A dozen braids sprang out from her head in all directions as a huge smile lit up her face. "Emma!" She waved frantically and raced down the walkway, shouting excitedly.

Tears filled Emma's eyes as she jumped out of the car. She met Mattie halfway, and swung her up into her arms, hugging the little girl fiercely. She hadn't seen Mattie for weeks, because the art class was over for the summer, and it felt so good to hug her. "How's my girl?"

Mattie beamed at her. "We're going to the fair, right?"

"We are."

"Can I stay overnight at your house?"

Emma hesitated. "I'm sorry, hon, but the rules say I have to bring you back tonight."

Mattie's face fell. "But I don't want to go back. I want to stay with you."

Emma hugged her tighter. "I know, sweetie. I want you to stay with me, too." She managed a smile that seemed to eat away at her very soul. "Your grandparents want you, too, you know. It's important to let family love you."

Mattie squirmed out of Emma's arms. "I don't want to talk about them." She ran over to the car and climbed into the back. She immediately shrieked with excitement when she saw the new princess booster seat that Emma had bought for her to ride in.

Emma bit her lip, her heart bleeding at the sight of Mattie's excitement. Grief filled her, and tears welled in her eyes. How had she messed this up so badly? How had she screwed up the one thing that mattered? How had she lost her chance for Mattie to live with her? Hands shaking, she got into the car, barely managing a smile as she handed Mattie a small plastic bag. "For you."

"Me?" Mattie took the bag and opened it. It was a book, *The Littlest Christmas Tree,* which Emma had stumbled across one day when trying to find an activity for her art class. It made her cry every time she read it. "It's for you. Your very own book."

"Wow." Mattie's gaze was reverent as she traced her hand over the glossy cover. "It's beautiful."

"I even put your name in it," Emma said, pointing to the

note she'd written on the inside cover. "And I signed my name, so you'll always remember who gave it to you."

Mattie opened the book. "Let's read it right now."

Emma glanced at the clock on the dash. "The pony rides start in an hour. Don't you want to make it in time for those?"

"No." Mattie climbed into the front seat and perched on the console next to Emma. "Read it to me." She tucked herself onto Emma's lap, and opened the book on the steering wheel, nestling her head under Emma's chin.

Tears filled Emma's eyes, and she kissed Mattie's tight braids. "Okay." She turned to the first page and began to read the story of the tiny Christmas tree that had only one Christmas wish: to find a family who would love it. Emma's throat tightened as Christmas grew closer and closer, and every family rejected the tiny tree, until Christmas Eve came, and the owner of the stand took it home for his little boy. And when the little tree stood so proudly at the end of the story, decorated with homemade ornaments while it presided over a tiny pile of presents, there was no way to stop the tears from sliding down her cheeks.

Mattie looked up at her, and then she brushed her finger over Emma's face. "Why are you crying?"

"Because it makes me happy to see that the tree found its family." She managed a smile. "Whenever you read this book, Mattie, I want you to remember that if you believe and don't give up, your wishes can come true as well, even if you're the littlest tree that no one wants."

Mattie's brow furrowed. "I'm not a tree."

Emma laughed and hugged her. "I know, sweetie, but someday, you might feel like one."

"I'm a butterfly," Mattie said seriously.

"Are you now?" Emma wiped her cheek with her sleeve.

"I am. Then, when I'm in South Carolina, I'll fly north with the other butterflies in the spring, and I will go to Birch

Crossing and find you." Mattie eyed her. "Did you know butterflies migrate?"

Alarm shot through Emma as she thought of Robbie's disappearance. Was Mattie planning to imitate him? "I didn't know they migrated, but it's awfully far for a butterfly to fly. Maybe..." she cleared her throat. "Maybe the butterflies in South Carolina should find some beautiful flowers down there to enjoy. Butterflies are so little that it would be a dangerous journey for them."

Mattie shrugged. "Butterflies are tough." Her face lit up, as if she'd had a sudden idea. "I think the littlest Christmas tree would have migrated if it hadn't found a family, don't you?"

Fear prickled at Emma. "Mattie, trees don't migrate—"

She held up the book. "This one would have. It wouldn't have given up. Isn't that what you said? Not to give up?" Mattie's face was so genuine and earnest that Emma felt her heart shatter. "I thought that was what you told me. Not to give up, right?"

How could she let this girl be shunted off to her grandparents? Sudden resolution flared through Emma. How could she tell Mattie not to give up, and then fail to fight herself? "Yes," she said. "I did say not to give up. Hop in back, Mattie. We have a stop to make."

Mattie scurried over the console into the back seat. "Where are we going?" she asked as she strapped herself in.

"To visit a friend." Emma started the car, gripping the steering wheel tightly. It was a suicide mission, she knew it was, but dammit, she was tired of living safely, because living safely sucked.

EMMA HELD Mattie's hand tightly as she hurried the little girl up the wood stairs of the somewhat decrepit building. Chloe met them at the door, pulling it open and looking nervously over her shoulder. "I can't believe you talked me into this," she whispered. "I could get fired for this."

"It would be worth it." Emma still didn't let go of Mattie's hand, so grateful that Chloe had answered her call on the way over to the courthouse. "Where do we go?"

"This way." Chloe hurried down a quiet hallway.

"Emma?" Mattie tugged at her hand. "What are we doing?"

"Not giving up," Emma said.

"Here." Chloe stopped outside a wooden door that was unmarked, but a shadow on the wood made it appear as though a name plate had once marked it, but had long since disappeared. "They're in here." She managed a quick smile. "Give me five minutes so it doesn't look like I let you in." Then she opened the door and ducked inside.

"Thanks." As Chloe disappeared into the room, Emma crouched in front of Mattie. "Mattie, baby, I want you to know that I will always love you."

Mattie nodded, her braids bouncing with each move of her chin. "I love you, too, Emma."

"I know." She swallowed, her heart pounding as all the warnings she'd heard from everyone else rang in her ears. She shoved them aside, refusing to listen to them. "Listen to me, sweetie. Inside that room, Dottie and the judge are talking about you. They're deciding who you're going to live with."

Mattie's gaze flicked to the door, and Emma saw wisdom in them that no five year old should have. "I thought I had to go to my grandparents."

"There is one other possibility, Mattie." Emma closed her eyes for a moment, Chloe's warnings ringing in her ears about making promises and breaking them. Should she really tell her? But when she opened her eyes and saw Mattie looking at her expectantly, she knew that there was something much worse than being disappointed by someone you love, and that was never knowing that you were loved at all. She had once been Mattie, and she had wanted nothing more than for someone, *anyone*, to say that they loved her. She'd spent her life craving the security of knowing that there was someone in this world who held her in their heart. Mattie deserved it, on every level, and there was one way for Emma to show her that she had it, even if it didn't work out. "Mattie, I want you to know that if you wanted it, and they agreed, I would take you home and have you live with me forever."

Mattie stared at her. "I thought you didn't want me," she whispered. "Every time I said I wanted to live with you, you didn't say you wanted it, too. You just said you couldn't, that I had to live with my grandparents."

Guilt surged through her at Mattie's interpretation of Emma's attempts to spare her. That was how she'd interpreted it? As Emma not loving her? Forget that. No way was she going to let Mattie live under that delusion for one more minute. She might have to go to South Carolina, but if she did, she was going to go knowing that she was loved dearly. "I love you, Mattie, and I've been trying to adopt you, but it's not easy. I want you to know that I love you dearly, like my own daughter. Do you understand?"

Mattie nodded silently, her eyes huge.

"Unfortunately, sometimes things don't work out the way that we want." She squeezed Mattie's hand. "Even if the judge decides that you should go to South Carolina, or even if you decided that you want to live with your grandparents, I will still love you just as much, forever. Nothing can change that, no matter what."

Mattie's eyes were wide, and she said nothing.

"People think that since you're only five, you don't know what you want, but I don't agree. I think you should be able to speak up." She knew she was breaking rules, but she didn't care. To be disempowered was heart wrenching, and Mattie deserved to be heard, to be taught that she had the right to speak up. She let go of Mattie's hand and knelt in front of her. "Do you want to talk to them?"

Mattie looked at the door again, then shook her head. "No," she whispered.

"No?" Disappointment flooded Emma, but she managed a smile. "That's totally fine, Mattie. You don't need to." She stood up and held out her hand. "Let's go to the fair, then. We'll ride some ponies."

But Mattie didn't take her hand. "I want you to talk to them."

Hope leapt in Emma's heart, but she kept herself calm, as she crouched again in front of Mattie. "What do you want me to say to them?"

Mattie lightly grasped Emma's necklace. "I want you to be my mom," she whispered.

Tears filled Emma's eyes, but she managed a nod, even while her heart leapt. "Are you sure, Mattie?" She met Mattie's gaze and spoke with pure truth. "I will love you no matter where you live. If you go to South Carolina, I will always be with you. Always." She drew an "X" over her heart. "Cross my heart."

Mattie made the same symbol over her own heart. "I want you," she said simply.

Emma managed a smile, even as resolution poured through her. She would not let Mattie down. "Okay, I'll go talk to them." She glanced at the door, debating whether to bring Mattie in with her, but then decided that it was important. Even if it didn't work out, Mattie needed to see that Emma loved her enough to fight for her. "You want to come with me?"

Mattie nodded and took her hand.

"Let's go." Emma squeezed her hand and pushed open the door. The shabby office was cluttered, with stacks of paper abounding. A gray-haired woman, presumably the judge, was sitting behind the desk. Dottie was sitting in a chair, her notebook open on her lap, and Chloe was sitting beside her, the three people who were responsible for deciding Mattie's future. They all stopped mid-sentence to stare at her and Mattie.

"What are you doing here?" Dottie asked.

"Breaking rules," Emma said, holding Mattie's hand firmly as she faced the judge. "My name is Emma Larson, and I want to be Mattie's mom."

CHAPTER EIGHTEEN

EMMA WAS SITTING in her living room on the edge of the couch, too tense to think. Clare was making their third pot of coffee, and Astrid was pacing the floor.

"They said they were going to call at two o'clock," Astrid said as she paced the living room, Rosie asleep in her arms "It's two-fifteen. Do they not have clocks in that building?"

"They'll call," said Clare calmly. "Sit down."

It had been five days since the meeting at the courthouse. After Emma had finished her announcement, the office had become ominously silent...but she could have sworn she saw a small smile playing at the corners of Dottie's mouth. It had been Dottie who had broken the impasse, asking Emma what had occurred to make her think that the case should be revisited.

Her only answer had been honesty, pouring out her heart as she hugged Mattie, as Mattie had wrapped her arms around Emma. The two of them together, fighting for a future they wanted. The discussion had gone on for two hours, and then they'd kicked her and Mattie out. Chloe had reported that they'd decided to table the decision about

Mattie for two weeks...and they were meeting today. Chloe had emailed yesterday to tell Emma that the meeting was scheduled to end around two, and at ten o'clock, Clare and Astrid had appeared at Emma's house to support her.

It had been the longest day of her life...except perhaps when she'd been waiting to hear if Harlan had died. She wasn't sure which was worse, but they were both torture. Harlan. Just the thought of him still made her heart ache. It had been three weeks, and the pain hadn't lessened. The betrayal of him leaving her, and the memories of that message he'd left her.

"Want some more coffee?" Clare asked, holding up the pot.

Emma hugged herself, her stomach churning. "I can't drink it. I'll throw up. You guys don't need to wait here with me."

Clare set a steaming mug down in front of her on the low table "There's no chance we're leaving you here alone to deal with this. If it's bad news, you shouldn't be alonc."

"It can't be bad news," Emma whispered, her belly lurching again. She checked her phone and saw that it still had five bars. "Astrid, try calling me again and make sure my phone works."

"No." Clare sat down next to her. "Your phone is fine. They'll call."

Astrid looked over at her as she patted Rosie's little back "Have you heard from Harlan since that day?"

"No." He'd clearly taken her rejection as truth and had not reached out. Silence had reigned between them ever since. "It's over." God, it hurt to say those words, to say aloud what she knew in her heart. She couldn't be the one to bridge the gap between them. It had to be him. He had to make the choice to try.

"Don't give up on him," Astrid said. "You should have heard his voice when he called me—"

"No!" Emma held up her hand, her heart twisting at Astrid's words. She had no energy left to hope for Harlan. She simply didn't. "It's done. It's over. It's—" Her phone rang. She yelped and dove for her phone, knocking the mug of coffee over and spraying it all over her floor. She stumbled to her feet, pressing the phone to her ear. "Hello?"

"Em?" Chloe was breathing heavily, as if she'd run all the way to her office...or was fighting back sobs.

She clutched the phone, barely able to breathe her chest was so tight. "What? Tell me. Please, just tell me."

"Emma...or maybe I should just call you Mom."

"What?" Disbelief poured through Emma, and tears flooded her eyes. "*What?*"

"Mom," Chloe repeated. "You've been approved. Foster to adopt. You're her new mother."

"Oh, God." Emma sank down onto the couch, her legs shaking too much to stand. She'd done it. All on her own, without a husband. Just her, alone. Her and Mattie. "You mean it? It's definite? They can't change their minds?"

"No, but—" she paused.

"But?" Panic ricocheted through Emma. "But what?"

"The adoption won't be final until you divorce Harlan. He's not part of the package, for obvious reasons, and they don't want him to have the ability to interfere in Mattie's life. But that should be fine in terms of timing, because you would have to foster her for six months first anyway. So the divorce should be final by the time you'd be able to adopt her."

Emma was too shocked to answer, her mind spinning. Divorce him? The words were like a sinking emptiness in her belly. Despite her brave words to her friends and to Harlan himself, she still hadn't done anything to initiate a divorce. She didn't know what she'd been waiting for, but she hadn't been able to do it. But now she had to, in order to adopt Mattie?

"Hello? Em?" Chloe interrupted her thoughts. "That's okay, right?"

She finally managed to catch her breath, and nodded. "Yes, of course." She looked at her friends, who were staring at her breathlessly, waiting for her to tell them what had happened. "I'll call the lawyer today."

"Awesome. I'll call you back in a little while with more details, and to see how quickly we can get Mattie moved into your custody. Congratulations!"

"Thank you," Emma said. "And thank you for all your help. I couldn't have done it without you."

Chloe laughed. "Actually, Emma, I owe you the thanks. You taught me a few things. I admit that I was wrong about how to handle this situation. I'm glad you didn't listen to me. Congratulations. I'll talk to you soon—"

"Wait!"

"What?"

"Can I be the one to tell Mattie?"

She could almost feel Chloe's smile over the phone. "Of course. Give me a little time to get the details and paperwork sorted out, and then we'll discuss it. I'm trying to arrange it so you can get her before the weekend."

Emma's heart stuttered. "This week?"

"Hopefully. Talk soon. Bye."

Emma disconnected and stared at her friends, who were waiting expectantly. Suddenly, as she stared into the faces of the two people who had stood by her, the enormity of it all seemed to descend upon her, and she started to cry.

"Oh, Emma," Clare dropped to her knees beside her. "I'm so sorry—"

"I got her," Emma managed to say.

"What?" Clare shrieked in astonishment. "You're going to adopt her?"

"Yes, but—" She looked at Astrid, feeling helpless. "I have to divorce Harlan first. It needs to be done within six months."

Astrid's smile faded. "He loves you," she said quietly.

"He left me. He left Mattie. He—" She thought back to that message he had left her, where he'd started to say the things she'd been dying to hear...and then he'd said, "Never mind," and hung up. What had he been about to say? She knew that message, that aborted message, was why she hadn't initiated the divorce yet. She'd been hoping, stupidly hoping, that there was still a chance.

Astrid shook her head. "He's broken, Em. Just like you. Just like me. Just like the rest of us. It's not easy to love someone who is broken, but when you do, you see through all their crap to the goodness inside."

"He's not broken—"

"He is!" Astrid set her coffee down. "Do you know how bad his father was? Harlan grew up surrounded by violence, with a mom who didn't want him, and a stepmother who wouldn't stand up for him. Do you think he has any clue how to be a father or a husband, or even to acknowledge he would want to do it? I know, because I was like him. Jason saw through that, and he made me see myself in ways I couldn't."

Emma lurched to her feet. "I know about his past," she snapped. "I know all about it, and I believed in him. I trusted him. But it wasn't enough. Don't you understand, Astrid? It's up to him. I can't do it for him, and I'm so tired of trying to make people be who I want them to be. It's not fair to me, and it's not fair to him." Tears trickled down her face again, but they weren't tears of joy. They were tears of loss, of grief, of the final abandonment of hope. The elation of being able to adopt Mattie felt tarnished by the hollowness that Harlan wasn't a part of it, that there was no chance he could be a part of it. "I can't live like this anymore," she said. "I'm not okay with a half-marriage, whether it's with a man like Preston, who is nothing more than glitzy poison, or Harlan, who brings my soul to life, but then shreds it with such ease."

"He needs someone to believe in him," Astrid said. "He can't do it alone."

"And what if I try again? What if I fight for him, and they let me stay married to him? What do I say to Mattie when she asks why this man who is supposed to be her father is never there? Why he doesn't love her?"

"He will come around!" Astrid said fiercely. "Tell them you won't accept that condition. Tell them that Harlan is part of the deal."

"Really? And what if they then change their minds and decide I'm not stable enough because of my infatuation with an unreliable man? I barely got them to agree. Is it worth the risk for a man who has shown no signs at all that he cares?"

Astrid hesitated. "They wouldn't change their mind just because you ask them—"

"No?" Emma sighed, suddenly feeling exhausted, just completely drained. "What if I asked, and they said no? You think I should give up Mattie to keep a man who left me?"

"I just think you should have fought for him. You didn't, did you? You just said yes. You're mad because Harlan hasn't shown up on your doorstep to fight for you, but you didn't fight for him either."

Emma wanted to scream with frustration. "Don't you get it? I did fight for him. I wore his damn ring! I waited for him. I cried for him. And he left—"

"He loves you!"

"Well, it's not enough!"

"It should be!" Rosie woke up suddenly and began to cry. Cradling the baby to her chest, Astrid whirled around and stormed out the door. It slammed shut behind her with a bang.

Emma looked helplessly at Clare, who was still sitting on the couch. "What am I supposed to do?"

Clare stood up. "The first thing you have to do is move your paintings out of your studio. I'll help." She started to walk across the floor, and Emma gawked at her.

"I didn't mean about that. I meant about Harlan."

Her hand on the door handle, Clare turned to face her. "Do you love him?"

Emma's heart constricted. "I can't afford to love him. I can't put myself out there again, Clare. I just can't."

"That's not what I asked. I asked if you loved him."

"I can't choose him over Mattie." Her chest hurt. Her throat hurt. Everything hurt. "I won't risk her."

"Then you'll have to divorce him, won't you?" Clare raised one eyebrow. "Unless you have a problem with that?"

Emma stared at her, and had no answer.

Finally, Clare smiled. "Don't let a man ruin the day," she said gently. "Your daughter is coming home. It's a beautiful, beautiful day, isn't it?"

"My daughter?" she whispered. *My daughter.* "I have a daughter. Mattie's going to be my daughter."

"Your daughter," Clare agreed, holding out her hand and gesturing Emma into the studio. "Come on, Emma. Mattie needs her mama. Don't let her down."

"You're right." But as Emma hurried across the small living room toward the studio, her heart aching with joy and love for Mattie, a part of her soul was slowly fragmenting. It hurt so much it was almost unbearable, and as she'd done so many times over the years, she started to will away the pain and close herself down. To harden herself so it couldn't hurt her.

Then she stepped into the studio and saw the roses that

Harlan had given her. They were dried and brittle, sitting on her bookshelf, but the sight of them made her heart ache. And suddenly, she was tired of being the woman who hid from pain and hurt, who was afraid to trust. She'd gotten Mattie by deciding to truly live. How could she go backwards and shrivel into a shell just because Harlan hadn't fought for her?

She walked over to the roses, and picked them up. The leaves crumbled in her hand, falling in withered fragments on the floor. She held them to her chest, and let herself mourn for him, for the loss of what she'd wanted from him. "I can't do it," she said.

"Do what?" Clare asked.

"Let him go."

Clare smiled. "You love him. I knew you did."

Emma looked at her friend. "For Mattie, I will let him go, if I have to. I made a promise to her, and I'll keep it."

Clare winked. "You have six months before you have to be divorced. He might surprise you. Men sometimes do that, you know?"

"They don't surprise me." But as she put the roses down, she couldn't stop the flash of hope, of desperate hope, that he would be the man she didn't expect anymore, that he would surprise her.

But if he didn't, divorce it would be.

HARLAN STOPPED outside the long-abandoned apartment building. The brick was cracked and broken. Most of the windowpanes lay in fragments along the sidewalk, and the plywood that had once blocked the front door lay in splinters on the crumbling front steps. The stench was strong, odors of death, rot, and mildew.

"This is it, huh?" Blue eased up beside him, studying the building. "If I ever get married, I think I'll honeymoon here."

Harlan snorted. "You'll never get married. You're too damned ugly."

"Ugly? My mug's my best selling point." Blue ran his hand down the faded scar that bisected the right side of his face. "Most people consider me pretty, you know."

"Prettiest damn sight most of our victims have seen in their lives," Harlan agreed, "when you show up to drag them out of there."

Blue said nothing, and Harlan glanced over at him. His partner's face was grim, as it had been more and more often lately. "You with me?"

Blue's gaze flicked toward him, and he flashed a grin that Harlan wasn't so sure he believed anymore. "Yeah. We going in or what?"

"Yeah." Harlan turned back to inspect their target. They were both on alert, knowing all too well the trouble that could come fast and unexpected in this part of Los Angeles. Needles and bullet casings littered the ground, and shadows moved too quickly in the corners. People. Animals. Nothing good.

It was dark out, almost three in the morning, and they'd been searching all night. For three weeks, they'd been searching, following false leads, coming up with nothing. Sleep had become a distant memory, tossed aside in favor of their relentless hunt.

"Tonight's our last night," Blue said. "Renée can't wait anymore. She needs us in the morning."

Five hours left until this shit was over? *Five hours.* A rising sense of desperation flooded him. It couldn't end like this. He couldn't fucking let it. With a low growl, he surged forward. "Come on." Not waiting to see if Blue followed, he carefully made his way up the decrepit steps, his adrenaline on high alert. They'd walked into too many bad situations in the last three weeks, and in Los Angeles, they didn't have the freedom to do whatever it took to ensure their safety, unlike when they were on some of their missions in other countries.

There had been close calls, and he had a bad feeling about this one. The building was too quiet, as if it were watching them approach. But at the same time, there was something about it that would not let him go. He had to see what was inside.

Blue caught up almost instantly, covering the rear as Harlan nudged aside the remains of the front door with his boot.

No movement from inside. No sound.

"I'm going in," he said. He eased into the entry and the boards creaked beneath his feet. The front room was empty, and there were massive holes in the floorboards, revealing dark pits beneath that would plummet him into a basement of hell.

"There's no way across that," Blue said. "No wonder the place is empty."

Harlan scanned the room, his eyes settling on a dark shadow in the far back corner. The shadow seemed too unnatural to be simply from the half-broken streetlights outside. Something was back there. "Check the corner," he said, easing a foot onto the nearest solid piece.

"The corner? Yeah, there's something there..." Blue swore as the floor shifted slightly. "Don't go out there."

"I have to." Harlan tested the board, and it creaked, but held. "Call for help if I go down."

"No help is going to come out here." Blue moved back to the doorway, out of range if the floor gave out. "Try not to die."

Harlan's mind flashed to Emma. *I will not cry for you,* she'd said. He'd replayed those words a thousand times in his head over the last three weeks, and every single time it felt like someone had hollowed out his chest. Worse and worse it had gotten, and the only thing keeping him going was his mission. A board cracked beneath his foot, and he jerked his foot off a split second before it thundered into the depths with a loud clatter that sounded deeper than a shallow death. If he fell, he knew it would be his grave.

"It's a bottomless pit down there," joked Blue. "I'll never find you if you go down."

"Good. Searching for me will keep you out of trouble then," Harlan replied as he edged forward again. Every board creaked and groaned, and two more broke beneath his weight. But still he edged closer to the corner, where the shadow still hung in silence.

He and Blue fell silent as he worked his way forward. He needed to feel the vibrations of the boards, to hear the creaks, to predict where it was safe to step and where it wasn't. Agonizingly slow progress taunted him, but he kept his gaze on his target.

Finally, he was almost there, and then his eyes were able to finally see into the shadows. It was a person. Adrenaline raced through him as his eyes adjusted, and he was able to discern that it was a teen boy huddled in a ball, with thin shoulders and ragged cornrows in his dark hair. His arms were wrapped around his legs, and his head was tucked against his knees. His white tee shirt was stained with dried blood, and his body was shaking. For a brief moment, Harlan was catapulted back into his past, to the countless hours and days where he'd been in that exact pose, hidden in the barn, hiding from his father, struggling to hold back tears and to be the man he was too young to be.

Outrage flooded Harlan, and he knew that this kid, unlike so many others, was not going to be left behind tonight. Even if he wasn't the kid Harlan was looking for, he was taking the youth out of there. Testing his footing, he crouched near the boy, not close enough to spook him, but close enough to grab him if he bolted. "Robbie," he said quietly, hoping that this time, after so many tries, he was right. "Mattie sent me to find you."

The boy's head jerked upright, his eyes wide. "I'm not going back!"

Holy crap. This was really the youth he'd been searching for? Harlan's adrenaline spiked, and victory raced through him. "You don't have to go back," he said, masking his sudden surge of energy behind a calm, casual voice.

Robbie stared at him. "Who are you?"

Harlan eased down beside him. "My name is Harlan Shea," he said conversationally. "I came to find you on my own, which means I don't have to take you back to your foster home. I break rules all the time."

Robbie turned his head to look at him, and Harlan swore at the haggardness of the kid's features. "What do you want?"

"I want to save your life. It's what I do." It *was* what he did. Go in. Rescue. Deliver to safety. Repeat. "You'll die out here, and then who will Mattie have to look out for her? She needs you, Robbie. Fuck the social workers and the foster homes. Who cares what they think? They don't matter. They really don't."

Robbie's brow furrowed. "You don't sound like them."

"Because I'm not them." As he said the words, he realized he spoke the truth. The complete truth. He was not a man who could play by the rules, or live a domestic little life. He belonged out here, doing shit that no one else wanted to do. "But I have a little sister that I wasn't around to take care of when she was growing up, and I wish I had been."

Robbie shook his head. "I can't help her." He held out his hand, and Harlan saw a small round burn on his palm, as if some bastard had shoved a lit cigarette into his flesh.

White-hot anger surged through Harlan, and he had to fist his hands to keep from erupting. Who the fuck hurt innocents like Robbie? But he knew who did. People like his father.

"If I go back to my foster home, I'll kill them," Robbie said quietly, his voice amazingly steady. "I'll kill them if they hurt my sister. I'll kill them if they hurt me again." His eyes were too burdened and too wise for a kid of fourteen. "Before my mom died, she told me I had to take care of Mattie. She said it would be hard, but I had to do it." He looked at Harlan, so much anguish in his young face. "If I go to jail, I can't help her."

Harlan tried to unclench his fists. "You won't kill them."

"Fuck you—" Robbie spat. "How do you know? No one believes me! No one believes what's inside me—"

"I do." Son of a bitch, it was like looking at himself again. The kid was exactly like he had once been. "I know exactly what's inside you because I killed my own dad."

Robbie's mouth dropped open. "What? Don't lie to me—"

"No lie." Harlan met his gaze. "I was fifteen. I didn't mean to do it, not really, but yeah, I did."

Robbie stared at him in awed silence.

"But *you* won't kill them because you're smarter than I was. I'll help you," Harlan said quietly. "But while you're hiding out here, your sister is suffering. You can't run away from her, from that."

"But I have to. I—" He looked at Harlan. "I'm really afraid of what's inside me," he whispered. "How do I make it go away?"

Well, hell, he didn't have an answer to that one. For a long moment, silence stretched between them as Harlan struggled to find an answer that he'd never been able to give himself. "You have to face it," he said finally. "Otherwise you'll be running from it your whole life. It'll never be safe to go back to Mattie, and you'll miss out on a whole lifetime with her."

Robbie was still staring at him. "Are you still running?"

Harlan looked down at the tattoo on his wrist, at the "E" nestled among the yellow roses. "Yeah," he said quietly. "I am."

CHAPTER NINETEEN

EMMA SHIFTED NERVOUSLY, her hands actually sweating as she waited by her car for Chloe to retrieve Mattie from her foster home. It had been two entire days since Chloe had called, two agonizingly long days in which Chloe had made her promise not to contact Mattie until all the details were confirmed. But today, today was the day. Today Mattie would know.

After what felt like an interminable wait, she saw Mattie and Chloe emerge from the front door. The moment Emma saw them, her throat tightened up, and a great sob caught in her chest.

Mattie let out a cry of delight and raced down the sidewalk.

Emma fell to her knees and scooped up the little girl, hugging her tightly, so tightly. "My dear, sweet Mattie," she whispered.

"Emma!" Mattie pulled back, her face heart-wrenchingly serious. "I missed you. Where have you been? What did they decide? No one will tell me!"

Her heart seemed to expand to fill her entire chest. "I'll tell you."

"You will?" Mattie stepped back, hugging her arms across her chest, withdrawing defensively into herself, already preparing herself for the bad news she was accustomed to receiving.

"They said it was okay," Emma said quickly, not wanting to make her wait. "They're going to let me adopt you. I'm going to be your mom."

Mattie's mouth dropped open in stunned silence, and she didn't move. Her dark brown eyes were wide, and she went utterly still, staring at Emma as if she expected her to vanish from sight and take the miracle with her.

Emma swallowed back the tears swimming in her eyes. "They're finishing the paperwork, but you can come live with me starting tomorrow. But I couldn't wait until then to tell you."

"Forever?" Mattie whispered.

"Forever," Emma agreed.

Mattie let out a shriek of jubilation and threw herself into Emma's arms. Emma laughed through her tears, hugging her tightly. "I love you, Mattie."

"Wait." Mattie suddenly pulled back, her eyes huge with worry. "What if you die, too? Then what happens to me?"

Emma's throat constricted at the question no five-year-old should ever have to think about. "I won't die."

"Mama said she wouldn't die either, but she did." Fear was thick in her voice, and she glanced over her shoulder at the foster home, as if it were a monster trying to sneak up on her.

Emma took her hands. "Mattie—"

A door slammed, and Chloe let out a gasp. "Oh, my God."

Mattie looked past Emma, and her whole face lit up with joy so vivid that there were no words to describe it. Emma spun around to see what had caught their attention, and saw a thin teenage boy climbing out of a black pickup truck.

"Robbie!" Mattie screamed, rushing past Emma and throwing herself into the boy's arms.

Robbie. Emma stared in stunned disbelief as Robbie scooped her up, hugging her tightly. Her chest ached with emotion as Mattie and her brother embraced, holding each other so tightly it was as if they would never let go.

Mattie was screaming excitedly, and Emma finally became aware of what she was shouting to her brother. "And we have a new mama," Mattie declared. "Emma is taking us home tomorrow!"

Them? Taking *them* home tomorrow? Both of them? Emma looked helplessly at Chloe, who lifted one shoulder. "I'll make a call," she said. "Be right back."

As Emma slowly stood up, a deep foreboding began to travel through her. A five-year-old girl, she could handle. But a fourteen-year-old boy, who had already run away? She'd never even met him before. How could she manage to give him what he needed? And would the judge even let her—

Then she froze as the driver got out of the truck. Her breath caught in her chest, and she suddenly went cold. "Harlan?" she whispered. He was unshaven and his hair was long. He looked worn out and exhausted, far worse than he'd been even after the time he'd almost died.

He leaned against the truck and met her gaze. "Found him," he said simply.

Emma's heart was pounding, her feet rooted to the sidewalk. He looked so drained that she wanted to rush into his arms, to hug him, to tell him how much she had missed him. Her entire soul screamed for him, but instead of rushing over to him, she folded her arms over her chest. "I thought you were gone." Her voice was shaky with emotion, trembling with the shock of seeing him, of realizing that he was the one who had gone to find Robbie and bring him home. How had that happened? Why had he done that? How did he even know about Robbie?

"I had to find him." He still made no attempt to close the gap between them. He just leaned against the hood of his truck, as if he was too tired to move even an inch.

Emma took a step toward him, as Mattie continued to talk excitedly to her brother. "How did you find him?"

He shrugged. "It's what I do. Search and rescue, right?"

He looked so forlorn, so weary, that her heart cried for him. "Are you okay?"

"No," he said, looking at her. "I'm not."

"Are you..." She could barely ask the words. "Are you staying? Or leaving?"

His eyes were dull and drained. "Renée has an assignment for me. I need to be on a flight in two hours."

"Oh." She closed her eyes against the pain, against the bitter assault of loneliness. In that moment, when he'd stepped out of the truck, she'd had a sudden, desperate hope for so many things. Of holding him again. Of waking up in his arms. Of Mattie growing up with a father who was so brave he risked his life to save others. Of being able to stop fighting so hard on her own and being able to finally, completely, put her trust in him. But it was not to be. Nothing had changed. "Okay."

She turned away, turning back toward Mattie and her brother. They were sitting on the sidewalk now, and Mattie was holding his hand, staring into his face with shining eyes. There was no judgment on Mattie's face, no recrimination for the fact that her brother had abandoned her. Just pure love that he had come back. Robbie was grinning at his sister, his young face creased into a smile that made him look sweet and kind, not the runaway who'd been arrested by the police.

"He's a good kid," Harlan said. "He didn't know how to come back."

Emma watched Mattie reach up and pat Robbie's cheek, and then she climbed onto his lap, pulling out a book. Emma realized that she was showing him *The Littlest Christmas Tree.* Robbie made a typical teenage boy groan, and then began reading it to her.

The tenderness of the moment made Emma want to cry at the pure acceptance of the two siblings for each other. Slowly, Emma turned to look at Harlan again.

He still hadn't moved, but he wasn't watching the kids. He was focused entirely on Emma. All of Astrid's words rang through her mind, claiming that Harlan was a good man who loved her, but was too broken to know how to fix himself. All those times when Harlan had brought her back to life when she'd thought she could never live again. She thought of the horror of his fifteen-year-old self standing over his father's body and realizing that he'd caused it. "You brought Robbie back because no one was there to help you when you were his age, didn't you? You wanted to be there for him so he didn't have to be like you were."

He shrugged. "The kid needed a hand."

Her heart pounding, Emma slowly walked across the side-walk toward him. As she got nearer, Harlan's eyes seemed to darken, but he didn't move. Not even an inch. He was rigidly still, watching her approach.

She stopped less than a foot from him. "I did it," she told him.

Fear flickered in his eyes. "Did what?"

"Got them to let me adopt Mattie."

A shudder ran over his body, and he closed his eyes for a brief moment. "I'm glad I didn't destroy that," he said. He opened his eyes, and they were bright with relief. "I'm so damn sorry for not being there that day."

She didn't want to talk about that day. "There's one condition, though."

He eyed her. "What is it?"

"I have to divorce you before the adoption is final."

The words hung in the air, and she searched Harlan's face for a reaction. For some hint that he didn't want it. For *anything*.

But his face was utterly impassive.

Neither of them said anything, and a feeling of helplessness seemed to flood her. "I don't know what to say to you," she snapped. "You make me crazy. I can't stop believing that any second you're going to tell me that you love me, that you're going to tell me that you want to try, that you're going to say that you want this to be a real marriage, that you're tired of running away, but you never say it. I can't keep waiting, Harlan. I can't keep believing in you."

A muscle ticked in his cheek, but again, he said nothing.

Frustration roared through her, and she stalked up to him, invading his space until she was so close that they were almost touching. "Before the night outside Astrid's when you kissed me, I was dying," she said. "Every day was like a great weight in my heart. I was living in fear, afraid to embrace life. And then I connected with you, and everything changed. You made me feel again. You made me cry like I haven't cried in so long. Because of you, I suffered loss like I never wanted to feel again, but you know what?"

"What?" His voice was thick and hoarse.

"You made me brave, because you made me realize that I can hurt so badly and still survive it. Because of you, I became brave enough to put myself out there and fight for Mattie." She glanced over at the children, and saw that Mattie had her head on Robbie's shoulder while he read to her. Mattie had the most supreme look of contentment on her face, utter peace in the moment. She didn't care that

STEPHANIE ROWE

Robbie had left her. She wasn't thinking about whether he would leave again. She was just happy, so happy, that he was there for her in that moment.

"Emma."

She tore her gaze off Mattie and looked at Harlan. His face was turbulent with emotions that she couldn't read. "What?"

"I—" He cut himself off, and the expression on his face was of such anguish and conflict that she finally realized the truth. He *was* broken, just like she was. He *did* care, but he couldn't close the circle of love and bind them. He might never be able to, either. He might never be the man she needed, but he was, and always could be, a man worthy of loving.

So, she stood on her tiptoes and planted a light kiss on his cheek. "I love you, Harlan Shea, but I now set you free. You don't owe me anything." She smiled through the tears brimming in her eyes. "You brought me back to life, and I will always hold you in my heart." She stepped back, her throat tight with all the emotions.

Something flared in his eyes, something so intense her pulse jumped. "Emma—"

"Okay, I'm back." Chloe hurried up. "Sorry for the delay. I had to talk to a few people."

Harlan shut his mouth at the interruption, and disappointment stabbed through her as she turned back toward Chloe. "What's up?"

"So, here's the deal." Chloe glanced at the kids. "They're going to have Robbie stay here with Mattie, even though he was in a different foster home before."

That wasn't what she needed to know. "What about the adoption?"

Chloe met her gaze. "The first question is whether you want to adopt him as well. If you do, then they have to go through a quick process to decide whether that makes sense. It will take a couple days. You only have space for Mattie, so you'd have to show that you can expand your house or buy a new one." Her gaze flicked to Harlan. "And are you staying? Because that will be an issue if you are."

Emma's heart seemed to hover in desperate hope as they both turned to look at him.

He looked back and forth between them. "Will it help if I'm gone?"

"Of course it will," Chloe said.

"Then I'll go." He met Emma's eyes. "I set you free as well," he said. "Let me just say goodbye to Robbie and give him my phone number."

Emma stared in shock as he walked away. He was leaving?

"Emma." Chloe drew her attention back. "I don't want you to decide right now about Robbie. It's a big deal, and it's a lifetime commitment. Take a few days—"

"But Mattie—"

"Will understand that things are on hold because of her brother." Chloe's gaze was steady. "You have to be honest with yourself, Emma. Taking on Robbie is a big deal. He's not an easy kid. I'm not sure if they'd let him go with you, anyway. Mattie was different because of your bond with her. Robbie..." She shrugged. "I don't know, but honestly, I think if you just want Mattie, the judge may be okay with that."

Emma stared at her. "Separate them?" Her voice was so choked up she could barely even utter the words. Break their bond? Tear them apart from each other forever? How could she possibly do that? But how could she give Robbie what he needed?

"At least one of them would have a chance, right?" Chloe's phone rang, and she glanced at it. "I need to take this call. I'll talk to you later." She put the phone to her ear and turned away.

Emma turned toward the kids. Harlan was crouched in front of Robbie and Mattie, talking quietly to them. Mattie's hand was on his knee, and Robbie was listening intently. It was clear that the youth had put his trust in Harlan, and it made her want to cry that Harlan had given Robbie someone to believe in. Both kids were nodding, and Emma's heart tightened as Harlan handed Robbie a simple cell phone, which she was sure was programmed with his phone number. He ruffled Mattie's head and then stood up, turning toward Emma.

"They're all set," he said, walking toward her. "I explained to Mattie that she had to wait on the adoption because of her brother. She's fine with that."

"It's only in your imagination, you know," she blurted out.

He frowned. "What is?"

"The dangerous man. The man who can't be trusted to care about anyone. He's not real."

Harlan stared at her, and for a long moment, she thought he was going to say something. But all he did was touch her cheek briefly. "He's a good kid, Emma. Take a chance on him." Then, before she could say anything else, he spun away and jogged to his truck.

Leaving all three of them behind.

◊

THE LAKE WAS STILL.

The night was quiet.

The water at night had always been his salvation, but Harlan felt no peace.

He'd been on the lake for hours, and he still could not stop the torment. The thoughts. The memories. Robbie. Mattie. *Emma.*

He slowed the boat as he drove past her cabin again, for

the twentieth time that night. The lights were out now, though they'd been on for hours. Astrid and Clare had been over, and he'd been able to imagine the discussion. Take the boy. Don't take the boy. Was Emma going to take him? What would happen to the kid if she didn't? If she took only Mattie?

No, she wouldn't do that. She'd never do that. She'd take them both. They were going to be okay. He'd done his job, like he always did. He'd rescued the boy, and that was all he was supposed to do.

But he couldn't let go. He just couldn't. He wanted to be in that cabin. He wanted to be the one sitting with Emma, making plans for their family, for their kids. They didn't need him though. Emma had taken care of everything. *They didn't need him*.

He idled the engine as he drifted past Emma's cabin, letting the boat coast, unable to drag himself away—

He suddenly noticed a motorboat cutting in close to her dock. The driver killed the engine and pulled up to her dock, a tall shadowed figure at the wheel. Frowning, Harlan circled around, watching closely as the driver tied up to her dock. Who would be at her place at three in the morning?

The driver got out, and Harlan instantly recognized the build. Preston. *Jesus.* "Hey!" Harlan gunned the engine, turning his boat toward shore as Preston stepped onto the dock. The man staggered slightly as he turned clumsily toward Emma's house. Jesus. The piece of shit was drunk.

The door slammed and Emma came racing onto the dock, the moonlight showing that she was wearing only a skimpy camisole and a pair of white shorts. She stopped instantly, when she saw Preston, but the bastard kept coming.

Harlan shouted again, but no one could hear him over the sound of his engine. Swearing, he gunned the engine as fast as he could safely go while he watched the scene unfolding on the dock. Preston lunged for Emma, and she ducked out of his reach. He grabbed her hair and yanked, jerking her back as his fingers went around her neck.

Fury exploded through Harlan as he slowed the boat. He couldn't afford to crash into the dock and knock Emma into the water. "Hey!" he yelled, standing at the wheel as his boat neared. "Get away from her!"

Preston ignored him, dragging Emma by her hair until she went down on her knees.

"Get the fuck off her!" Harlan was coming in too fast, and he hit reverse, slowing the boat. His reflexes were bellowing in helpless frustration as he coasted in with agonizing slowness. "Emma!" He was frantic now, consumed with fear for her. His boat neared her dock, and Harlan bolted to the bow of the boat. It was still five feet away when he leapt off. He crashed onto the dock with a violent thud and sprinted across it. He grabbed Preston and flung him aside. He didn't even hear the man land as he fell to his knees beside Emma. "Emma, sweetheart, are you okay?"

She was clutching her throat and coughing, but she grabbed for Harlan's hand. He gripped it tightly, his free hand checking her frantically for injuries. "Are you hurt? Tell me what's hurt. Talk to me, sweetheart." He felt like he couldn't breathe. "Emma?"

"I'm okay." Her voice was raspy and thick, and she was still holding onto him.

"You're okay? You're sure?"

She nodded, still coughing, still gripping him as if he were her salvation. *She was okay.* Intense relief cascaded through him. *She was okay.* He closed his eyes and pulled her into his arms, desperately needing to feel her against him, to hold her, to protect her. She melted against him, her body trembling and cold. He kissed her forehead, her cheeks, her nose...and then froze as she lifted her face toward him.

He stared at her mouth, his instincts screaming at him to kiss her, but he went rigid, fighting the urge. He couldn't cross that line. He couldn't. He couldn't do that to her again—

She smiled suddenly. "You're thinking about kissing me."

He ground his jaw even as his arms tightened around her. "I'm not going to—"

She raised her eyebrows. "Just for the record, you do realize that you were so worried about me that it didn't even occur to you to hurt Preston, don't you? Once you got him off me, all you were thinking about was me, not hitting him or killing him. Do you even know where he is?"

Harlan looked over his shoulder in time to see Preston surge to his feet in the shallow water, stumbling as he tried to find his boat. "I guess I threw him off the dock."

"You guess?" Emma started laughing, and she framed his face. "See, Harlan? See what happens when you let yourself really care? You were so focused on making sure I was okay that you forgot to hurt him. Loving me made you think about saving me, not hurting him."

Harlan stared at her, as her words sank in. He looked over his shoulder again as Preston tried to climb over the rim of his boat, and promptly fell back in the water. He waited for the hate, the anger, and the need to kill him, but those urges didn't come. He was too tired of those emotions. It felt like too much effort to want to kill him. He simply didn't have the energy, the focus. He just wanted Emma. He just wanted to hold her, kiss her, and be with her.

Son of a bitch. She was right. The anger...the violence...the need to hurt... it was gone.

He looked back at the woman still in his arms. Her smile had faded, and her brow was furrowed. "Why are you here?" she asked. "Weren't you supposed to be on a plane this morning?"

"I couldn't make myself get on the plane." And now he knew why. "I had to give you something."

"Give me something?" She sat up as Harlan dug his hand into the pocket of his jeans. His fingers closed around the circle of gold that he'd kept in his pocket for weeks.

He held it out to her, and the moonlight glittered on it. "I took two rings from Astrid's that night," he said. "I took the plain one, because I didn't want to make promises. But this is the ring I wanted to give you, the one that I chose for you, the one I didn't dare offer to you." He held it out to her.

She looked at it, but she didn't take it. "What is it?" she asked. "It's too dark to see it clearly."

He knew every detail on the ring. "It's gold," he said. "It has three roses engraved around the outside. Three roses, for you, me, and Mattie." His voice seemed to stick in his throat. "They're all intertwined, so you can't see which leaves or stems go with which rose. They're three separate roses, but at the same time, they're one."

Her face softened in the moonlight. "Why'd you pick it?"

"Because—" Shit. He didn't even know how to say it, but he wanted to. The sound of Preston still splashing around in the water behind him was like this great liberation, a symbol of release from being the man he dreaded.

The words that had floated around inside him for so long...he could finally say them. Breathe them. Live them. And, most importantly, *share* them. "Because I want to be that man for you. I want to create a family with you. I don't want to just save the day and then walk away. I want the aftermath. I want the recovery. I want to be there to pick up the pieces every day, for as long as it takes for them to stop falling."

As Emma stared at him, a look of disbelief on her face, he rose to one knee, holding out the ring. "Emma Larson, I love you. I love your smile. I love your heart. I love how you are so brave, and so vulnerable at the same time. I love that you saw in me what I didn't even see." He grinned. "And I love that you left me that message and said you wouldn't cry for me, because I needed that." His smile faded as the weight of his words settled on him. "I don't know how to be a husband, or a dad, or even the guy who knows how to sit at the same dinner table every night, but I swear that I will love you every second of every day, and I will love our kids, because we're going to adopt both of them no matter how much red tape we have to get through, and I will never, ever walk away again, not even for one damn night."

Emma smiled, a slowly-growing beautiful smile that seemed to light up the night, the earth, his world. "So what are you saying?"

"I'm saying that I want to be your husband. Forever." He held out the ring. "Marry me, Emma, marry me for real. Give me one more chance. Please."

The night seemed to pulse in anticipation, and he couldn't take his gaze off Emma's face. He was a man who had never had time for prayer, and he knew he didn't deserve another opportunity, but nevertheless, he found himself whispering a fervent prayer that she grant him that second chance.

"Harlan?"

His heart started to pound. "What?"

"I love you."

He grinned stupidly, his heart leaping in disbelief. "You do?"

"Yes, and I will marry you on one condition."

She was going to marry him again? For real? His grin got wider, a big ass shit-eating grin that felt like it was going to take over his entire face. "What's that?"

"You need to ask your sister to add one more rose to my ring. For Robbie." Then she smiled, a smile that seemed to melt the final pieces of steel still lodged in his heart. "Welcome home, my darling husband."

And home he was.

He took her hand and held up the ring. "We never said our vows before, so here are mine." He met her gaze. "I promise to love you with every bit of my heart for all our days," he said. "I promise that I will always love our children unconditionally. I promise that I will never leave any of you, ever, for any reason. I promise that I will never break your trust in me, and I will never hurt you. I also promise that I will never strike any of you ever, no matter what. *Ever.*"

Emma touched his face. "You don't need to promise not to hit us. I know you'd never do that—"

"I always told myself I would never get married unless I could make that promise and know I spoke the truth." He kissed her hand. "You gave me that truth, Emma, a truth that I thought was impossible, until I met you." He started to slip the ring onto her hand, and she stopped him.

"My turn." She met his gaze, her face so earnest that emotions threatened to overtake him. "I promise to never run away and hide, no matter how hard things get. I promise to always believe in you, and in myself. And I also promise to love you, and our children, with every bit of my heart for all my days."

He grinned, his heart soaring as he took her hand and slid the ring onto her fourth finger. It fit perfectly, glittering in the moonlight, so beautiful. "One more thing before I kiss the bride." He pulled her to her feet. "Come on."

"Where are we going?" Her hand slipped perfectly into his as he led her to the edge of the dock, where his boat was now bumping gently against the reeds a few yards from shore.

"Patience, my dear." Harlan jumped off the dock, landing in water up to his hips. He held up his arms. "Come on."

She didn't hesitate as she tumbled into his arms, trusting

him completely. He carried her across the water and then set her in the boat. With nothing but a mysterious grin, he shoved the boat back into deeper water, then hauled himself on board, dripping wet, but neither of them cared. Within minutes, they'd left Preston and her cabin behind, the wind whipping past them just like it had the night of their first boat ride.

As he drove, he pulled Emma in front of him, trapping her between his body and the steering wheel, just like the night they'd gotten married. He drove to the exact spot in the lake that he'd avoided ever since, and cut the engine. "Do you recognize where we are?"

"It's where we were the first time you asked me to marry you." She turned to him, her face glowing. "You're a romantic, aren't you?"

"Turns out, there may be many hidden facets to my personality that can be brought out only by the love of a good woman." He slid his hands through her hair, tangling his fingers in the golden tresses.

Emma smiled. "You can grab my hair if you want. It doesn't scare me anymore." She draped her arms around his neck. "Nothing about you scares me, even giving you my heart."

"That is very good to know," he said, as he bent his head. "But I don't want to do the he-man grab-your-hair thing anymore. It's not my style." Then he kissed her, showing her exactly what his style was now. A kiss that promised forever. A kiss that promised love. A kiss that promised that the floor of his boat was going to get a little bit of action under the moonlit sky.

He might be married. He might soon be a dad. But he was also a man who had waited too damn long to make love to his wife the way he wanted to, and the way she deserved. Tonight, he was going to make her his.

"Harlan," she whispered as he lowered her to the carpet, their kisses becoming more intense and passionate as they both finally lowered the barriers they'd lived with for so long.

"Yeah?"

"Why did you leave me roses the second time?"

He braced himself above her, supporting himself on his hands as he looked down at her. Her hair was tousled, her smile happy, his ring sparkling on her hand. "Because I wanted you to be right about me."

She grinned. "Me, too."

He settled himself on top of her, basking in the feel of her beneath him as he lightly grasped her wrists and stretched her arms above her head.

"Make love to me, Harlan." She grinned suddenly. "The kids probably arrive tomorrow. We won't make love again until we're both sixty."

"Screw that." He let out a low growl that made her giggle. "I'll be claiming you every damn night of our lives, woman. I've got a lifetime to make up."

She smiled. "So do I."

Then he kissed her, and that new lifetime finally began.

CHAPTER TWENTY

"WHICH WAY AROUND THAT BUOY?"

Shielding her eyes against the afternoon sun, Emma glanced over her shoulder to look where Robbie was headed. "Stay to the left. That marks a reef in the middle of the lake. You have to stay on the shore side with that one."

"That's Moose Reef?" The youth was wearing sunglasses, and his Red Sox cap on backwards, already faded from the sun. It had been only two months since that day Harlan had arrived with him from California, but he had already come so far. He'd ditched his tee shirt and shoved it under the dash so it didn't blow away, showcasing ribs that were getting less visible and the ragged scar on his side that she was sure would never completely go away. "I gotta learn this lake. I don't want to crack up the boat."

"You're doing great." Smiling at his innate sense of responsibility, Emma leaned against the windshield, playing spotter for Robbie while he drove. Behind the boat, at the end of a thirty-foot rope were Harlan and Mattie, who were scrunched together in the tube that Harlan had come home with two days after Mattie and Robbie had moved in. Her pink princess life jacket was practically around her ears, but her broad smile lit up her face. She waved at Emma, and Emma waved back.

Robbie glanced quickly over his shoulder to check on his load.

"Hey," Emma corrected him gently. "Since you're the driver, you have to watch the lake. You have to trust your spotter to keep an eye on the people you're towing. There are too many shallow areas for you to take your eye off the water."

Robbie grinned, and turned his attention forward. "You're kind of bossy," he observed.

Emma smiled. "I'm only bossy when it matters, like keeping you and Mattie safe." Robbie was pulling the tube slowly, so the engine wasn't so loud they had to shout. "Remember to take a wide turn so you don't jerk the tube."

"I got it." He executed a long, slow turn that kept the tension on the rope constant, just as they'd been practicing. It was an unseasonably warm fall day, one of the last ones before it would be time to retire the boat for the winter. "So, I was thinking..."

She gave a thumbs up to Mattie. "You should start heading toward the beach. It's getting late."

"Yeah, okay." He looked around, and she could tell he was trying to figure out the way to the town beach. She waited, and eventually he turned the boat south. She smiled, and she saw him glance stealthily her way to see if he'd chosen correctly, then the corner of his mouth turned up and he pulled his shoulders back ever so slightly.

"What were you thinking, Robbie?" she prompted, not wanting to lose the connection of the moment.

He kept his gaze on the lake ahead. "So, yeah, Harlan showed me some of your paintings last night when we were moving stuff into your new studio."

She raised her brows. "Did he?" The addition to her cabin was almost complete, though it could hardly be called an addition since the new part was bigger than the original. But since Harlan had sold his place, they'd been able to turn her small cabin into a four-bedroom home that even had the most beautiful, natural-light studio she'd ever dreamed of.

"Yeah, so, um...I was wondering whether maybe I could like borrow some paint or something, sometime." He wouldn't look at her.

Emma studied him for a minute. "Do you like to paint?"

He shrugged. "I don't know. Maybe sometimes, you know?"

She was surprised by his admission. He'd been very reticent since he'd arrived. Only on the lake had he opened up, apparently having the same connection with water that she and Harlan had. "I was going to do some painting tomorrow morning before you guys got up. If you want, I can wait for you and we can do it together. I have an extra easel and brushes." She eyed him thoughtfully. "I could show you some techniques."

He didn't look at her, but he shrugged. "Yeah, okay, if you want."

She couldn't keep the smile off her face as she leaned toward him and put her arm around his shoulders. "I definitely want, Robbie."

There was no mistaking his smile this time, and she wasn't sure who was smiling more.

HARLAN KEPT his arm tight around Mattie as he watched Emma lean in and chat with Robbie while he was driving. He grinned when he saw Emma put her arm around him. *Yes*. It was finally happening. Robbie hadn't wanted to trust anyone except Harlan, and it hadn't been easy for Emma to reach him.

But progress was being made. When they'd received the initial paperwork from Dottie officially approving both he and Emma to adopt both kids, something had changed in Robbie. He was still guarded, yeah, but the tough edge was slowly beginning to dull ever so slightly. The kid still had nightmares, and Harlan had sat out with him on the dock at three in the morning on many nights, but even those were getting less frequent.

As he thought it, Robbie glanced back at him, and Harlan inclined his head toward the teen, reminding the youth that he wasn't going anywhere. Not ever. How could he? Between his family and the troubled youths he had started working with through Dottie, he had enough missions right here to occupy him for the rest of his damn life, and he loved every minute of it.

"Harlan." Mattie tugged at his arm.

"Yes, sweetie?" Harlan watched as Robbie carefully and flawlessly navigated the approach to the town beach, driving the boat up onto the sand beside the roped-off swimming area with perfect precision and care. It had been hard as hell handing over the keys of his boat to a fourteen year old, but Robbie had thrived under the responsibility.

As the boat came to rest on the shore, Harlan saw Eppie race over to start lecturing Robbie on the fact he was late and she needed his help cooking the burgers. The kid barely had time to throw down the anchor before Eppie was hauling him across the beach to the grill... where Clare and Griffin's teen daughters were shucking corn. The minute he saw them, Robbie stood taller and shoved his sunglasses on his head as he approached, swaggering just a little bit more. Harlan chuckled softly as the girls waved at him, their giggles and secret smiles made it very clear that they were happy to see him.

"Harlan!" Mattie banged on his hand.

"Sorry, sweetie. What is it?" Harlan untangled his legs from the tube as Mattie squirmed on his lap and turned to face him. Emma had woven pink ribbons into her braids, and she was beyond adorable. Just looking at her made his whole world slow down. "Are you my daddy now?"

Something tightened in his chest, and his throat seemed to become clogged. "Yes, I am."

"Forever?"

"Of course forever."

"And what if Emma died?" Her dark brown eyes were riveted on his. He saw in those five-year-old depths a fear bred of a life too tough for such a small child. "What would happen to me?"

Harlan met her gaze, and knew this wasn't the time to dismiss her concerns with a placating statement that Emma wasn't going to die. Her fear was real, and it was created from what had already happened to her. "If Emma died, then you and Robbie would keep living with me."

"And what if you died then?"

He turned her and pointed to the beach, where Astrid and Noah were helping Emma tie up the boat. "Then you would live with Aunt Astrid, Uncle Jason, Noah, and Rosie."

She studied them. "I like them."

He smiled. "They love you."

She turned back to him. "And what if they died?"

He pointed her to Clare. "You and Robbie would live with Clare and Griffin and their daughters."

Mattie studied them, and finally she turned back to him. "Would I ever run out of people to live with?"

"No, baby, you wouldn't." He gestured toward the beach, which was full of people from the town. It was the end of the summer barbeque, just for the locals, and Mattie knew almost everyone present. "See all those people? They are all your family. You and Robbie won't ever be alone again, no matter what." As he said it, he realized he wasn't speaking only for Mattie and Robbie. He was speaking for himself. This was his town, and he belonged.

She looked at the beach again, and then back at him. "Can I call you Daddy, then?"

"Can you—" He was startled by the question, and touched so deeply he couldn't answer for a moment. Something seemed to come to life inside him, and he nodded, his throat too tight for words.

She smiled. "And now I want to go look for frogs with Noah. He said he knows where some really big ones are. 'Kay?"

"Okay." Harlan lifted her out of the tube, and helped her take her life preserver off. She was just starting to run off when he grabbed her wrist. "Hey, I love you, bumpkins!"

She gave him a huge hug. "Love you, too, Daddy!" And then she ran off through the water, shouting for Noah, her mermaid swimsuit the cutest damn thing he'd ever seen.

Daddy. She'd called him *Daddy*. His vision seemed to blur, and he looked over at Emma, who was organizing their contribution to the picnic in the back of the boat. Her hair was tangling around her shoulders in a ponytail that had been ravaged by the wind and the sun. Her shoulders were a pale gold, just barely kissed by the sun, and on her hand sparkled the same ring he'd given her that night on the lake. His wife. The mother of his children. The woman who had saved his life.

She looked up as if she'd felt him watching her, and she smiled and held out her hand to him. Wordlessly, he waded through the water toward her. As he neared, her smile faded. "What's wrong?"

"Nothing." His voice was husky as he reached for her over the edge of the boat and wrapped his arms around her waist. He hauled her close, burying his face in her belly. Emma wrapped her arms around his head and held him, as she had done so many times over the last two months, so many times when it had simply become too much for him to process.

For a long moment, neither of them moved. The craziness of the picnic and the crowds seemed to fade away, and the moment became simply about them. He breathed in the scent of sunscreen and soap, he felt the soft cotton of her cover-up against his cheeks, the warmth of her body against his.

Emma tapped his arm, and he loosened his grip enough for her to kneel down in the boat so that her face was level with his. Her green eyes were like the purest emerald as she smiled at him. "It's okay, Harlan. It's all okay."

"No, it's not okay. It's more than that. So much more." He tucked a strand of hair back from her face. "It's the most beautiful gift I ever could have received."

"What is?"

"You. Mattie. Robbie. This town." He had no words, but he tried. "I never thought I would leave my job. I liked rescuing people, and I liked being on the move. I never thought I could stay in one place, but these last two months of waking up with you in my arms, and Mattie and Robbie fighting in the living room have been the best two months of my life."

She searched his face. "You don't miss it? Because if you did—"

"No, sweetheart, no. This is my world. I'm done saving other people's families. I'm needed here, with my own family."

Her smile widened. "Yes, you are."

"Hey, Harlan!" Eppie's voice rang out over the beach.

Emma chuckled as he rolled his eyes. "Yes, Eppie? What can I do for you?" he called back.

"Preston and his obnoxious friends just showed up at the other end of the beach. You need to do a walk-by to scare him off!"

Emma laughed as Eppie began to call for bets on how many seconds it would take Preston to sprint back to his car upon sighting Harlan.

Shortly after the incident at Emma's cabin, Preston had received an anonymous envelope documenting the number of people Harlan had killed in the line of duty. He'd put his Birch Crossing house on the market the next day. No one had taken responsibility for the package, but Emma had quietly pointed out that Eppie had known about the letter before anyone else had...even Preston.

Eppie was officially involved in Harlan's life, which left no doubt about his role in the community. His roots were down. He was going nowhere ever again. Except possibly, on the honeymoon they'd never had...which would, of course, include the kids.

A honeymoon with kids as his next trip? He chuckled as he swept Emma up in his arms to help her out of the boat. He grinned at her as he carried her through the water. "Just so you know," he said, "when the kids go to bed, I'm going to have to make love to you until you scream my name."

She smiled, the devilish gleam in her eyes that he'd grown to love so deeply. "I accept that dare."

He laughed. "I know you do. I love that about you. In fact, I love it all."

And he did.

∼

Will Blue ever find the peace and love that Harlan found with

Emma, or are his shadows too deep? When Blue and a spunky social worker discover they've accidentally rented the same lakeside cabin, things get complicated in a hurry. Find out more by grabbing your copy of Irresistibly Mine right now!

Get your copy now!

"A beautiful romance that touched me deeply."
~Madison F. (Amazon Review)

SNEAK PEEK: IRRESISTIBLY MINE

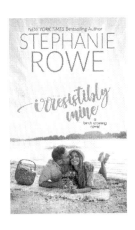

"I can't find the words to adequately express how much I loved this book." ~Elizabeth N. (Amazon Review)

When an ex-military hottie and a spunky social worker discover they've accidentally rented the same lakeside cabin, things get complicated in a hurry.

IN THIS MOMENT, Blue knew exactly what he wanted. He wanted to help her. "Give me a chance to make it up to you, Chloe." The moment he said her name, Chloe's face softened, as if the sound of him saying her name had meant something to her.

Still watching him, she put the phone back to her ear, resuming the conversation with her friend. "Hi, Emma. Blue said that he'll fix my car or drop me off, so I'm all set. But if he can't fix it, I'll need the name of a mechanic for the morning."

Something inside Blue loosened when he heard her accept his offer, almost as if the chance to be with her for a little while longer made the tension inside him ease its relentless grip on his gut.

She listened for a moment. "Okay. I'll stop at Wright's for some food on the way. See you soon. And... Emma? Thank you. I don't know what I would've done without you." Her voice choked up, and Blue looked at her sharply. Her eyes were shiny, and she was gripping the phone so tightly that her knuckles were white. She cleared her throat, and nodded, clearly listening to something Emma was saying. "Right, I know. I'm fine. Really, I am. I'll see you soon. Bye."

As she hung up the phone, she closed her eyes, bowed her head, and pressed her phone to her forehead. She took a deep breath, and then another, as if she'd forgotten she wasn't alone. Blue watched her, noting the paleness of her skin, and the way her shoulders were tucked up toward her ears ever so slightly, in the protective posture he'd seen many times when a newly rescued kidnap victim had hunched in the corner of the helicopter, unwilling to believe the nightmare was really over.

Instinctively, Blue walked over to her and crouched in front of her. "Hey."

She opened her eyes and quickly lowered the phone,

sitting up straighter in a posture clearly designed to make sure no one knew the weight she was carrying inside. She met his gaze for a split second, then her attention dropped to the beer he was holding. "Is that for me?"

Silently, he handed it to her, still watching her. "It'll be okay," he said. "Whatever the nightmare is, it can't get inside you unless you let it." Of course, he knew all too well about the damage nightmares could do, but just because he couldn't shield himself from his own baggage didn't mean he was unaware of how it could work if someone had their shit together better than he did.

She narrowed her eyes. "It's that easy to let it go? Really? I had no idea." She sounded a little annoyed, as if insulted he would reduce all her problems to some philosophical resolution.

He got that. He inclined his head in acknowledgment. "Theoretically, yeah, it's that's simple. In reality, it can eat away at you until you're so dead on the inside that life stops mattering. Until all you can do is run as hard as you can, hoping that you can escape the darkness before it consumes you."

She froze with the bottle of beer halfway to her lips, her eyes widening in surprise. Belatedly, he realized what he'd said and what he'd revealed about himself. Grimacing, he shrugged, and took a sip of his own beer. "Or so I've heard."

Chloe angled the mouth of the bottle toward him as if pointing at him. "You, my friend, are a wealth of complexity, aren't you?"

Blue grinned. "Nah. I drink beer. I shoot guns. And, after tonight, apparently I can add terrorizing women to my list. It's pretty simple and basic. I'm just your normal, upstanding boy-next-door kind of guy. I'm exactly the type that mothers fantasize that their daughters will fall for."

Her gaze flicked to his cheek, and he suddenly remembered

the scar that bisected the side of his face. He never thought about it much. Who the hell cared about a scar? But Chloe was soft, gentle, and sensitive. What would she think about a six-inch scar that belied every claim he'd just made? The thought made him tense, and he didn't like that. He didn't like worrying about his scar, or what someone would think about it.

Scowling, he stood up and paced away from her. He leaned against the tiny kitchenette counter and folded his arms over his chest. "So, tell me, Chloe Dalton. Why were you barging into this cabin at ten o'clock at night in the first place?"

She raised her eyebrows. "I felt as though my life was too tame and predictable. I thought that getting the living daylights scared out of me would make my day more interesting."

He felt himself grin again, but he was learning not to be surprised by the fact she could coax a smile out of him. "Any other reasons?"

She took a drink of her beer, wrinkling her nose as the bitterness drifted across her tongue. "First of all, you're kind of nosy. Second of all, the beer is kind of horrible."

He grinned wider, amused by her inability to school her face into impassive, neutral expressions. "You know, the problem with trying to avoid questions with me, is that I'm an expert on not telling anyone anything that I don't want them to know, so I see right through that façade. So yeah, I'm nosy. Yeah, the beer sucks. But I still want to know what's going on that made you show up at this cabin and sprint into it without checking to see if anyone was here."

She cocked her head, studying him. "Why do you want to know so badly?"

He shrugged. "I don't know. I just do."

She smiled then, a gentle smile that made him want to

grin. "Fair enough." Her gaze flicked away from him, drifting over the bare walls of the rustic cabin, before coming back to rest on his face. "In addition to losing my job yesterday, I also got evicted from the place I've been living in for the last ten years."

Her voice was tight and calm, but he could instantly sense the depth of grief at her words, grief she was absolutely refusing to succumb to.

Respect flooded him, but also empathy. She was tough, refusing to be broken, but something really shitty had crashed down upon her. "Sorry about that."

"It's fine." She shrugged, tracing her fingers over the condensation on the bottle. "I was a little desperate, so Emma said I could stay here until I figure things out, because it was empty." She glanced at him, and cocked a sassy eyebrow at him. "She didn't realize, however, that Harlan had given you the keys. That phone call I just answered? That was Emma calling to warn me that you were already living here. Of course, being the intelligent woman that I am, I had already figured that out."

"You were planning to stay here?" Guilt shot through Blue. There was no chance in hell he was stealing her safe house. He stood up. "No problem. It'll take me five minutes to pack, and the place is all yours." He set his beer on the counter of the kitchenette, and strode across the room to where his duffel was stashed. "I've already been here two days, and I told Harlan I wasn't staying any longer than that—"

"Whoa." She stood up just as quickly, her hand going to his arm as he passed.

He froze, his senses flashing to awareness at the feel of her touch. Her fingers were gentle, barely there, and yet he couldn't move away from her. He took a breath, and turned his head to look at her. "It's okay," he said softly. "The place is yours—"

"No, I don't need it. Emma found another place, one that's in town, which I would prefer anyway." She rolled her eyes. "I was never a huge nature girl, but after tonight, I think I'd lie in bed all night waiting for the boogie man to get me if I stayed here. It's all good."

"But you'll have to pay for that one, right?" He didn't move away from her touch, and she didn't take her hand away either.

Her face softened. "It's very sweet of you to be concerned about that, but the answer is no, actually. You know how Harlan is a real estate agent in his spare time?" At his nod, she continued on. "He has a vacant listing that's for sale, but the owners said I could stay there for free while it's on the market. They figure it'll help sell if the windows are opened and the mustiness is aired out, so I'm good. That's where you're driving me tonight, unless you can work magic with my car."

He grimaced. "I don't want to complicate things for you—"

"It's not complicating anything," she interrupted. "Seriously, this works out better for me." She patted his arm. "But I appreciate your willingness to surrender the cabin to me." Her smile faded. "It's nice. Nice is good."

He still didn't move. "I'm not nice."

She raised her brows. "No?"

"No." Her face was so close to his. Only inches away. Her mouth...it was insanely tempting. He imagined brushing a kiss over her forehead. Across her cheeks. Against the corner of her mouth.

Her eyes widened, and she caught her breath. Suddenly, that same tension that had been strung so tight when they'd first walked in was back, only this time, it hummed with higher intensity, like the eerie silence when a night was too still, indicating that all hell was about to break loose.

He brushed his fingers along her jaw, and she froze, not even breathing. "Would it be inappropriate to kiss you right now?"

"Yes." She blurted out the answer before he'd finished asking the question. "Don't kiss me." But she didn't retreat, or even turn her head away from the brush of his fingers along her jaw. "Don't even think about it."

He shrugged. "Can't help thinking about it."

"Well, find a way." She swallowed hard.

"Can't." Silently, he moved his hands so his fingers were resting on her throat. The frantic fluttering of her pulse was like a butterfly beneath his touch, delicate, untamed, and beautiful. "You could stay here instead of going into town tonight."

Her eyes widened. "Stay here? With you?"

"Yeah." He ran his fingers along her collarbone, tracing the delicate curve of her body.

She closed her eyes, inhaling sharply at his touch, leaning into him ever so slightly. "Never."

"Why not?" He wanted to kiss that fluttering pulse in her throat. He wanted to trace it with his lips, and his tongue. He wanted to taste her lips.

"Because—" She stopped, her breath catching again as he bent his head and pressed a feather-light kiss to the delicate skin of her throat. "Oh, God. Really? You had to do that?"

"Yeah, I did. Your throat was calling to me. Didn't you hear it? It was whispering my name. *Blue, kiss me. Blue, kiss me now.*"

She made a strangled noise that sounded like a cross between laughter and disgusted, skeptical scorn. "My body would never beg for a man's kiss. Ever. You're delusional."

"Probably." He pressed another kiss to her collarbone, and

her fingers tightened on his arm, where they were still resting from her initial contact. "But as delusions go, it's an extremely pleasant one, so I'm just going to go with it." He pressed a kiss to her forehead. "Can you hear it? Now it's your cheek whispering to me. *Blue. Kiss me.*"

"My cheek is not saying that—" He brushed a kiss over her left cheekbone. "Damn you," she whispered.

He bent his head, so his lips were hovering over hers. "What about your lips? Can you hear them whispering?"

"They're telling you to stop bugging me." But her fingers continued to grip his arm, and she didn't pull away.

"What about the corner of your mouth? Right here?" He kissed the spot in question.

She tightened her grip on his arm. "Oh, yeah, maybe there. That might have been saying something to you."

"And this corner?" He tried the other.

She made a small noise of pleasure that made him grin. "It's a distinct possibility," she muttered. "But only because that particular corner of my mouth is stupid, irresponsible, and a glutton for situations that would leave it strewn across the highway in a thousand shattered pieces."

He slid his hand into her hair, tangling his fingers in the strands. "No need for shattered pieces," he said gently. "I can't have any of that when I'm around. I'm a sucker for picking up broken pieces and trying to glue them back together. I can't ever leave them scattered around. It's against my nature." His lips brushed hers, barely, just a whispered touch that made visceral longing course through him, tightening every muscle in his body. "I need to kiss you, Chloe. Like my life fucking depends on it."

Her eyes snapped open, and she searched his face. He knew he'd sounded too desperate, but he didn't pull back. He let her see the raw, brokenness of his soul. He let her see it, because she'd already ripped away his shields, leaving him with no defenses.

"Kiss me, Blue," she whispered. "Kiss me, now."

"*Chloe.*" With a low groan, he closed the distance between them, and claimed her mouth with his own.

Like it? Get it now!

A QUICK FAVOR

Did you enjoy Harlan and Emma's story?

People are often hesitant to try new books or new authors. A few reviews can encourage them to make that leap and give it a try. If you enjoyed Unintentionally Mine *and think others will as well, please consider taking a moment and writing one or two sentences on the eTailer and/or Goodreads to help this story find the readers who would enjoy it. Even the short reviews really make an impact!*

Thank you a million times for reading my books! I love writing for you and sharing the journeys of these beautiful characters with you. I hope you find inspiration from their stories in your own life!

Love,
Stephanie

STAY IN THE KNOW!

I write my books from the soul, and live that way as well. I've received so much help over the years from amazing people to help me live my best life, and I am always looking to pay it forward, including to my readers.

One of the ways I love to do this is through my mailing list, where I often send out life tips I've picked up, post readers surveys, give away Advance Review Copies, and provide insider scoop on my books, my writing, and life in general. And, of course, I always make sure my readers on my list know when the next book is coming out!

If this sounds interesting to you, I would love to have you join us! You can always unsubscribe at any time! I'll never spam you or share your data. I just want to provide value!

Sign up at www.stephanierowe.com/join-newsletter/ to keep in touch!

Much love,

STAY IN THE KNOW!

Stephanie

BOOKS BY STEPHANIE ROWE

Do you know why I love to write?

Because I love to reach deep inside the soul, both mine and yours, and awaken the spirit that gives us life. I want to write books that make you feel, that touch your heart, and inspire you to whatever dreams you hold in your heart.

"This book has the capacity to touch 90% of the women's lives. I went through all the fears and anguish of the characters with them and came out the other side feeling the hope and love. I would even say I experienced some healing of my own." -cyinca (Amazon Review)

All my stories take the reader on that same emotional journey, whether it's in a small Maine town, rugged cowboy country, or the magical world of immortal warriors. Some of my books are funnier, some are darker, but they all give the deep sense of emotional fulfillment.

"I adore this family! ...[Wyoming Rebels] is definitely one of

my favorite series and since paranormal is my usual interest, that's saying something." -Laura B (Amazon Review)

Take a look below. See what might strike your fancy. Give one of them a try. You might fall in love with a genre you don't expect!

◞

CONTEMPORARY ROMANCE

WYOMING REBELS SERIES
(CONTEMPORARY WESTERN ROMANCE)
A Real Cowboy Never Says No
A Real Cowboy Knows How to Kiss
A Real Cowboy Rides a Motorcycle
A Real Cowboy Never Walks Away
A Real Cowboy Loves Forever
A Real Cowboy for Christmas
A Real Cowboy Always Trusts His Heart (Sept 2019!)

A ROGUE COWBOY SERIES
(CONTEMPORARY WESTERN ROMANCE)
A Rogue Cowboy for Her, featuring Brody Hart
(Coming Soon!)

LINKED TO A ROGUE COWBOY SERIES
(CONTEMPORARY WESTERN ROMANCE)
Her Rebel Cowboy

BIRCH CROSSING SERIES
(SMALL-TOWN CONTEMPORARY ROMANCE)
Unexpectedly Mine
Accidentally Mine

BOOKS BY STEPHANIE ROWE

Unintentionally Mine
Irresistibly Mine
Mistakenly Mine (Coming Soon!)

MYSTIC ISLAND SERIES
(SMALL-TOWN CONTEMPORARY ROMANCE)
Wrapped Up in You (A Christmas novella)

CANINE CUPIDS SERIES
(ROMANTIC COMEDY)
Paws for a Kiss
Pawfectly in Love
Paws Up for Love

PARANORMAL

ORDER OF THE BLADE SERIES
(DARK PARANORMAL ROMANCE)
Darkness Awakened
Darkness Seduced
Darkness Surrendered
Forever in Darkness
Darkness Reborn
Darkness Arisen
Darkness Unleashed
Inferno of Darkness
Darkness Possessed
Shadows of Darkness
Hunt the Darkness
Awaken the Darkness (Oct 2019)

ORDER OF THE NIGHT
(AN ORDER OF THE BLADE SPINOFF SERIES)
(DARK PARANORMAL ROMANCE)

Edge of Midnight, featuring Thano Savakis
(Coming Soon!)

HEART OF THE SHIFTER SERIES
(DARK PARANORMAL ROMANCE)
Dark Wolf Rising
Dark Wolf Unbound
Dark Wolf Untamed (Coming Soon!)

SHADOW GUARDIANS SERIES
(DARK PARANORMAL ROMANCE)
Leopard's Kiss

NIGHTHUNTER SERIES
(DARK PARANORMAL ROMANCE)
Not Quite Dead

Writing as S.A. Bayne

NOBLE AS HELL SERIES
(FUNNY URBAN FANTASY)
Rock Your Evil

IMMORTALLY CURSED SERIES
(FUNNY PARANORMAL ROMANCE)
Immortally Cursed
Curse of the Dragon
Devil's Curse (Dec 2019)

THE MAGICAL ELITE SERIES
(FUNNY PARANORMAL ROMANCE)
The Demon You Trust

DEVILISHLY SEXY SERIES

(FUNNY PARANORMAL ROMANCE)
Not Quite a Devil
The Devil You Know (Coming Soon!)

ROMANTIC SUSPENSE

ALASKA HEAT SERIES
(ROMANTIC SUSPENSE)
Ice
Chill
Ghost

YOUNG ADULT

MAPLEVILLE HIGH SERIES
(FUNNY CONTEMPORARY ROMANCE)
The Truth About Thongs
How to Date a Bad Boy
Pedicures Don't Like Dirt
Geeks Can Be Hot
The Fake Boyfriend Experiment
Ice Cream, Jealousy & Other Dating Tips

BOXED SETS

Order of the Blade (Books 1-3)
Protectors of the Heart (A Six-Book First-in-Series Collection)
Real Cowboys Get Their Girls (A Wyoming Rebels Boxed Set,
with bonus novella!)

For a complete list of Stephanie's books, click here.

ACKNOWLEDGMENTS

Special thanks to my beta readers, who always work incredibly hard under tight deadlines to get my books read. I appreciate so much your willingness to tell me when something doesn't work! I treasure your help, and I couldn't do this without you. Hugs to you all!

There are so many to thank by name, more than I could count, but here are those who I want to called out specially for all they did to help this book come to life: Alencia Bates, Jean Bowden, Shell Bryce, Kelley Currey, Holly Collins, Ashley Cuesta, Denise Fluhr, Valerie Glass, Heidi Hoffman, Jeanne Hunter, Dottie Jones, Janet Juengling-Snell, Deb Julienne, Bridget Koan, Felicia Low, Phyllis Marshall, Jodi Moore, Judi Pflughoeft, Emily Recchia, Kasey Richardson, Karen Roma, Caryn Santee, Dana Simmons, Julie Simpson, Summer Steelman, Amanda Tamayo, Nicole Telhiard, Linda Watson, and Denise Whelan.

And lastly, thank you to Kelli Ann Morgan at Inspire Creative Services for another fantastic cover. Mom, you're the best. It means so much that you believe in me. I love you. Special thanks also to my amazing, beautiful, special daughter, who I love more than words could ever express. You are my world, sweet girl, in all ways.

Made in the USA
Middletown, DE
22 June 2020